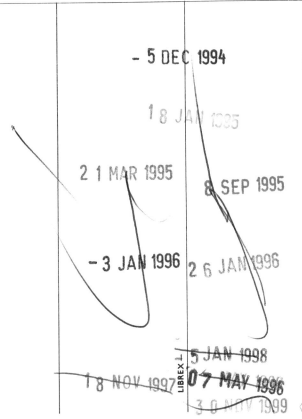
ns in Architecture:

ology of Beginning Design Projects

D1612701

Foundations in Architecture:
An Annotated Anthology of Beginning Design Projects

OWEN CAPPLEMAN • MICHAEL JACK JORDAN

 VAN NOSTRAND REINHOLD
NEW YORK

Library of Congress Catalog Card Number 93-7262
ISBN 0-442-00764-7

I(T)P   Van Nostrand Reinhold is a division of International Thomson Publishing.
         ITP logo is a trademark under license.

Printed in the United States of America

Van Nostrand Reinhold
115 Fifth Avenue
New York, NY 10003

International Thomson Publishing
Berkshire House, 168-173
High Holborn, London WC1V7AA
England

Thomas Nelson Australia
102 Dodds Street
South Melbourne 3205
Victoria, Australia

Nelson Canada
1120 Birchmount Road
Scarborough, Ontario
M1K 5G4, Canada

Interanational Thomson Publishing GmbH
Königswinterer Str. 518
5300 Bonn 3
Germany

International Thomson Publishing Asia
38 Kim Tian Rd., #0105
Kim Tian Plaza
Singapore 0316

International Thomson Publishing Japan
Kyowa Building, 3F
2-2-1 Hirakawacho
Chiyada-Ku, Tokyo 102
Japan

16 15 14 13 12 11 10 9 8 7 6 5 4 3 2 1

Library of Congress Cataloging in Publication Data

Cappleman, Owen.
        Foundations in architecture : an annotated anthology of beginning design projects / Owen Cappleman, Michael Jack Jordan.
        p.   cm.
        Includes index.
        ISBN 0-442-00764-7
        1. Architectural design—Study and teaching. I. Jordan, Michael Jack
    II. Title
        NA2750.C37 1993
        729—dc20

93-7262
CIP

for J.C. and S.J.

We wish to express our gratitude to the thirty-two contributors, and the twenty-five universities they represent, for making this book possible. Special thanks go to Tim McGinty both for originating the idea that we have three times purloined, parlaying it finally into this book, and for his continued support in our efforts; and to Hal Box, Dean of the School of Architecture, the University of Texas at Austin, 1976–92, without whose help in providing facilities and staff the Foundations in Architecture conference could not have happened.

—O.C. & M. J.

Foundations in Architecture
*An Annotated Anthology
of Beginning Design Projects*

CONTENTS

Foundations in Architecture
*An Annotated Anthology
of Beginning Design Projects*

PREFACE

*If you have built castles in the air, your work need not be lost;
that is where they should be. Now put the foundations under them.*

–Henry David Thoreau

It has been a long road to get to the major juncture that is Foundations in Architecture. One might say that this book was a dozen years in the making. The three volumes of *Best Beginning Design Projects,* spanning nearly a decade, were essentially insider commodities exchanges, much like underground newsletters, or virtual chain letters. Going back to Tim McGinty's trailblazing first efforts in 1979, the history of a free exchange of information between beginning design educators became firmly established.

In the intervening years we have witnessed a proliferation of national organizations and conferences dedicated to the beginning design student. These groups forged long-standing bonds that defied geography. Their get-togethers, at first dominated by self-congratulation and mutual commiseration, were nonetheless electric and memorable events that gradually elevated the status of first-year architectural studies from that of tolerated stepchild to one of a recognized and crucial specialization within design education.

Over time, however, it became evident that as valuable as beginning design conferences were, and as enhanced as their value was by the subsequent journals and written proceedings, there was still something missing. Somehow the measured, almost clandestine swapping of working documents, unfettered by the need to "dress up" with formal papers, travel anxiety, stage fright, and the like, seemed still to be the means to fill such a void. So five years after its predecessor, Volume 2 of *Best Beginning Design Projects* was produced by Michael Jordan in 1984. Its expanded format and circulation generated such positive response that after another four years the present authors collaborated on Volume 3 of *Best Beginning Design Projects*, arguably the most ambitious and comprehensive example of this genre to date.

Comprehensive, perhaps, but Volume 3 also sounded its own death knell. The methodology used in producing the series had been pushed about as far as it could go in its present form; it was still too private and exclusive, and cried out for both broader participation and wider circulation. The next logical steps, then, were to enter the international arena, search for a range of pedagogical approaches and techniques, exercise more stringent editorial judgment in the competitive selection process, and, finally, confer with the selected contributors in a forum that would allow their ideas to guide us in the making of this book. Thus the Foundations in Architecture conference convened in Austin in March 1992, attended by those educators representing schools worldwide who were willing to contribute their ideas and their work to this project. The proceedings of the Foundations conference recharted the path of groundwork toward the realization of this book, which had already been proceeding for more than a year. The challenge now is to test our gamble, and see if the many constituencies we are counting on are really out there.

Yes, the road has been long, and twisted. And fun. It seemed like potential bad luck, or maybe pretentiousness, to call this book Volume 1. But we hope sincerely to see a Volume 2 a few years down that same long road.

Image 1. Foundations in Architecture Conference, Austin, Texas, March 1992. Above, clockwise from lower right: Leonard Newcomb, Laura Joines, David Yeomans, Alan Stacell, Robert Hermanson, Joseph Lim, and Nicholas Markovich. Opposite page, left to right: Desmond Hui, Jonathan Friedman, Laura Joines (standing), Michael Jordan, David Covo, Mary Hardin (head down), and Leonard Newcomb.

USER'S GUIDE

This book is organized so that different readers can use it in different ways, or the same reader can use it differently on various occasions.

Following the insightful Foreword by Tim McGinty, the text proceeds from the broad to the specific. In the first section, "Foundations in Architecture," an overview and history of beginning design education is provided, with illustrations of projects from the students of our contributors. The second section, "An Annotated Anthology of Beginning Design Projects," gives two-page synopses of all the projects in the book. The projects appear in alphabetical order by author's names, with more illustrations, and feature marginal annotations drawn from various sources, including our own editorial observations and ideas generated during the Foundations conference. Along the bottom of each double-page spread in this section is a band of text, the "Systematics," indicating the various typologies of the project.

The next three major sections, or Annexes, contain more specific data. Annex 1 provides detailed program notes and supplementary

for professional practitioners who have little or no opportunity for interaction with educational institutions, to gain a sense of the current direction of architectural education

for beginning design students themselves, to allow them to observe and evaluate just where their own program "fits in" on a global scale, and as a means of supplementing and enriching their own local studies

for potential architecture students, and for their high school counselors, to see if the realities of beginning design education match their expectations;

and, finally, for the parents of architecture students as an aid in understanding the idiosyncratic nature of design studio education.

It is to these, and untold others, that we offer this book. In the coming years, the authors would enjoy comments and criticisms, which will help us make Volume 2 of *Foundations in Architecture: An Annotated Anthology of Beginning Design Projects* a yet more useful and enjoyable book.

Owen Cappleman
Austin, Texas

Michael Jack Jordan
Norman, Oklahoma

information about each project, and includes more illustrations; Annex 2 gives brief biographies of the authors of the projects; and Annex 3 explains the Systematics concept, and how it can be used by various readers. Finally, Annex 4 brings the book full circle, with a quizzical essay by David Yeomans. Following the text are the Matrices, two indexed graphs keyed to the Systematics taxonomy in Annex 3.

One way this book may be used is to scan the summarized projects in Section 2 as an easy means of locating a project of interest, and then to move directly to that same project in Annex 1 for a deeper, more detailed understanding. Another tack might be to study Annex 3 to gain an understanding of the Systematics approach to project typologies, and then move to the Matrices to cross-reference projects of specific types, or those that address particular kinds of issues. Of course, the reader could simply read the book from beginning to end, a tactic we highly recommend.

Foundations in Architecture, while written with the beginning design educator uppermost in mind, should have broad appeal and usefulness for a number of other potential readers:

for the advanced design instructor, as a bridge of understanding regarding the preparation his or her current students have received, and as an informed means of providing counsel to the first-year staff to improve and enrich the beginning educational environment for future students;

FOREWORD

I Love Beginnings

By Tim McGinty

The title phrase belongs to Louis I. Kahn, the honored architect and teacher. He said it often, and he said it with enthusiasm. A wonderful, healthy, optimistic view. A gift to me as one of his new graduate students. A view I hadn't felt deeply since I was a freshman. The message has staying power; nearly thirty years later, I still love beginnings—at school, in practice, in life.

This book shares Kahn's love of beginnings. Its projects are imaginative; some are amusing; most are adaptable, and could be modified and used effectively in many schools. The projects, the text, and the annotations are an offering to everyone who loves teaching beginning students. My goal in this foreword is to broaden the scope of discussion and complement the history of architectural education contributed by the book's authors with a more general discussion of beginnings in higher education.

COLLEGE IS A BEGINNING THAT MATTERS

Not every moment is equally a "beginning." Some are more important than others; beginning college is one of those moments. For our students, their first month at college, their first days in graduate school, the first week of a job after graduation, are all special beginnings. But beginning college is a particularly significant event for young adults, as notable and stressful as other life markers such as leaving home for the first time, joining the military, or beginning a marriage. These beginnings are moments when emotions and decisions strike chords that reverberate for many years, and shouldn't be wasted. As teachers, we are privileged participants in one of these moments, and as their first professors, we automatically become champions of higher education, as well as champions of "the cause of architecture," to use Frank Lloyd Wright's phrase. It might be seductive to think that only architecture matters, that the responsibility of introducing students to the ideals, rigors, and ethics of higher education belongs to someone else, to someone who teaches the required university core curriculum, or to the student's living group, or to the students themselves. But whether we want to be or not, we are active participants in the drama. We affect student success, and we are interested in their success and growth as individuals, not because we pretend to be their parents, but because we are their teachers.

THE VERY BEGINNING MATTERS

The first semester in college is crucial for most students. In fact, the very beginning—the first five to ten weeks—matters very much for all entering students, not just for recent high school graduates, but for transfer and adult students as well. There are so many questions demanding answers.: "How am I supposed to behave?" "How am I supposed to use my time?" "What is really valued by my peers?" "What am I supposed to learn?" "What is really expected of me?" "Which assignments are important, and which are not?" Answers to these questions matter and set the tone for the student's entire college experience.

If, after the first few weeks, the values and habits learned do not match faculty expectations, the student probably will not survive in school. Losing students, not because of lack of talent, aptitude, or intelligence, but because of a mismatch between their expectations *about* college, learned *at* college, is not acceptable. As faculty, we cannot dismiss our responsibility and claim that the student, as a young adult, is solely responsible for charting his or her own course. This is too easy. And when students do not succeed, it is too great a loss in an era when the quality of an institution is measured, in part, by retention and graduation rates. Dropping out is painful to everyone, not just the student, the parents, and the institution. We cannot do their work for them but we can at least be frank in explaining our expectations. It turns out that it is more important for students to understand what is expected of them than it is for them to agree.[1] The question for us becomes: "The first weeks: How are we doing?" And "Are we part of the problem or part of the solution?"

FIRST TEACHERS MATTER

Several instructive patterns have been recognized in studies of the careers of prodigies in sports, music, and science.[2] According to the studies, the most important lessons taught by first teachers and coaches is their love and enthusiasm for what they teach. The individual attention they give their students is also critical, but their own mastery is not as important as their ability to share their enthusiasm. It takes a lot of enthusiasm for students to persevere given the drudgery of practice and the inevitable setbacks ahead. Other questions: "Is our enthusiasm evident?" "Do our projects nurture enthusiasm in our students?" "Are we willing to take that risk?" The best teachers take the risk of being enthusiastic and know when to "release" their students and send them on to a more advanced level, a gift both to the student and the next teacher.

TEACHING BEGINNERS TEACHES TEACHERS

Teaching beginners is useful to all teachers. Unfortunately, at many schools teaching beginners only represents an entry ticket to architectural education. Then, as quickly as possible, many "escape" and rise to the presumably loftier mission of teaching more advanced students. A few continue to teach at all levels. Fewer still specialize exclusively in teaching at the beginning. We, however, are the lucky ones. Teaching beginners continually tests one's mastery of what really is fundamental in architecture. The clarity of your thinking is tested. If your thinking is fuzzy, what you say will not make sense to them. But, if you think clearly, your insights may last a lifetime.

Regularly teaching beginners is also a wonderful position from which to test the wisdom and truth of one's thoughts. The teacher's ethics are tested. Beginning students might actually believe you! The teacher's vocabulary is tested. Beginning students are innocent cynics and suspicious of fancy words. The teacher's powers of communication are tested. Beginning students are still close to "the real world," still close to "mass culture." The jargon and rituals of architecture do not yet mean anything to them. More questions: "Can our students understand us?" "Are we *learning* as well as teaching?"

A DIVERSITY OF BEGINNINGS

Motivation, learning styles, personality types! Cultural backgrounds, ambitions, ideals, values! Gender, race, nationality, academic preparation, family traditions! Beginning students are an elite group simply because they qualified for college. But, they are a very diverse elite. For example, students learn in different ways. Some students may only need to briefly hear an idea explained to catch on. For others, a few vivid examples are all that are necessary to confirm their understanding. For many, nothing is clear until they have practical firsthand experience with a concept. Our students represent a variety of learning types, both abstract and concrete, to use the jargon of educational psychology. We teach both, and, surprisingly, both are valid modes. Experienced teachers know being a concrete learner at this stage is no better or worse a predictor of future success than being an abstract learner.[3] We also teach different personality types. The student who never speaks or makes eye contact with the teacher may be paying attention and be as committed to the class as the outwardly judgmental cynic asking all the questions.

Managing a diversity of learning styles, personality types, cultural backgrounds, and levels of motivation creates powerful dilemmas for teachers—the ethics of grading for example. As part of teaching, we assign grades, we evaluate, we pass judgment on progress. We write our projects to reveal "potential" as well as "performance." Grading studio courses raises special problems. Are our judgments premature? Are brightly burning stars rewarded disproportionately compared to those who slowly reveal steady long-term growth? Excellent teachers are skilled in balancing teaching as an encouraging and nurturing endeavor with teaching as a standard-setting judgmental endeavor. More questions: "Are our projects and curricula maximizing growth and understanding or are we rewarding previous experience and current agility?"

More dilemmas. At most schools only a few of the students we see in our beginning classes will graduate in architecture. How do we keep from winnowing out all those least like ourselves and our colleagues instead of seeding, cultivating, and waiting for growth and blossoming? Whom do we anoint and what proof do we have that we have earned this right? I still remember an image from a lecture about architectural education from many years ago. It included a drawing of students being poured into a meat grinder—the old-fashioned kind with a crank handle. Instead of hamburger emerging from the sieve, students popped out, each one exactly like the other. Diversity was gone. In its place was a presumably higher level of homogeneity.[4] Are we truly cultivating diversity, merely accommodating it, or systematically eliminating it?

ARCHITECTURAL EDUCATION AS UNDERGRADUATE EDUCATION

So how are we really doing? How good an education is an architectural undergraduate education? According to one report we are doing a very good job. In a comprehensive University of Tennessee self-study assessing how much a student grows (or regresses) during college, the architecture program stood out on two counts: first, because their entering students had the highest average rating in the study compared to other entering students; and second, because the study showed that their students gained more during college and by the time they graduated, both absolutely and relatively according to their tests, than students in other fields.[5]

We are doing a good job according to other studies as well. How we teach fulfills many of the recommendations noted in a Harvard University self-study of quality in higher education. The Harvard report advises that student satisfaction with undergraduate education is tied to "being involved." This includes being involved in campus activities like drama, singing, newspapers, and service. But more important, they mentioned being involved with peers who are focused on academic projects that the students feel are worthwhile. I remember my delight when, during the first semester in my first architectural history class I suddenly realized that, for the first time, I was in a room with fifty peers, each of whom was interested in architecture! In high school I was the only one who wanted to become an architect. My delight was that I no longer had to apologize for talking and arguing about what interested me! In contrast, according to the Harvard study, students who feel that they have not "found themselves" report that they have not developed academic peer relationships, especially relationships which focus on accomplishing things the students feel are "substantive" and that "stretch" them.[6] "Substantive stretching" is commonplace in the studio; it's something we do every day.

MEASURING CURRICULUM QUALITY

One criticism of beginning design educators, and perhaps implicitly of this book, is that by seeking recognition from our peers, we are missing a truer measure of our efforts. Our successes should not be based merely on what our peers think, or even what our students think. Instead, the quality of a program for beginners should be measured against the contribution it makes to the curriculum as a whole.[7] The building blocks—the individual projects—must be sound, but the gestalt, the whole program, should be considered first. An appropriate measure is the quality of the linking and joining, the reinforcing, the enriching that happens during a student's career at a school. But how do we measure this? A pragmatic measure might be the number of projects regularly offered in advanced courses that expand on projects offered at the beginning. Another measure might be whether or not the vocabulary introduced at the beginning is regularly used by reviewers at all levels. Perhaps the best measure would be the number of senior faculty who regularly teach beginners: the larger the number, the stronger the integration. Can a fifth year critic complain that the students "know nothing" when, in fact, that same critic helped teach those same students as freshmen?

WHAT IS IMPORTANT REALLY IS QUITE SIMPLE

My father asked me a simple but provocative question as I was packing to drive from St. Louis to Lincoln, Nebraska, for my first teaching job: "Do you know what your job as a teacher really is?" My response was a pedantic, "I guess it's to teach the courses I'm assigned to the best of my ability," or something to that effect. "No, it's to get them in the habit of working." Indeed.

A few years ago I had the pleasure of team-teaching with Dick Williams, who headed the graduate program at the University of Illinois for many years. His observation about teaching beginning students: "It's to get them committed to quality." Yes.

Recently I watched several of the PBS programs in the series on ethics. The aphorism the moderator used as his closing for the last

show of the series stuck in my mind: "Make the agony of the question so intense that the only way out is through thinking." The implication, of course, is "Get them in the habit of thinking."

Perhaps what is important really is quite difficult. As a guest lecturer I was asked, during an open discussion, "What is the hardest thing about teaching beginning students?" A surprising question (I like surprising questions almost as much as I like beginnings), and after few moments it occurred to me—the most difficult thing is patience.

As I remember these questions and answers, I also remember that they are not subtle, and every day in my teaching there are subtleties of diversity and subtleties of motivation that I consider. Still, they make good everyday reminders that I measure my thoughts and actions against.

THIS BOOK IS A BEGINNING

The first few weeks count. Setting standards counts. Patience counts. Ultimately, however, teachers and students have to get on with the business of teaching and learning, experiencing, testing, reviewing, applying, and internalizing lessons. This book celebrates the rigors and satisfactions of orchestrating day-to-day accomplishments What we must also address are the strategies and politics that maximize each project's contribution to a whole education.

T. McG.
Arizona State University
Tempe, Arizona

[1]This argument was vividly made by Dr. Harman, professor of psychology at Haverford College, at a lecture given for Danforth Associates at Geneva, Wisconsin, in the early l980s. As a consultant to colleges and universities he discovered that new students, in the first five weeks, learn values and attitudes that last them through the rest of their undergraduate careers. If these values are at odds with those held by the faculty and the administration then the student and the school end up being unhappy with one another. The consequence for small private colleges can be disastrous. Students drop out or only marginally succeed, and the school develops a bad reputation and receives fewer and fewer applications from qualified students and faculty.

[2]The Talent Development Project, headed by Professor Benjamin S. Bloom, at the University of Chicago. The New York Times, March 30, 1982.

[3]Ibid.

[4]This is an image Philip Thiel of the University of Washington-Seattle and others have used to remind teachers of the difference between education and indoctrination. (Editors' note: It is interesting to obvserve that Professor Thiel figures prominently in the closing essay of this book as well.)

[5]Jon P. Coddington (University of Tennessee), "Architecture and the Liberal Arts: A Case Study in the Acquisition of an Education," in the proceedings of *The Liberal Education of Architects*, November 8-9, 1990. Dennis Domer, Ph.D. and Kent F. Spreckelmeyer, Arch. D., AIA, Editors

[6]Richard J. Light. *The Harvard Assessment Seminars: Second Report 1992—Explorations with Students and Faculty about Teaching, Learning and Student Life*. Harvard University, Graduate School of Education and Kennedy School of Government, Cambridge, Massachusetts.

[7]This was essentially the argument made by Professor Juan Bonta, University of Maryland, as the invited respondent for the 1980 ACSA-AIA Teachers' Seminar at Cranbrook.

Foundations in Architecture

Foundations in Architecture

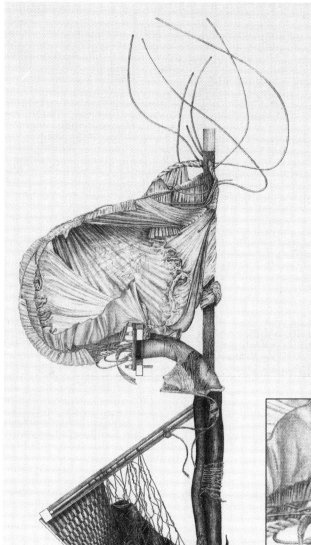

Seen from the outside, universities are monoliths, similar in that regard to like bodies in government, business, or religion. From the inside, though, from the point of view of either faculty or experienced students, such similarities with other insular institutions are less apparent. On close examination, the structure of universities dismantles into fluid hierarchies of administration and individual academic units—often into single personalities—as a clear reflection of the immense diversity of disciplines, emphases, and resources found there. The forces that hold these disparate elements together and allow a university to function are indistinct at best, depending as they often do on the particulars of the separate disciplines and the singular concerns of the participants in those disciplines.

For the beginning university student, this complexity often proves daunting, yet most survive the confusion to become active participants in the academic community. For the beginning student in architecture, however, normal collegiate bewilderment is compounded by unfamiliar teaching methods, especially in the studio; by the requirements of a

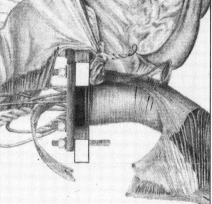

Image 2. Home for the Master of Flemalle. Section and detail by Jane Thompson, student of Lorna McNeur, Cambridge University.

professional curriculum, both mandated and assumed; and by the general mystery surrounding the implications of architectural study on future professional practice. Again, over time students sort these issues out, and, as they progress through the course of study, find answers to most of their questions.

While students choose to study architecture for a variety of reasons, many of them ill-informed (architecture is glamorous, architects are rich), most, if not all, come to their first studio experience thinking they will learn to design buildings. This expectation was fulfilled during the early history of organized architectural education, relying as most North American institutions did on European pedagogy. But for a substantial, and very influential, portion of this century, beginning students were instead assigned problems that seemed more directly related to art, or graphic design, or typography, than to architecture. Only in advanced studios were the principles of architectural design introduced, typically with little or no apparent reference to the earlier studies. Traditions, however, are malleable. Within the past two decades what was at first a subtle shift toward foundation studies in building design has now become a virtual landslide, coming full circle in the history of organized architectural education, each step in the evolution reflecting the spirit of its time.

A BRIEF HISTORY . . .

In the United States, the opening and settling of the West brought with it a wealth of opportunities for adventurous architects from the Eastern Seaboard. Few of them, however, were trained in any formalized context. In general, basic training for architects was conducted under the tutelage of a "master," employing the traditional pattern of apprenticeship common in Europe and elsewhere for centuries. Neophyte architects also came to the profession from allied fields as diverse as furniture making and stonecutting.

The Morrill Act of 1862, which established "land grant" colleges, marked the beginning of the end for this system. The colleges established under this act were to provide a "practical" education. This was in marked contrast to the European tradition, which historically differentiated between "education" and "training." This practical bent proved quite durable, and was most influential in the southern and western regions of the country.[1]

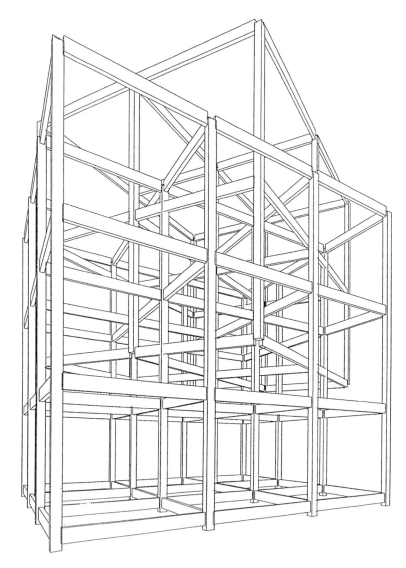

Image 3. Nine-square cube, computer-generated perspective by student of Bruce Lindsey and Paul Rosenblatt, Carnegie Mellon University.

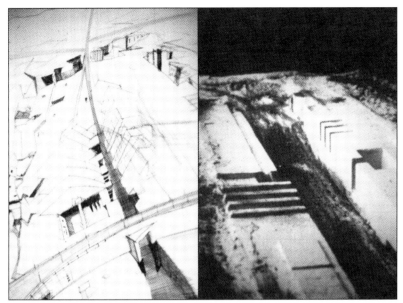

Image 4. Images of "Gateway Project" at Coober Pedy, Australia: left, perspective drawing; right, expressive model. By Danny Heerding, student of John Andrews, Royal Melbourne Institute of Technology.

The formalized, institution-based study of architecture in the United States began in 1865 at the Massachusetts Institute of Technology, following by many years an unrealized proposal in 1814 by Thomas Jefferson for such a program at the University of Virginia. MIT's lead was followed two years later by the University of Illinois at Urbana and in 1871 by Cornell University. Two schools in Canada, at Toronto and Montreal, followed suit in 1876. Standardized professional programs, typically five years in length, were initiated at Cornell in 1922, and had become a standard by 1940.[2] Today there are more than a hundred institutions in North America offering professional programs in architecture, each with its own flavor, each affected by the unique qualities of its history, its faculty, and its setting. Many more programs exist elsewhere in the world. They are quite varied in detail (length of program, emphasis, accrediting procedures and the like), but are remarkably similar in their intent and method—the imparting of shared architectural theory and process in an orderly, consistent, and professional manner.

The Eurocentric Tradition

While an institution may have its own unique character, in the West it is typically built upon a foundation of shared educational method derived in large part from two European models. One model was from nineteenth-century France, the Ecole des Beaux Arts; the other, early twentieth-century and German, the Bauhaus. While the tenets of neither were adopted universally, their influence was pervasive. Schools of architecture throughout the world retain and employ vestiges of these traditions, both essential and trivial, to this day.

The architecture program at the Ecole des Beaux Arts, a uniquely Parisian institution, dates from 1819, and survived until 1968. The Ecole proper came into existence between 1793 and 1819 from the union and transformation of two existing academies, the Académie Royale de Peinture et de Sculpture, founded in 1648, and the Académie Royale d'Architecture, founded in 1671.[3]

The aim of the Académie Royale d'Architecture, a true product of the Age of Reason, was to " bring forth a more exact knowledge and a more correct theory"[4]; in short, a true and perfect architecture. Principles based on classical forms (initially Greek and Roman; later from other sources, especially French) were devised; when properly applied, so the theory ran, they could not help but result in perfection.

Once established, the Ecole des Beaux Arts became a world center for architectural study. Foreign students were common; during the course of its existence, over 500 Americans undertook its program of study. There they found a system physically external to the Ecole modeled in part on the tradition of the guild—the master and his apprentices—and a hierarchical student body. The pinnacle of the student ranks was occupied by the best student, who was the current winner of the Grand Prix, a design competition held among the most advanced students. The base of the hierarchy consisted of beginning students, the aspirants.

In contrast to today's universities, students were admitted to the Ecole proper only after first undertaking extended study with the "patron of an atelier,"[5] the studio master, and then passing entrance examinations for the Ecole "which tested mathematics, descriptive geometry, history, drawing, and, most important, architectural design."[6] Students in the atelier not only benefited from contact with the studio master, but formed what was for all intents a self-governing community of peers, typically directed by the oldest student. The more experienced students tutored the novices; in turn, the novices assisted the advanced students with their work. There was no set number of years for progress through the program; the only limitation was one's thirtieth birthday. Finally, there were no degrees awarded. Only the winner of the Grand Prix "graduated"; the rest simply left the Ecole.

The atelier, or the studio, was the heart of architectural education at the Ecole. The ateliers were "off campus," on the river Seine's Left Bank. The Ecole itself offered lectures on a variety of subjects including history, mathematics, and construction. But the student learned to design in the autonomous ateliers, which were, in essence, "private schools of design."[7] The more famous or influential the master of the atelier, the more students he attracted; the most prized positions were in the studios of former Grand Prix winners.

From the first day in the atelier students were thrust into the mysteries, and the facts, of architecture—the study of materials, the response of those materials to natural light, the ordering of architectural space, the necessities of structure, and, most important, the study of classical architecture.

The principal teaching method of the Ecole centered on monthly design competitions, the concours. The problem for each competition was written by the senior professor of theory, and subject matter alternated between the esquisse, the sketch solution, and projets rendu, rendered projects. Concours in construction were posed, as were similar problems in mathematics and a variety of drawing techniques. The éléments analytiques, designed to introduce the student to classical motifs, was introduced in 1876. The duration of the concours varied from twelve hours for the esquisse to four months for construction. While participation in the various concours was voluntary, promotion was based on successful completion of a specified number of concours covering a given set of issues. Evaluation of student submissions to the concours was conducted in private reviews by the faculty of the Ecole, a closed jury of experts. In effect, these reviews were interim examinations; the Grand Prix was the final examination.

The philosophy and method of the Ecole became the core of architectural education in the United States during the early part of this century. This was accomplished via the importation of Beaux Arts professors, who were often Americans returning home from study in Paris. These same graduates of the Ecole founded the Beaux Arts Institute of Design in New York under the direction of Lloyd Warren, the first American to receive a diploma in Paris. Schools throughout the country were affiliated with the Institute, and sent the products of their concours to New York for evaluation. The winners of the American

Image 5. Analytique and other Beaux Arts drawing techniques by Thomas L. Sorey, Massachusetts Institute of Technology, July and August 1921 (courtesy of College of Architecture Archives, University of Oklahoma).

version of the Grand Prix were, in turn, sent to Europe for further study and travel.

While the Beaux Arts method per se, especially its reliance on classical models, is no longer a prominent feature of architectural education, its legacy is certainly visible. Most architectural curricula are organized around a core of design studios, where students study under a particular teacher—in effect, the patron. The teacher sets problems for the studio. But unlike the Ecole method, participation is not voluntary. The problem solutions are usually evaluated in review by a jury, which is open to students and is considered an essential educational event. There continue to be companion courses in the essentials of the discipline—construction, mathematics, and history, for example—and in some schools the mentoring of neophytes by more advanced students is encouraged. Finally, there is direct contact with the teacher, and a sense of community in most architecture schools rarely seen in other university disciplines.

The second of the European traditions, that of the Bauhaus, began in 1919 (exactly a century after the founding of the architecture program at the Ecole) in Weimar, Germany, a city with a rich artistic heritage that included Bach, Goethe and Liszt. Like the Ecole, the Bauhaus was the product of a merger, this time between the Grand-Ducal Academy of Art, founded in the eighteenth century, and the Arts and Crafts School in Weimar, headed by Henry van de Velde, a leader in the Belgian Art Nouveau movement.

The Bauhaus, which translates as "house for building," was first headed by Walter Gropius, the scion of a family of architects and painters and a prominent architect in his own right. While the ideals and ideas of the Bauhaus were markedly different from those of the Ecole, the organizational lessons of the Ecole had been heeded. Here too the master-directed studio, or workshop, was the core of the curriculum. Here too the design problem was the chief means of imparting architectural wisdom. Here too the sense of community was profound. But here the similarities end, for Gropius, in the rubble of post–World War I Germany, had other ideas about the future of architecture.

Gropius was not only a "tough administrator and shrewd politician" but also "an idealist and a visionary."[8] His concept, as delineated in a manifesto marking the opening of the Bauhaus, was built around the idea of the building as the ultimate expression of all creative activity. He maintained that "art cannot be taught, but craftsmanship can, and that architects, painters and sculptors are craftsmen in the fullest sense of the word."[9] His ultimate goal, and the organizing principle

behind the curriculum, was the uniting of craft with industry. To that end the curriculum was structured around a series of workshops in various materials—wood, metals, textiles, and the like—taking advantage of the facilities established in Weimar by van de Velde. The workshops were preceded by the Preliminary Course, required of all students. Studies in architecture followed successful completion of the workshops, and were approximately the equivalent of today's graduate school.

To put the ideals of the Bauhaus in proper perspective, it must be remembered that there were undeniably powerful forces at work in the world of 1920's Europe. Not the least of these was the war and the reconstruction that followed. Einstein's theory of relativity was published in 1905. In Paris (again) Picasso and Braque were hard at work developing the methods of Cubism, and artists from across Europe were making what amounted to pilgrimages to their studios. Some of these pilgrims ultimately became faculty at the Bauhaus (especially those connected with the Dutch movement de Stijl and the Constructivists of Russia and Eastern Europe), bringing with them radical new ideas about the visual world. The work of Frank Lloyd Wright, which proved an enormous influence on the development of European Modernism, was better known in Europe than in America. Mass production, especially in America, was having a profound effect on traditional means of production in Europe, and in general there was a delight in the "modern" and a barely constrained anticipation, in some quarters at least, of a new order. The Bauhaus proved to be a key player in this drama of transition, soon becoming a focal point for the study and practice of modernist ideals.

Gropius's first faculty appointment was Johannes Itten, a Swiss painter. Hired to formulate and implement the Preliminary Course, which he insisted on calling the Basic Course, Itten proved to be a brilliant and charismatic but eccentric teacher. Robert Hughes, in The Shock of the New, describes Itten as "a 'faddist' who would have been quite at home on the coast of California in the seventies."[10]

Itten's program for beginning students consisted of three elements: (1) a detailed study of nature, consisting of both representation of materials and experiments with them; (2) compositional and textural studies with various materials; and (3) analysis of "old master" paintings.[11] His students were encouraged to delve into the emotional content of the materials in order to "liberate" their creative abilities. Itten described their efforts as "a mad tinkering,"[12] the products of which were, in the context of the Beaux Arts or apprenticeship tradition, quite revolutionary.

However effective his method, Itten's manner was, at least to some, subversive, and Gropius relieved him of responsibility in 1923. Prior to Itten's departure Wassily Kandinsky, a Russian-born painter, graphic artist, and writer, joined the faculty. He taught two fundamental courses parallel to the Basic Course to all Weimar students, one in the basic elements of form, another in color. In 1923 Gropius made two additional faculty appointments—Josef Albers, the first Bauhaus graduate to (eventually) assume the role of master, and Lazlo Moholy-Nagy, a Hungarian Constructivist. Their educational methodologies were distinctly different, and often at odds, leading ultimately to the division of the Basic Course into two elements, the first taught by Albers, the second by Moholy-Nagy.

Albers's course, like Itten's, was focused on experiments with materials. Gone, however, was the quirkiness of emotional issues. In its place was a program based on economy of means: "[He] limited himself to a minimum of means but not a minimum of meaning."[13] Moholy-Nagy's projects, as a companion to those of Albers, were concerned with more concrete experiments in the explication of form and the complex development of space. Given his additional responsibilities in the photography workshops, as well as his own work, his projects were intimately concerned with the interaction of form and light . To quote from Moholy-Nagy's writings, "Today spatial design is an interweaving of shapes; shapes which are ordered into well defined, if invisible, space relationships; shapes which represent the fluctuating play of tensions and forces."[14]

In 1925 the Bauhaus relocated from Weimar to Dessau. This move was precipitated by the city fathers of Weimar, who were, in essence, quite unhappy with the strange goings-on at the Bauhaus. Dessau was more receptive of the avant-garde, and there Gropius, with funding from the city, built one of the icons of modern architecture—the Bauhaus building. Kandinsky, Albers and Moholy-Nagy, among others, moved with the school, and continued their work in the Basic Course. Moholy-Nagy left in 1928 and Kandinsky in 1932. Albers remained until 1933, when the school was closed by the Third Reich for being "degenerate."

An exodus to the United States by many of the most prominent faculty followed the closing of the school in Dessau. Walter Gropius joined the faculty of Harvard. Albers first relocated to Black Mountain College in North Carolina and then to Yale. Moholy-Nagy went to the New Bauhaus in Chicago, and Mies van der Rohe, the last director of the Bauhaus, to the Armour Institute in Chicago (now the Illinois Institute of Technology).

Image 6. Typical latter-day post-Bauhaus "basic design" studies, by David Harriss, student of Owen Cappleman, University of Texas, c. 1966.

Naturally enough, they brought with them—intact—the methods of the Bauhaus. Schools across America made wholesale changes in curricula in response to these new and extremely seductive ideas, away from the puritanical classicism of the Ecole and toward the puritanism (some would say, from the vantage point of hindsight) of the new modernism. The Preliminary Course in its various incarnations became "Basic Design," and its methods, again minus Itten's requirement of emotion, were adopted verbatim not only by schools of architecture, but by fine arts programs as well. In fact, for a time, foundation courses in art and architecture were identical. Abstract studies, later typified derisively as "spots and dots," became the rule. Only a few schools, the University of Oregon among them, adopted the entire Bauhaus program of collaboration between art, craft and

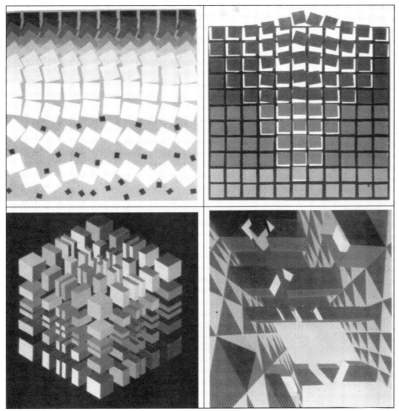

Image 7. Four recent Bauhaus-inspired color studies by students of Munehiko Taniguchi, Kogakuin University.

architecture. It must be kept in mind, however, that these momentous changes in substance in no way modified the organizational lessons learned from the Ecole.

The influence of the pedagogy was pervasive, and continues in diminished form to this day. The results of Bauhaus methodology, as translated and interpreted by schools everywhere, has permanently colored our perception of architecture, and has had, for better or worse, a profound effect on world architecture.

The United States 1950–1980

The years 1950 to 1980 were essentially a period of stasis followed by rapid growth and change, a description not only of architectural education but of the world at large. The Journal of Architectural Education, the official voice of the Association of Collegiate Schools of Architecture, remains the primary record of this period in education, and there is little to be found in its pages relating to the beginning study of architecture. This may be a product of a consistently held pedagogy based on the principles discussed above. There are exceptions to this silence, however. In a 1957 article in The Journal of Architectural Education titled "An Introduction to the Study of Architecture," William Shellman of Princeton notes: "Once a student sees that architectural forms can only be conceived as the activity of giving form to feeling, he is aware that architecture, like the other arts, is a humanistic discipline."[15]

Shellman goes on to describe the role of drawing, especially in the "study of artistic structure in works of art, painting, sculpture and architecture."[16] These quotations reflect, it seems, the ambiguity of the age, simultaneously recalling the tenets of the Bauhaus and pointing to the concerns of the next decade.

As world conditions changed radically during the late 1960s and early 1970s, chinks began to appear in the ramparts of the historically unassailable Bauhaus method. Broad and ill-focused awareness of the architect's role in social and environmental problems appeared, as did the idea of "design process"—essentially the employment of scientific method as a means for solving architectural problems. "Process" became an important buzzword of design education, spurred by the publication in 1964 of Christopher Alexander's Notes on the Synthesis of Form. In this book Alexander proposed a method for "systematically structuring physical design problems,"[17] a process that relied on intensive, and often protracted, analysis of factors affecting an architectural solution. M.A. Milne and C.W. Rusch, in an extended dialog titled "The Death of the Beaux Arts" and published in 1968, note that "The method [of architectural education] is being changed to fit the man, and architectural education is more and more training students in scientific techniques." They also comment that "architects have not been trained as scientists, and they don't expect their work to have that character." While they were essentially in support of Alexander's method (which Alexander himself was in the process of modifying), they observe toward the end of the discussion that "this whole approach can only go so far in producing architectural reality," and that "subjective judgments still must be made in the face of uncertain or incomplete information."[18] These comments reflect in large part the difficulty of a hybrid pedagogy, which was to be at once scientific and intuitive. The methods of process and analysis, however, as components of a design solution, continue to be of importance today in the majority of design curricula.

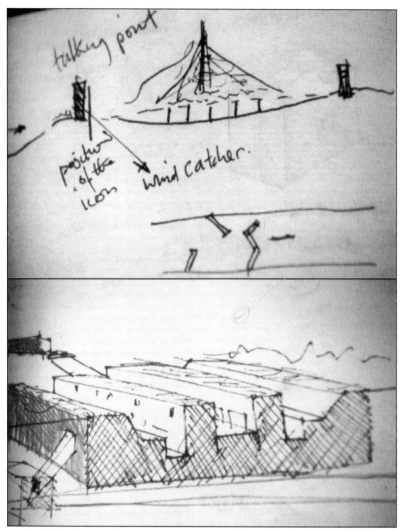

Image 8. Concept sketches for the "Gateway Project" by Danny Heerding, Royal Melbourne Institute of Technology.

Recent History

Through the course of this often difficult period, the regard formerly given to beginning studies—"basic design"—declined steadily in the face of mounting pressures from the public, from the profession, and from within the university. The relevance of beginning studies based on "spots and dots" was widely questioned, both by teachers, the majority of whom were products of the method, and by students, who often could not relate beginning studies to more advanced, building-focused work. A contributor to this book, Professor Jonathan Friedman, sums it up best:

> So. . . teaching beginning design in architecture is in one sense the lowest of the low: At the bottom of the rank in instruction in studio, which is lowest in the architecture school program, which has little status within the profession, which itself stands low in the eyes of the general public.[19]

While The Journal of Architectural Education continued to be the official organ of the universities, other voices were beginning to be heard as a consequence of the frustration inherent in Professor Friedman's summation. In 1979 Professor Tim McGinty, then of the Univer-

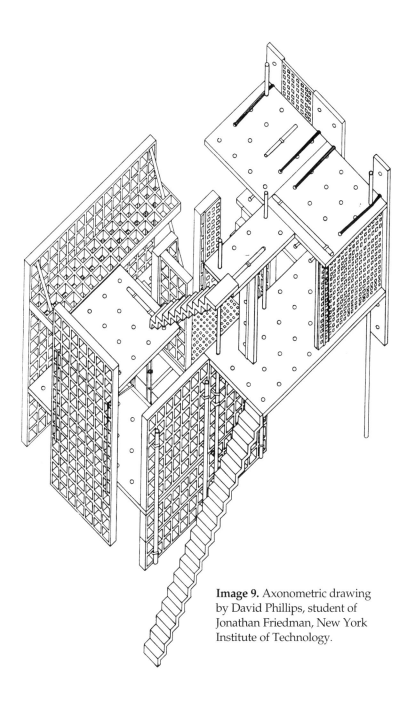

Image 9. Axonometric drawing by David Phillips, student of Jonathan Friedman, New York Institute of Technology.

sity of Wisconsin-Milwaukee, advertised nationally for contributors to an informal collection of beginning design problems, which he called Best Beginning Design Projects. The contributors were promised, in return for the use of their work, a complete set of submissions in return. The final document served as the first reasonable record of the status of beginning design education in nearly thirty years, and marked the beginning of an awareness that change was in the air. Of the thirty-nine projects submitted, eleven fit within the general outlines of the Bauhaus model. The real surprise, and the harbinger of change, was that the balance of the projects were concerned with a broad array of architectural issues, and five were written around an authentic building design problem, completely forgoing tradition in favor of direct admission to the mysteries of architecture.

Following McGinty's lead, at roughly five-year intervals, the authors of this book assembled two more collections of Best Beginning Design Projects, expanding the scope with each step, and including fledgling efforts at analysis of the submissions. The results were clear: Each successive edition illustrated the decline in purely abstract studies in favor of building design, or "architecture" issues. The second edition, for instance, contained only five projects that were Bauhausian in character; thirty were architectural, fifteen of which were concerned with the design of a building. Of the thirty-eight projects in Volume 3 of Best Beginning Design Projects, published in 1988, eleven were abstract, eleven studied a range of architectural issues, and sixteen were purely building design. The collection of work contained in this book includes only two projects that fit squarely within the Bauhaus model, although vestiges of the Bauhaus remain in a few others. While there are some bumps in the raw quantities of abstract problems in these collections, the indications are that the European traditions that have held sway for the past fifty years, particularly those of the Bauhaus, are receding into history at a majority of schools of architecture. And, some would say, perhaps not a moment too soon.

ON TO THE MILLENNIUM . . .

This discussion has been intended to be simply an outline; the reality of the matter was not nearly so tidy. There were important and often quite influential alternative views, as well as traditional values, within each of the directions described. Recent history, for instance, has seen the rise of first Postmodernism, now Deconstruction. Attending these has been a focus on historical and theoretical issues. These radical alternatives have arisen within the context of essentially traditional—and professional—curricula, not to mention within an even more traditional—and conservative—profession. While changes in academia, especially in the beginning years, are slow in coming, the shift toward the design of buildings, or at least the study of architectonic issues, is in some way a response to these new ideas. The authors of this book had hoped that some hints of new trends might emerge from the collection of work that follows, as indeed they have. There are, for example, a number of projects that recognize what is coming to be the central role of computers in architecture. There are several projects based on social and cultural issues. For instance, one project is an extended and intense involvement in the traditions of aboriginal Australia, and another concerns the plight of the homeless in America. There are projects that continue to delve into the relationship between architecture and the arts, be they visual or written, and there are continuing paths in more traditional arenas such as structures and the

landscape. Finally, there are projects that are poetic in nature, and question the limits of what architectural education is all about.

It must be remembered that the work contained in this book is merely a sampling, albeit an international one. Like any sample, it indicates only broad directions, not explicit tracks. But most important, there is plurality. If consensus is the grist of historical traditions, a fierce independence seems to be the rule of the near future, as we rush ineluctably into the next century and the dawn of a new millennium.

NOTES

1. Richard E. McCommons, AIA, ed., Guide to Architecture Schools in North America (Washington, D.C.: Association of Collegiate Schools of Architecture Press, 1991), p. viii.
2. Ibid.

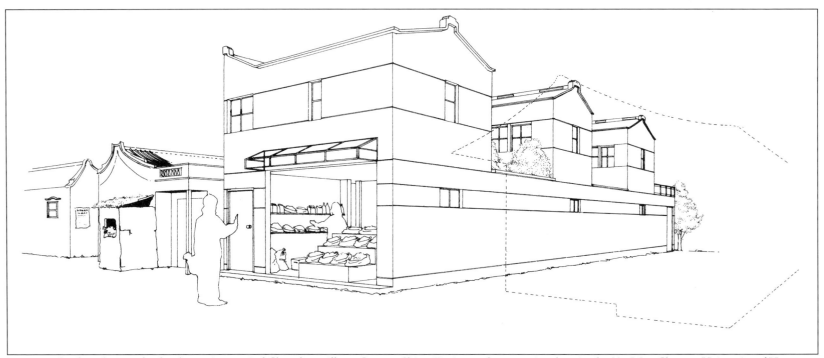

Image 10. Student design of a shophouse in a typical Chaozhou village, Canton, China. Design and perspective drawing by Yat Man Cheong, University of Hong Kong.

3. Arthur Drexler, ed., The Architecture of the Ecole des Beaux-Arts (New York: The Museum of Modern Art, 1977), p. 62.
4. Ibid.
5. Ibid., p. 82.
6. Ibid.
7. Ibid., p. 89.
8. Gillian Naylor, The Bauhaus Reassessed: Sources and Design Theory (New York: E. P. Dutton, 1985), p. 53.
9. Ibid., p. 55.
10. Robert Hughes, The Shock of the New (New York: Alfred A. Knopf, 1991), p. 194.
11. Herbert Bayer, Walter Gropius, and Ise Gropius, eds., Bauhaus: 1919–1928 (Boston: Charles T. Branford Co., 1952), p. 30.
12. Naylor, p. 78.
13. Ibid., p.156.
14. Bayer, Gropius, and Gropius, eds., p. 122.

13

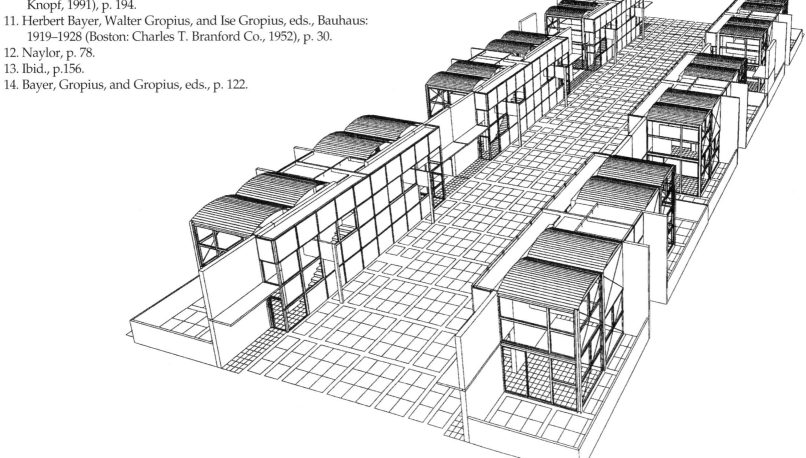

Image 11. Computer-generated aerial perspective drawing of "Main Street" by student of Charles Graves, Jr., Kent State University.

15. William Shellman, "An Introduction to the Study of Architecture," Journal of Architectural Education, vol. XII, nos. 2 and 3 (Summer 1957), p. 21.
16. Ibid.
17. M.A. Milne and C.W. Rusch, "The Death of the Beaux Arts: The Cal-Oregon Experiment in Design Education," Journal of Architec-tural Education, vol. XXII, nos. 2 and 3 (March 1968 and May, 1968), p. 22.
18. Ibid., p. 27.
19. Jonathan Friedman, "Playing with Blocks: An Overview from Underneath." Keynote speech: 7th National Conference on the Beginning Design Student, Santa Fe, New Mexico, April 5, 1990.

14

Image 12. Computer-generated ground level perspective drawing of "Main Street" by student of Charles Graves, Jr., Kent State University.

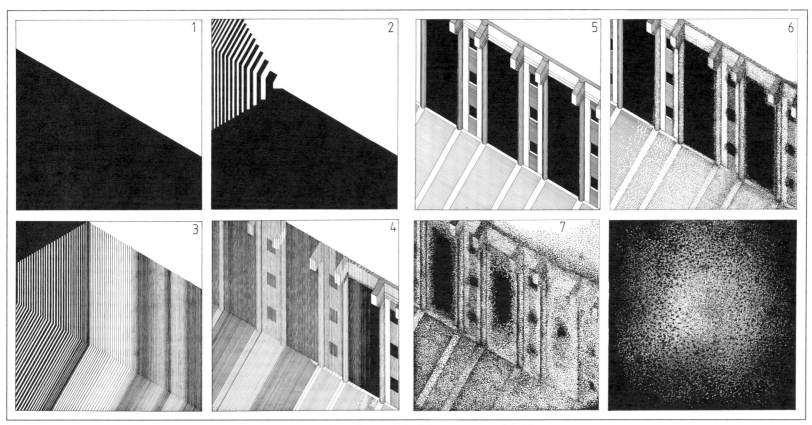

Image 13. "Upwards, Downward and Away" by Alen Bauer, student of Janez Suhadolc, University of Ljubljana.

15

An Annotated Anthology
of Beginning Design Projects

17

This section features condensed versions of the twenty-six projects contributed to this book. It includes some illustrations of student solutions to each project, and marginal annotations drawn from various sources, primarily the Foundations in Architecture Conference and the book authors' editorial observations. For a lengthier, more detailed study of these projects, and supplementary information about them and their schools of origin, please see Annex 1, "Project and Program Details." Also appearing in Annex 1 are more illustrations of student solutions and other pertinent details.

Along the bottom of each double-page spread appears a single band of text with selected words italicized. This band represents an abbreviated version of the "Systematics," and their specific reference to the project at hand. For more understanding of the systematics concept, what it means, and how to use it, please see Annex 3, "Systematics: A Taxonomy of Educational Design Objectives." Also note the Matrix that follows the text at the end of the book. This device allows the reader to cross-reference all projects based on specific taxons.

The Journey

John Andrews
Royal Melbourne Institute of Technology
Melbourne Australia

Projects that concern themselves overtly with the emotional and social, not to mention cultural, development of students are very rare. The norm is that a student "grows" as an architect in the studio and as a human being elsewhere. This norm is clearly challenged at Royal Melbourne Institute of Technology.

While the "field trip" is not uncommon, an extended venture such as this certainly is. It is tantamount to foreign travel, and is no doubt equally complex to organize and conduct; the voluminous preparatory materials given the students — from exotic insect-bite remedies to shelter-making instructions — attest to this.

Mining the treasure-lode that is Australia.

The primary concern of "The Journey" is not isolated formal building blocks of design, but rather an accumulative "journey" of creative imagination that raises design issues in the course of its path. It exists as an inquiry that moves inward into spaces that provoke students' creativity. It begins on the exterior — recording and observing existing environments — then guides students to start exploring within themselves, and within a building's fabric, ultimately to delve within an environment's form and structure to identify, explore, and create spatially. "The Journey" covers four areas of emphasis: Perception and Measured Drawing, Travel, Objectives, and Synthesis. Each area culminates in an exhibition.

PERCEPTION AND MEASURED DRAWINGS

This part of the program provides a framework for direct experience of existing city surroundings, and an introduction to the language and concerns of the built environment. Through developing abilities to sketch, draw freehand perspectives and work in different media, students begin to hone individual observations, and to move beyond attempts to make "exact" recordings. Yet at the same time, the formal qualities of the buildings are also explored with measured exactness. Conducting measured surveys and drawing plans, elevations, and details introduces students to the precision and the conventions of measured drawings, and establishes opportunities for conversation, through drawing, with related disciplines.

TRAVEL

The exploration of known built environments now develops into an investigation and engagement with the landscape. The design program always includes a travel studio to afford this option. These long and far-ranging trips provide an opportunity for students to meet each other and the lecturers in a relaxed atmosphere, and to move from being observers of an urban environment to consciously locating and positioning themselves within a landscape.

Exercises focused on "the camp" lead from developing a personal understanding and awareness of the environment to beginning to translate — and to abstract — experiences and impressions in sketches and in built form. In addition, groups work toward a definition of their collective place in, and response to, the landscape.

Through the use of sketches and maps, students identify borders around the campsite, a process that begins to analyze and define the reality of the campsite area. Students map personal interpretations of

SYSTEMATICS TAXON ONE: *Conceptual. Analytic.* Nonobjective/Compositional. Compositional/Architectonic. *Architectural* TAXON TWO: *Poetic. Metaphoric.* Literary. *Human Concerns. Environment.* Visual Vocabulary. *Procedural.* Programmatic. Tecthe area, such as light, rock formations, sound, or atmosphere. Sketches often examine small details in the landscape as a version of the universe in micro. These reveal forms that can be examined, interpreted, and abstracted as a catalyst for design. Locating personal spaces, students respond to these spaces in poetry, and also built form, creating temporary sculptures as representations of themselves in the landscape.

OBJECTIVES

The study area "objectives" seeks to loosen up thinking, to question, explore and experiment with possibilities, and to propose new forms and thoughts with respect to everyday objects. It extends ideas of designing via the landscape and personal reference, begun in the travel studio, to include other areas of reference such as history, culture, and function.

Focusing on the "object" is central to this study area, introducing creative exploration in three dimensions, and exposing students to formalized design tools, related disciplines, and the idea of visualizing nonreality. The students' task is to design and produce an object to meet a set of parameters. A series of day *esquisses* support the development of the object by exploring the many levels beyond the functional one at which the objects most obviously exist. Through the *esquisses* students are encouraged not only to research design precedent and to record existing forms, but also to work beyond these. They are asked to challenge their prejudices and to reveal the hidden possibilities that can generate and support their design. Finally, the objects develop a "precious" status with the advent of a curated exhibition.

SYNTHESIS

"Synthesis" offers the opportunity to integrate understanding from the previous studios in the design of interior environments. The studio works through a process leading from object to space in a series of conceptual shifts that work toward an unpredicted endpoint. The exercises transfer focus from personal expression to questioning the dynamics of the physical space our bodies occupy.

The final exercise is a synthesis of these explorations, developing nine consecutive images of a creative and physical narrative within their imagined spaces. This process empowers the students as they translate their space in scale and medium, taking control of what is seen and the space that is viewed. The students create a narrative of vision and experience, and in maintaining control of "nonreality" they define themselves as designers.

Image 14. left side: group expression, "Ocean"; right side: personal sculpture, "River," by Leon Lopata.

The extraordinary range of scales and activities engaged in "The Journey" is truly remarkable.

The pedagogical approach employing a series of seemingly self-contained exercises leading to an unexpected accretive "whole" at the end is found elsewhere in this book. What is unusual here is the breathtaking scope of such engagements.

Recognition of the final exhibition as a significant learning experience transcending mere "show-and-tell" is a clear indication of the teacher's understanding of cognitive growth.

19

Nine Square Matrix

James Bagnall, William Benedict, and Laura Joines
California Polytechnic State University at San Luis Obispo
San Luis Obispo, California

The nine-square problem has a rich history. It has been employed by architects as diverse as Palladio and Hejduk, and is the foundation for other projects in this collection.

The inclusion of visual "research" is a particularly valuable component of this exercise. While often included through preliminary studies for solutions, its explicit use as research is far less common, much less its use in the final presentation.

The "Nine Square Matrix" project shares objectives with the other fundamentals problems at Cal Poly. Specifically, it supports communication objectives in the areas of model building, layout, and concept diagramming, and draws on general design principles previously introduced and explored. The project's theoretical focus is the definition of architectural space. Its key objectives include being able to define a hypothesis or strategy for investigating complexity in spatial definition; being able to consciously manipulate the number, attributes, and organization of architectural elements to create spatial compositions of relative complexity; and being able to communicate in words and diagrams the hypothesis investigated, concepts employed, and discoveries made in the investigation. The project provides students a formal format for exploring basic issues of architectural design related to simplicity and complexity, proportion and scale, and the defining of sets of relationships between parts and the whole.

In this exercise the student is to design and construct a total of nine architectonic compositions of spaces, each illustrating combinations of floors, walls, and roofs defined in a matrix provided by the faculty. The horizontal edge of the matrix consists of three "continua" of simple-to-complex solutions. The vertical edge establishes the combinations of the basic architectural elements of floor, walls, and roof to be investigated (see Investigation Matrix, p. 79). The use of the matrix and continua ensures that the models—the externalization and representation of ideas—become sources of understanding and discovery. Design decisions are seen not as right or wrong but appropriate given the context and goals.

The project is given an explicit research or investigation orientation. It requires the student to consciously identify a set of factors to be investigated, and to explicitly communicate them to others. This process builds both vocabulary and the ability to translate ideas into words and diagrams. It also aids in building an understanding of the difference between a concept and a specific manifestation of that concept. The project's meaningfulness grows in direct proportion to the degree to which students invest themselves in some discovery.

The solution to each continuum is to exhibit three clearly different and evenly spaced levels of complexity, with a smooth gradation across the continuum. Each composition within a continuum must contain a minimum of three visually accessible, inhabitable spaces, as well as scale human figures.

Solutions to the exercise are presented in models constructed of white or colorless opaque, translucent, or transparent materials. The models must be accompanied by a two-dimensional presentation that communicates in words and diagrams the complexity hypothesis; the specific concepts employed in its exploration; and observations on the successes, failures, and discoveries of the investigation. This component of the presentation is an essential part of the research orientation of the project. Its role is to make explicit the hypothesis or positions that the investigation is exploring, identify the specific concepts being manipulated and reflect on the exploration's discoveries. The process of making project-thinking explicit facilitates conscious decision making and meaningful learning.

Image 15. Nine-Square Matrix model by student of Will Benedict.

Mapping Tools

Peter Beard
Architectural Association
London, UK

There are too few projects that challenge students to actually build. Firsthand experience is essential regardless of scale.

Approaching a traditional convention (in this case, surveying and mapping) in an unconventional way can provide meaningful cognitive insights for the students.

Some of the projects in this book stress the importance of a specific, visitable site, while others with site-sensitive issues employ a figmentary site. How does the reader regard this distinction?

This is a study of how perception is framed by the instruments and methodologies we adopt for looking. Consideration is given to the distance and relation between the means of representation that architects use to develop proposals and the real, lived-in space of buildings and places. The study also looks at the relationship of perceived reality and its representation, the correspondence between paper and land, between a map and real space. At the same time, it is about mastering techniques of making and craft, tested in the construction of a working instrument of measurement; representing qualities of a place (site) in a drawing (map); and relating a built artifact (the instrument) to a site and to a set of conceptual intentions.

Central to the project was the making of a tool with which to effect this correspondence. This involved detailed issues of working with materials, jointing and construction, dimension and scale, all of these being considered in relation to the operation and use of the tool. The tool acts as a mediator between the body of the surveyor and the site surveyed. It frames the surveyor's perception and actions, and in so doing uncovers a hidden text; it simultaneously blinds and speaks.

From the original project brief given to the students: "Primary tools of your own devising will be used to make and measure land—staking out and scratching the earth's surface, then mapping and recording using the techniques of the archaeologist, surgeon, surveyor, draftsman, navigator, physicist, tailor, and geographer. . . ."

The project was originally seen as the starting point for a building proposition on the chosen site, a piece of wasteland at Canning Town, East London. The act of mapping the site in this direct and individual way was meant to provide a singular and detailed perception of that place. This could then be exploited as a theme for the building proposition. However, what was originally seen as preparatory work—the design and building of the instrument—became a project in itself, and the building proposition was abandoned.

The project was introduced to the students with a visit to the Whipple Museum of the History of Science in Cambridge, England, which has an extensive collection of surveying devices dating from the eighteenth century and earlier. These surveying devices suggested a range of approaches to the idea of measurement, and provoked a consideration of the way tools frame a perception of space. The project brief did not ask for the re-creation of such tools, nor did it ask for a measurement of the site in the same terms, i.e., spatial dimension.

The tools that were constructed challenged the land surveyor's perception of space. The proposition is that many things in a place contribute to its qualities and conditions; thus, every reading of a site is subjective. What is to be measured is open to question.

The tool, as the students were asked to devise it, is a highly condensed architectural piece of its own. A specific site was chosen to focus attention on an actual rather than an imagined situation. The tools become specific to an individualized rather than a generalized perception. It is important that the earth of the site be touched; the state of the wasteland site was such that digging, marking, and other forms of intervention could be made freely.

The process of accurate fabrication naturally demands a parallel document of drawings and notes. Firsthand experience reinforces awareness of the necessity of these documents in the construction process. The relatively small-scale nature of the pieces enabled working drawings to be made at a 1:1 scale for the most part, and with this, the relation of artifact to a simple set of working drawings is clearly made. In a similar way, knowledge of materials is developed through direct experience. The use of steel or brass demands a visit to the supplier for the purpose of investigating possible raw materials. Once selected, the materials' properties are explored through their working.

Test pieces were made prior to fabrication of the final piece to enable the refinement of construction techniques. Finally, the building of the instruments took on a life of its own, becoming an extended process that ultimately resulted in significant modification of the problem—the cancellation of the building design phase.

It is interesting how, at times, a project—or here, a piece of a project—can take on a life of its own. It is equally interesting, and admirable, that a teacher can have the flexibility to "let it happen" and the courage to effect a mid-course correction that abandons preconceived plans.

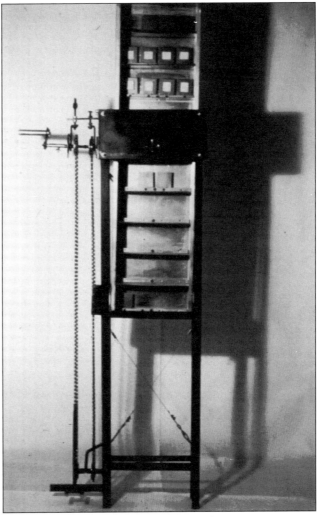

Image 16. Full-scale model of mapping tool by Laurence Liauw.

A Commemorative Pavilion for Joseph Cornell

Owen Cappleman
University of Texas at Austin
Austin, Texas

Might this be too large a project for five weeks? Is there the danger of superficiality?

Deconstruction, indeed...

Part 2 seems excellent, drawing on the best of the Bauhaus tradition in a new and fresh manner.

Very rich. Perhaps the richest part of the project.

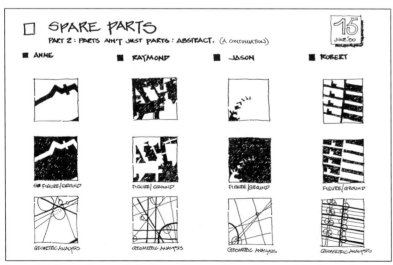

Image 17. Figure/ground studies and reversals, and geometries. From the sketchbook of teaching assistant YewKee Cheong, who drew each student's oeuvre during review.

The intentions of the Cornell project are many and varied, but three common threads run through the entire process: broadening the students' horizons through the abandonment of stereotypes and clichés, learning not to be precious with one's work, and developing the habit of seeking the unexpected.

The Cornell project was specially designed for the intensive five-week summer first-year studio at Texas, and although the project is very much about Joseph Cornell, the actual working title of the project is "Spare Parts," due to the particular methodology employed. The pavilion itself is the last of the five parts of the course, and is only realized at the very end of the summer session.

The first part is humorously referred to as "Deconstruction." Each student brings a model kit to class, separates all the pieces, and, after editing them, places them in a common pile. This pile becomes the "bank" of parts, from which all students freely draw their initial source materials for the next phases of the project.

Part 2, "Abstract Analysis," explores figure/ground relationships, tonality and color, and geometric analysis. The first figure/ground studies, based on a typology of figure/ground conditions, are created by projecting silhouettes of various arrangements of selected parts on an overhead projector. These studies, done in black collage on a white field, are then "reversed" in ink on vellum. The reversal process is simply exchanging black for white in each image, but the meaning becomes evident when the students see new shapes and relationships in the reversals, and experience for the first time the "seeking of the unexpected." Following the reversals, the figure/ground compositions are translated first into gray tones, then into specified color harmonies. The final phase of this part, which is also a "hinge" piece into the next phase, is a rigorous geometric analysis of selected studies using drafting instruments.

Part 3, "Reconstruct," takes place after students discuss the life and artistic intentions of Joseph Cornell and view slides of his work. The students then create their own shadowboxes "in the manner of" Cornell. They have three resources to work with in this phase: (1) another student's geometry from Part 2 (which again seeks the unexpected, as they must select the work of another rather than their own as a working tool); (2) a metaphor that the student develops from a literary source drawn at random; and (3) the bank of model parts, freely supplemented with found materials. The geometry serves as a compositional guide, the metaphor as subject matter, and the parts plus other "stuff" as working materials.

SYSTEMATICS TAXON ONE: Conceptual. *Analytic. Nonobjective/Compositional. Compositional/Architectonic. Architectural.* TAXON TWO: Poetic. *Metaphoric. Literary. Human Concerns. Environment. Visual Vocabulary. Procedural. Programmatic.* Tec-

Part 4 begins with an act of destruction that again seeks the unexpected, with the added lesson of not being precious with one's work. The shadowboxes are taken to the shop and sawed with the bandsaw into two pieces along a major axis. After this, the student peers inside one half of the box, gaining an unanticipated view, which is drawn in orthographic section. This not only teaches the convention of the architectural section drawing, but provides a new resource with which to proceed. A series of low reliefs are created, the first being a direct translation of the shapes seen in the section drawing done in a carefully chosen color scheme. The remaining reliefs explore various formal and coloristic permutations.

Part 5, the "Synthesis" phase, is at last entitled "A Commemorative Pavilion for Joseph Cornell." It is here that an actual site is introduced and studied, a program is developed that addresses both quantitative and qualitative issues, and the pavilion is designed. The rich lode of resources created earlier, the series of reliefs, plays an important role in the design process, as do notions of materiality, sequence, human experience, and a meaningful response to a sylvan site.

How brutal! Professor Cappleman says that the students take this act in stride, but one wonders if the negative aspect might not outweigh the positive intentions

The question may be asked whether this process focuses too heavily on formalism. Despite this concern, an exciting project indeed.

25

Image 18. First relief "translation" from the section drawing of the sawed box, by Diana Huang.

The Novel and Architecture

Elizabeth Patterson Church
(formerly of Mississippi State University)
VermontCollege of Norwich University
Montpelier, Vermont

This project joins several others in this collection in employing sources for design external to architecture. The unique connection here, however, is to the students' prior academic experience, one that enlightened them, perhaps, regarding the nature of abstraction.

How rare it is to see an architecture teacher who actually knows about and understands, at more than an intuitive level, the development of cognition in design ("The novel was used to build a cognitive bridge . . .").

Yet another noteworthy attempt at breaking down preconceptions.

The student whose work illustrates this project used Huxley's Brave New World for resource material.

t seems odd that a project which derives from such a rich reservoir as literature—and is handled in such an exciting manner, it may be added—would result in such relatively subdued solutions. It might be good to try to infuse some of the exuberance implicit in the preliminary study into the final product.

"The Novel and Architecture" was designed to address beginning design students' need for critical thinking by challenging their preconceptions about what a building should be. The vehicle of literature was chosen because these former high school honor students had already been exposed to a process of critical thinking within the framework of high school or college literature courses. The students' familiarity with the concepts of metaphor/symbolism/abstraction, the interpretation of information on a variety of levels, and the juggling of simultaneous pieces of information would have been available to them in the context of an English class. The novel was used to build a cognitive bridge from critical thinking in the written word to critical thinking in the design studio. This project was given in the first semester of the first year, following studies in figure/ground, proportioning systems, and geometry in two- and three-dimensional compositions.

"The Novel and Architecture" was devised to address the notion of breaking down boundaries of preconception. As a second goal, the project was to be an assimilation of the entire semester's explorations—figure/ground, proportion, geometry, two-dimensional composition, use of drawing and model material, and last but not least, formulating a convincing response to the given program. Third, the project sought to promote reading, writing, and critical thinking in the context of the design studio. The fourth goal of the project was to introduce a new ordering methodology—order through an abstract idea.

The novel seemed a particularly good point of departure because it is a crafted form composed of abstract ideas, and so might be an area in which the students had already begun to employ the process of critical thinking. Students read either To Kill a Mockingbird, The Great Gatsby, or a selection of their choice with approval from their critic. They were then asked to select three passages that best exemplified the development of a character, and to write a short essay about each of their choices. This segment of the process was intended to push the students into making explicit their implicit selection of the passages, thus taking the abstraction of the project's "program" further away from a superficial reading of the text.

Finally, the students developed a three-dimensional spatial response to all three passages. The response had to distinguish between the three spaces, but be united within one structure. Furthermore, the response was to be generated primarily via a study model that used only linear and planar components of a certain size. Draw-

26

ings were done after the design had reached a level of completion using just the study model. The entire project took a week and a half, and culminated in the customary end-of-semester juries.

Image 19. "The Fall," elevation drawing by Muse Davis.

tonic. TAXON THREE: Hermetic. Artifact. Individual. Personal. Social. *Edifice.* Monumental. Neighborhood. City. TAXON FOUR: No Scale. Ambiguous. Relative. *Referential.* Full. TAXON FIVE: Nonvisual. Electronic. Actualized. Expressive. *Descriptive.*

Spatial Apotheosis for Apollo and Dionysus:

A Study in the Dichotomy of Order and Disorder

Alan R. Cook
Auburn University
Auburn, Alabama

One week seems far too short a time for any significant comprehension of the wealth of issues in this project, both explicit and implicit. Surely much of the time must be given simply to production of the model.

One wonders why this opportunity to address issues of scale was not seized.

It is not clear exactly what role information theory played in this project. However, using the project as a means of exploring the fourth dimensionality of architectural space is notable.

In this one-week exercise the student is to design and represent, in model only, two domains: one each for the Greek gods Apollo and Dionysus, who symbolize order and disorder, respectively. One domain is to be dominantly additive geometry, the other dominantly subtractive. While they are to be separate places, they are to share a common connecting path that functions as a means of transition and arrival between domains. There are additional limitations regarding scale, size of final product, and color palette (achromatic). The final design is without representational imagery, using abstract elements only.

The source of the project lies in the author's reading of architectural historian Ronald Ramsey's notion of the Apollonian and Dionysian pendulum, which Ramsey observed seemed to swing historically back and forth between the stylistic tendencies of (noble) simplicity and (frenzied) complexity. These observations are incorporated with the author's personal experience with serial vision exercises and his reading of Gordon Cullen's Townscape and Rudolf Arnheim's Entropy and Art.

"Apollo and Dionysus" is for first-term beginning students. It requires no mature graphic skills since it is presented completely in three-dimensional model form. Model-building skills, however, are critical. This project is typically preceded by simple two-dimensional abstract studies of composition involving gestalt figure/ground and grouping principles, and a three-dimensional construct involving similar principles.

The intent of the exercise is to focus attention on the question of the nature of order. The study is devised so as to force inquiry into the attributes of "order," and into the differentiation of these attributes into a continuum polarized by simplicity and complexity. During this one-week exercise students come to realize the importance of context and relativity when comparing the level of complexity and/or simplicity of a pattern. They should also begin to understand the value of a theme as a device for establishing a datum of reference for evaluations. The issue of syntax is given priority over that of semantics in an attempt to increase focus on the role of basic design as a universal (i.e., not culturally limited) system for evaluating order.

The immediate goals of the projects are quite broad, and include an enhanced understanding of basic design principles and patterns and their expressive implications; the introduction of principles of information theory, serial vision, and spatial sequence, and the roles these theories play in the development of architectural messages; an investigation

28

of simplicity versus complexity; the introduction of a (symbolic) theme as a design issue; and, at a practical level, the further development and improvement of model-building skills. The long-range goals include an increased awareness of the potential value of abstract expression as an unavoidable design issue, the employment of a Design Pattern Checklist—a generic preliminary methodology for generating likely starting points in a design process, as an evaluative procedure (see p. 98)—and the development of conceptual abilities in the expression of "sense of place," i.e., identifiable domains of distinct character.

The Design Pattern Checklist could prove an extremely useful tool beyond beginning studies, but only if its use is reinforced in studios that follow.

Image 20. Model of student solution to "Spatial Apotheosis for Apollo and Dionysus."

tonic. TAXON THREE: Hermetic. Artifact. Individual. Personal. Social. *Edifice.* Monumental. Neighborhood. City. TAXON FOUR: No Scale. *Ambiguous.* Relative. Referential. Full. TAXON FIVE: Nonvisual. Electronic. Actualized. *Expressive.* Descriptive.

Working with Piranesi

David Covo and Derek Drummond
McGill University
Montreal, Quebec, Canada

The idea of working beyond the limits of the space visible in the original image is far richer than projects that merely work "in the manner of . . ."

The "borrowing" process is a many-for-the-price-of-one kind of deal, in which the student—although just doing one drawing—becomes intimately familiar with the whole portfolio.

It would be interesting to see the ancillary, or auxiliary, drawings the students spun off as problem-solving aids, instead of only the admittedly beautiful final products.
It is good to see drawing unabashedly used as a design project, without the need to "justify" it with a follow-up.

This project is formulated to develop design skills by confronting students with the power of drawing; perspective is presented as both a medium for the exploration of ideas and a process in which images of places that exist and places that do not are generated with equal enthusiasm and conviction.

The exercise is based on the series of sixteen etchings by Giovanni Battista Piranesi in the Second Edition of his Carceri, published in 1761, and calls for the design of an expansion of the space described in any single plate. Following a lecture in which they are introduced to Piranesi and the Carceri etchings, students are provided with 11" by 15" photocopies of the sixteen plates (the original plates measure approximately 16" by 22"). Each student selects a plate, analyzes it, formulates a strategy for expansion of the space, and then prepares a larger 24" by 36" perspective drawing of the expanded space, incorporating within this new drawing the original plate at 11" by 15". Working entirely within the perspective framework and in Piranesi's graphic language, students draw the new expanded space by simply extending the original image. All pretensions to, and preconceptions about, technique and personal style are laid aside as they lose themselves in the apparently resolved world of the selected plate.

Students quickly learn that valuable sources of ideas and inspiration are, in fact, other plates in the series, from which they freely "borrow" props for addition to their own drawings; these props include objects like hanging lanterns, bollards, a fall of rope or chain, and mysterious bits of machinery, and they invariably add a certain narrative content to the images. Rendering techniques adopted are in many cases based on Piranesi's own handling in the original plates of material, light, and shade.

Work is executed in soft pencil, conté, or charcoal on white card, and is completed in one week. The results are visually stunning. Drawings are large and bold, vigorous and highly imaginative. When forty-five students draw at this size, the studio resonates with the sound of cross-hatching. The act of drawing is seen and heard. The energy in the room is palpable and infectious.

Students experiment with a variety of strategies in their first attempts to understand Piranesi's visions. Some use color to separate and identify major compositional forms and structural elements; many construct schematic plans based on horizontal sections taken at different elevations in the original plate. Almost everyone at some point lays a large sheet of tracing paper over the plate in order to isolate and extend the governing perspective lines, and many students find their first cues for the expansion of Piranesi's space in the forgiving wire-frame world of these perspective grids.

The results of these and other investigations are invariably surprising. Vanishing points that ought to coincide do not; they seem to drift, sometimes along the horizon, sometimes above or below it. The horizon line itself is often low, near the bottom of some plates and even outside the bottom edge of others. The temptation to treat the original plates as fragments of larger visions becomes irresistible, transforming the exercise for some individuals into a special kind of searching for clues to this larger image.

The exercise with Piranesi's Carceri does not seem to require a follow-up assignment; it develops skills in drawing and design and, more important, the beginnings of a true understanding of the relationship between the two. It engages the student in a process of exploration and discovery and reveals in a most constructive way the importance and the power of perspective drawing in the consideration of architectural ideas.

The project seems to encourage the development of both analytical and creative skills through cognitive self-discovery, the "ah-ha!" experience.

It is good to see drawing unabashedly used as a design project, without the need to "justify" it with a follow-up.

Image 21. Expanded version of Plate XIV, "The Gothic Arch," 21 1/2" x 34," graphite, by James McLaughlin, 1990.

Image 22. 11" x 15" fragment of Image 21; detail shows the student's version of the original plate.

Exhibition Area at Cappadocia

Zafer Ertürk, Ph.D.
Karadeniz Technical University
Trabzon, Turkey

While this surreal landscape would certainly provide profound inspiration for some students, might it not overwhelm or intimidate others? Given its place in the students' history, and its cultural linkage to them, perhaps not.

Although the architectural program is minimal, the cultural program for this project is profound. In that it joins several others in this collection in being unique to its context.

Even for those who do not know the author of this project, his love for and lifetime dedication to the region of Cappadocia should be apparent.

The goals of this project are numerous: the development of a sense of spatial dynamism, rather than creating defined volumes in a stiff manner; the search for a sensible approach for more confident and sound utilization, interpretation, and realization of the value of environmental data; the development of a proficiency in molding the possibilities of contemporary technology with cultural and social patterns; and the formation of an ethos of aesthetics that makes use of the harmony of contrasts within similarities, while trying to ensure integration with the context of the surroundings.

The site for this project is in the Göreme Valley in the Cappadocia region of Turkey. Cappadocia lies in central Anatolia within the boundaries of the towns of Kayseri, Kirsehir, and Nigde. Geologically, Cappadocia is renowned as a region of unique landscape: nowhere else in the world can its geological elements be found. Surrounded by volcanic structures, and in recent geologic time prone to volcanic convulsions, Cappadocia's atmospheric conditions have caused the formation of compact and complicated geologic patterns in which isolated pinnacles, called "fairy chimneys," rise to a height of 40 to 45 meters.

It is not known when it began to be used, but the local stone— "tufa," which is porous and easily worked—provided settlers in Cappadocia with a convenient building material from which to hollow out dwellings. Today we can see the two- and three-story houses, churches, mosques, underground cities, and cold-storage depots that have been hollowed out over the last thousand years, at least. For the Turkish people the region of Cappodacia embodies the geographical and historical heartland of their rich cultural history: the uniqueness of their history here is actualized in this distinctive natural environment.

It is virtually impossible to exaggerate the historical richness of this region. It is part of one of the three coeval Mediterranean "cradles of civilization"—the Hittite civilization, which flourished between 3000 and 1000 bc, along with the neighboring Minoan and Egyptian civilizations. A Hittite text circa 2300 bc, contains the earliest reference to an urban settlement in Cappadocia. From that time onward Cappadocia was to exist under the hegemony of the Assyrian Empire, the Medo-Babylonian Realms, the Persian Empire, Alexander the Great, the Roman Empire, the Eastern (Byzantine) Roman Empire, the Seljuk Turks and the Ottoman Empire until it became part of the Republic of Turkey in 1923. In looking at the succession of empires in Anatolia one can imagine the extent of the migrations of its populations and the foreign influences that trade, particularly the trade of an empire, would bring. Artifacts from Anatolia reveal a broad diversity of influence reflecting the cultures of the Hittite, Greek, Hellenistic, Roman, and Byzantine empires, as well as that from cultures based on shamanism, Manichaeanism, Buddhism, and, of course, Islam and Christianity.

The project proper called for the design of a series of open and/or semi-open and/or enclosed exhibition spaces as a part of one of the open-air museums of Cappadocia, using a formal vocabulary that would be harmonious with the natural silhouette as a contemporary architectural piece within the historical site. Solutions were studied and developed in three-dimensional models of various materials, and evaluated by concentrating on the general concepts and fundamental principles of architecture.

One wonders if the constraints of "open and/or semi-open and or/enclosed," being so broad and inclusive, are actual constraints at all.

Image 23. Exhibition area, design, and drawing

Image 24. Exhibition area, design, and model.

Harmony

Jonathan Block Friedman
New York Institute of Technology
Old Westbury, New York

In Supplementary Information (p. 110) Professor Friedman refers to the source of this project as being in part the nine-square work of Hejduk and others at Cooper. In this it joins a host of others influenced by this effort, several of which are contained in this volume.

The "bag of tricks" idea is a variant on the "kit of parts" methodology found in other projects in this book. Many of those, it must be said, are derived from Friedman's earlier work.

It is good to see a cogent discussion of the importance of light, especially when not addressed as an isolated issue. Incorporation with other design concerns when talking about "illumination, circulation and space-making" relationships fosters a more holistic view of architecture.

"Harmony" is one of four major studies given in the second semester of a beginning design studio course for architecture majors. It is intended to demonstrate to the student who has already mastered the essentials of organizing void through the placement of mass that there is another aspect of spatial design that cannot be understood simply through the juxtaposition of solid blocks. The common Boolean operations of union and intersection reveal the architectural possibilities of shared spaces, zones that belong to more than one other volume. Thus the program is deliberately simple— the definition and organization of two similar volumes, 16' cubes, within a site, a 24' cube, that forces their intersection, creating a third volume, an 8' cube. The pragmatic characteristics and uses of these spaces suggest architectural implications.

"Harmony," which occurs in the second design course, titled Dynamics (the first course, Architectonics, is documented and elaborated on in the author's textbook, Creation in Space Volume 1: Architectonics), makes major use of a set of design elements, the "Bag of Tricks," to organize specific spaces to an architectural program. The Bag of Tricks is the available supply of construction materials. Their combinations and connections become an important substudy—as do the possibilities of vertical and horizontal circulation. The students are encouraged to explore ways to contrast the two major cubes as much as possible, through material, orientation, light/dark, etc. The question of joint, from smallest constructional to largest architectural scales, is also a major consideration. The students learn to model space through a perforated topology, in which light is modulated rather than completely excluded or contained. Students learn the interaction of concerns about structure, material, construction, circulation, and program in developing and resolving a problem of volumetric requirements. The program has been reduced to an essential relationship between two given volumes and how they may generate additional spaces.

The positive outcomes of this project include a marked increase in students' ability to visualize plastic solutions through a continuity of interior and exterior volumes; a clearer understanding of the relationship between illumination, circulation, and space-making; and an insight into the unique property of architecture to make a volume "read" as part of more than one spatial order. As these areas are emphasized, some students are also able to grasp the way detailing of joints and material relationships can enhance a project, while other students find that they begin to lose control of their earlier simple and clear partí notions through the detailing.

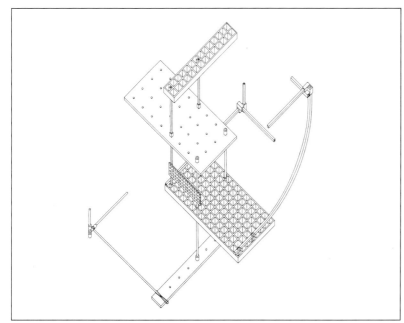

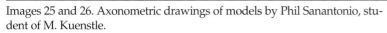

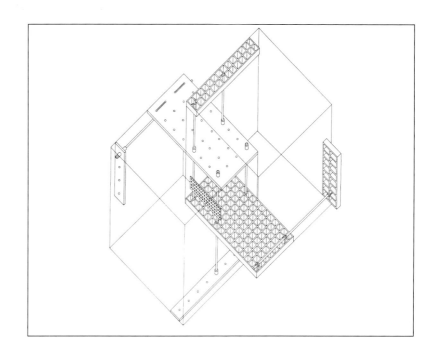

Images 25 and 26. Axonometric drawings of models by Phil Sanantonio, student of M. Kuenstle.

House to Street

Charles P. Graves, Jr.
Kent State University
Kent, Ohio

This is the only exercise in this collection that is based solely on the computer, and develops procedures that are at once unique to the computer and yet familiar to the nonexpert.

"House to Street" is a multipart exercise given at the beginning of the second semester of the first year. It is preceded by a series of accretive projects that begin in the Bauhausian tradition and proceed into more inclusive architectural issues. The exercise was devised to employ the street as primary spatial definer. It introduces students to the capabilities of the computer, which facilitates the conceptualization and design of three-dimensional forms and spaces, the design of a single-form housing unit, and basic street typologies. The exercises are designed to give students a quick understanding of the CAD software (MacArchitrion) and hardware (Macintosh SE30). As the students progress through each exercise they are exposed to more complex traits of the software and hardware, and thus advance in gradual but expedient stages.

The first exercise teaches basic computer techniques. For an introduction to the modeling software, all students are required to use the computer to construct a gridded rectangle that has outside dimensions of 21' wide x 31' deep x 21' high, and is subdivided into twelve cubes of 10' x 10' x 10'. The architecture of the cubes is founded on the application of a tartan grid, which allows great freedom in design while serving both to control the abstract space of a design in a rudimentary but meaningful way and to act as a safety net, preventing a student from falling beyond the grid into utterly unstructured chaos.

The second exercise requires the student to design a single housing unit based on the gridded rectangle described above. The square footage for one unit falls within the boundaries of the twelve 10' x 10' x 10' cubes. The program for the single unit includes a double-height living space, one 5' x 10' x 10' cooking area, a dining area, a staircase, one 2' x 4' x 15' fireplace and flue, a study area, a sleeping area, one 5' x 10' x 10' shower room, and a garden space.

No particular site is given for the design of the single housing unit, which allows the student to view the object from any direction. The object-house may be viewed as a microcosm of solid to void relationships, and thus a prelude to the street.

The third exercise, a basic introduction to a street setting, asks the student to investigate multiple configurations of the single unit in groups of twelve, creating three basic prototypical street settings. They are labeled, for purposes of classification, "Main Street," "Elm Street," and "The Strip." Main Street is defined as a dense urban fabric with buildings sharing party walls that create a solid facade. On Elm Street there exists a balance between solid and void. The structures are separated by the minimal distance needed to signify individuality, yet they tend to share repetitive guidelines of setbacks and porch sizes. The final setting, The Strip, presents images of buildings that occur as objects randomly placed in space.

Throughout the four-week program a number of basic urban issues are addressed in lectures. Parallel with the first exercise—the construction of a gridded rectangle on the computer—the history of the grid as either a construction device or an abstract, mathematical tool is presented. During the second exercise—the single housing unit—the lecture covers precedents for buildings seen as objects. Their internal-to-external relationship, public and private spaces, solid and void, and issues of context are compared. In the final lecture, the history of the street is presented, with discussions on the relationship and proportion of the following items to each other: the building height, the width of the street, the building setback from the street, the spacing of the buildings, and the use of repetitive elements.

The exercises described above create a "self-generating" architecture that begins to establish basic guidelines for the transformation of single-form objects into urban space. By the very nature of inputting commands into the computer, the user becomes cognizant of a process of design through which the how of design is revealed. Ultimately, however, designers must face what has been created on the computer and consider the phenomenal implications of their designs in the built environment.

The possibilities of creating a "self-generative" architecture originating from the technological capabilities of the computer are indeed exciting, yet often result in the creation of autonomous objects that deny any real sense of physical context. However, if "self-generative" means the potential for the computer to generate solutions independent of a human author, who serves as editor after the fact, then altogether new horizons for design appear.

37

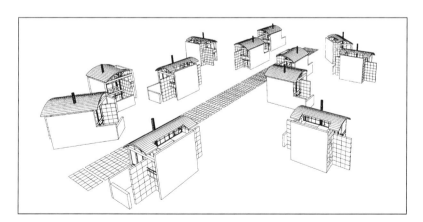

Image 27. Aerial perspective of "The Strip."

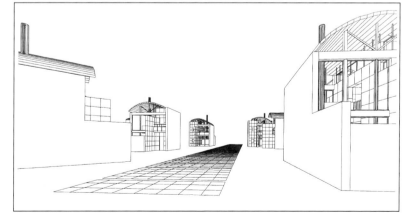

Image 28. Ground-level perspective of "The Strip."

A Nomadic Shelter

Mary Hardin
Arizona State University
Tempe, Arizona

An important early lesson about a standardized world in which there are few, if any "standard" people.

. . . and another lesson on the "lost-in-translation" syndrome, a source of frequent heartache for the designer...

. . . and finally, the lesson that the elusive goal of a "flexible" architecture is rarely realized.

In this exercise students are asked to join forces to conduct research, create the design, and ultimately construct and test a portable dwelling. While there is no known specific history of this project, it may have derived unconsciously from "snippets of countless 'Instant City' projects witnessed by the author in the early 1970s." "A Nomadic Shelter" was conceived as a way of introducing students to the issues of anthropometrics as a generator of a building's form, size, and spatial layout. It also served as a bridge between a series of two-dimensional graphic design exercises that characterize the first semester of a design fundamentals course, and a subsequent series of three-dimensional architectonic projects that constitute the second semester of studio.

The requirements for a satisfactory portable dwelling are deceptively siple. It must house one adult of ordinary size, accommodating both sleeping and sitting. It must be fashioned from cardboard and string ony, and must be portable. Finally, it must provide shelter from sun, moderate breezes, and light rain. Students begin by researching other human "containers" designed for a tight fit, such as space capsules, tent, sleeping bags, coffins, and cockpits. They searched for architectural precedent as well, and discovered a legacy of huts, teepees, and lean-to structures that had served as portable shelters for nomadic populations throughout history. Additionally, student teams measured their own physical dimensions through a range of activities and compared their findings with the averages found on anthropometric data charts. The differences between an individual's dimensions and those of the "composite man" were suddenly perceived as the root cause of discomfort in the world of standardized vehicles, furniture, and appliances.

Measurement and accommodation of the human body were the aspects of the problem that were most easily solved. Human dimensions, reach, and posture characteristics were the primary determinants of the shelter's scale, proportion, and form. The requirement of portability, however, proved to be the sticking point. Ideas that seemed like sure winners on paper were disastrous when translated into cardboard. Even the teams that experimented with small-scale models made of index cards were disappointed to find that rigidity was not a property that translated accurately from one material and scale to another.

Results of the "Nomadic Shelter" project were quite diverse; structures resembling everything from solar yurts to Dymaxion race car bodies were in evidence. Some rolled up into compact backpacks for transport, while others could never be assembled a second time after breakdown (even by the designers). For some, the restrictions on the materials and the insistence on portability had led them down serendipitous paths that ended well. For other participants, the value of research was underscored. For all, an unexpected lesson was learned regarding the potential impact of architecture on society's ills.

The aspirations of this project are admirable. We hope that students will not be discouraged from future activism by their unsuccessful gestures toward the homeless of Tempe, Arizona.

Image 29. Nomadic shelter in portable mode; student wearing dismantled shelter as a "backpack."

tonic. TAXON THREE: Hermetic. Artifact. Individual. ***Personal.*** Social. Edifice. Monumental. Neighborhood. City. TAXON FOUR: No Scale. Ambiguous. Relative. Referential. *Full.* TAXON FIVE: Nonvisual. Electronic. ***Actualized.*** Expressive. Descriptive.

Between Tradition and Modernity

Desmond Hui and Lye Kum Chew
University of Hong Kong

Investigation into one's own unique cultural roots is an excellent cognitive launchpad into the design process.

What a rich and wonderful intercultural experience.

40

Field work of all sorts, from that described here to actual construction exercises, is an all-too-rare component of beginning design studios. It is noteworthy that other projects in this book have their beginnings in, or revolve around, a field trip.

Feng shui, or Chinese geomancy of ancient Taoist origins, concerns itself with propitious alignments. It is found in all parts of Asia that have significant Chinese populations, and in some multicultural regions it insinuates itself into other societies. In fact, some Westerners are beginning to take note of feng shui as a potent design determinant.

Perhaps the rationale and significance of this project can be summarized in the words of the French philosopher Paul Ricoeur, who urges one to go back to one's own origins so as to be worthy participants in the great debate of culture. This project is an attempt to translate Ricoeur's ideas into architectural terms in order to discover an architecture that relates to the cultural origins of the Chinese, while partaking at the same time of the positive offerings of modern universal civilization. The immediate intention of the exercise is to develop students' sensitivity toward the physical and social environment of their cultural origin, and to solve an architectural design problem based on the development of this sensitivity. The long-term goal is to investigate the problems arising from the confrontation and integration between tradition and modernity, and to formulate an approach through the direct and experiential interaction of fresh and ideologically unbiased beginning design students.

Prior to beginning "Between Tradition and Modernity" the students completed fifteen weeks of studio work, which included short exercises on architectonics, ergonomics, color, and geometric studies, plus projects that introduced architectural concepts dealing with site and program issues. They also learned sketching, both Chinese and Western painting, and Chinese calligraphy, as well as other visual and graphic techniques. Concurrent courses included Chinese and Western history of architecture, structure, construction, and environmental science.

The students and teachers carried out a one-week field trip to the Shantou and Chaozhou area of Canton in mid-November 1990. They visited the traditional houses and examined their architecture for an understanding of the context and heritage in terms of building forms and techniques. They then selected for further study a typical Chaozhou village settlement, one still intact in terms of the building fabric and unaffected by modern technology. A survey was conducted so as to understand (1) the history and development of the village; (2) feng shui and siting; (3) social hierarchy; and (4) conformity of design techniques and vocabularies with the general tradition established in the neighboring regions. Students were divided into groups and each measured a typical shophouse and documented the history of its particular household. In the end, a specific site was chosen for redevelopment, from which students gathered the necessary data, details, and field measurements.

Studio work on the project was divided into phases. The first phase was assembling the data and information from the field trip into

SYSTEMATICS TAXON ONE: Conceptual. *Analytic.* Nonobjective/Compositional. Compositional/Architectonic. *Architectural.* TAXON TWO: Poetic. Metaphoric. Literary. *Human Concerns. Environment.* Visual Vocabulary. Procedural. *Programmatic.* Teca report. Measured drawings were prepared and a 1:200 scaled site model was built. The design program called for a shophouse in the village. Students were free to compose their own scenario for the project, i.e., the type of shop (a variety of which they all had the opportunity to observe during their trip), the ownership of shop and house, the size and nature of the family living and working there, the characteristics of the occupants, and the spatial and physical requirements of the rooms and areas. They were also free to choose, with qualifications and negotiations, one of the twelve selected sites in the village. In developing their design concept, they were also required to observe the importance of the idea of "environment," which has been chosen as a philosophical theme for the design approach of the whole department of architecture at the University of Hong Kong.

To quote the words from one visiting critic to the final jury of the project: "All in all, it was exciting to see the diversity of designs and the imaginative effort brought forth by what must have been a most wonderfully edifying trip. The students came upon their roots and obviously became aware that materials and shapes formed part of the living environment. They sensed that there were reasons for these to be what they are and that the living environment is, even in so remote a village, a part of a cultural link. . . ."

Shophouses are row buildings of two or three stories sharing party walls, and are found throughout Asia. Business is conducted at ground level, with the family that owns and operates the building using the upper level(s) as living space.

41

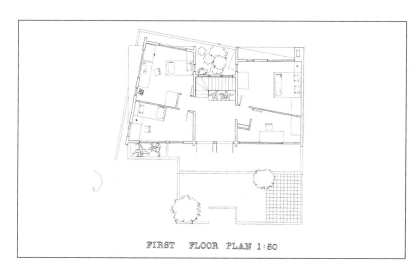

Image 30. First-floor plan of a shophouse in a typical Chaozhou village settlement by Lawrence Mak.

Image 31. Model of shophouse by Lawrence Mak.

tonic. TAXON THREE: Hermetic. Artifact. Individual. Personal. *Social. Edifice.* Monumental. Neighborhood. City. TAXON FOUR: No Scale. Ambiguous. Relative. *Referential.* Full. TAXON FIVE: Nonvisual. Electronic. Actualized. Expressive. *Descriptive.*

The Metaphysical City

Michael Jordan
University of Oklahoma
Norman, Oklahoma

This is one of many projects in this book to use works of art, either visual or literary, as external source material.

It is an acute observation to note that all of de Chirico's piazza paintings depict a single figmentary piazza.

At its base this project is intended as an exploration of the relationships that exist, or might exist, between architecture and painting. It delves into a wealth of issues, including development of an understanding of the work of an artist; color theory and application, the solving of both architectural and architectonic problems; the integration of graphic and modeling skills; and, to no small extent, the development of interpersonal skills as part of a group. It consists of numerous accretive phases connected both thematically, through study of the work of Giorgio de Chirico, and by a vision of the ultimate goal, the realization and habitation of his Metaphysical City.

The exercise begins with the selection of a single painting by de Chirico from the period between 1910 and 1919. Each painting is subjected to a three-part analysis. First, the painting is reduced to a line drawing describing its essential geometry. Particular attention is given to the role of perspective in these images, and to how and why de Chirico distorted the rules of perspective. Next, the color structure of the painting is analyzed. The product is a diagram of essential color interactions, relative proportions of colors, and their spatial implications. Finally, the painting is studied for its spatial cues, which often contradict those found in the color study. The product of this effort is a bas-relief, in white only, illustrating the physical facts of the space of the painting.

The second phase centers on the study of an existing Italian piazza. The initial work involves library research and the collection of documentation on a specific piazza. Each piazza is dissected through diagrams to reveal its underlying geometry and partí in a manner similar to the analysis of the painting. Kevin Lynch's Image of the City, particularly his discussion of paths, edges, districts, nodes, and landmarks, serves as the source for further analysis. Finally the piazza is studied in model.

Next, the source painting is again scrutinized, this time for literal architectural elements. Each student produces a set of scaled orthographic drawings—plan and related elevations—of her or his fragment of the city. They are instructed to use their knowledge of a real piazza to imagine the portions of the fragment hidden from view.

In a frenzy of group activity, the orthographic fragments drawn above are collaged into a plan of the town. This is not an altogether ad hoc event, although there is certainly the element of invention. Each painting contains clues to its position in the town. Once completed (generally in a single class period), the plan is subdivided and each student is assigned the task of constructing models of the buildings in one segment.

In the final phase of the project each student is assigned a piazza or open space within the Metaphysical City. The objective is the design of an architectonic event celebrating de Chirico's birth, a sort of surreal fair pavilion. At a minimum it is to contain three spaces, one each for Enigma, Melancholy, and "the lyric significance behind the surface appearance of mundane objects." The final product is built to scale in full, de Chirico-esque color and inserted into the city model. In addition, it is documented with a standard set of architectural drawings, including a "walkthrough" of perspective vignettes.

The range of scales of concern in this project is phenomenal, from artifact scale (painting) to the scale of a city. There is also an aspect of special imagination and mystery in the notion of a "lost" de Chirico painting (see long version of the project in Annex 1) being "found."

There is something complete, consistent, and satisfying about this project, which is composed of a series of seemingly disparate procedural steps. Other such projects, with a similar attitude or orientation, can be found in this book.

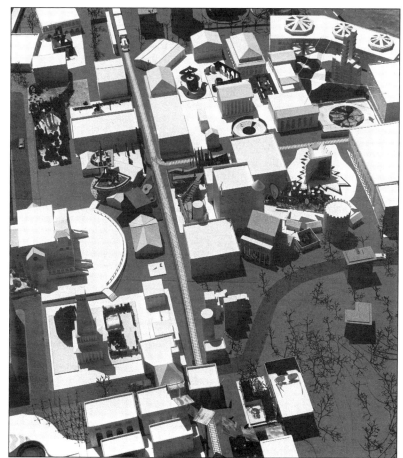

Image 32. General view of the final version of Metaphysical City, including the Centennial pavilions.

Teaching Structures for Architectural Application

Joseph Lim
National University of Singapore

The creative, even poetic, use of structure in this project series is exemplary.

These three interrelated and sequential student projects focus on the use of structure in architecture as a response to the gaps between the intangible ideas in architecture and the craft of object-making. In the design process, students are encouraged to develop an understanding of structures in architecture, far beyond the technical realm, both to break the existing divisions between art and technology and to allow for architectural ideas that determine technological application.

This set of projects is given in the second studio semester of the second year. It is preceded by an initial two weeks given to the development of the design brief and usage specification—including seminars on design process, structural types, and applications—and case studies and their relationship to architectural form, space, and use. The seminars relate structural behavior to structural form, and illustrate how variations in the character and scale of interior and exterior spaces may determine structural configuration. This approach to teaching encourages the development of structural understanding beyond the technical, and attempts to break the existing divisions between art and technology.

PROJECT 1: A MILITARY OBSERVATION POST

This is an exercise in space, form, and structural idea in response to use and place in a military context. The observation post is intended for exhibition at a military expo, and for eventual use in peacetime military maneuvers. Actual combat specifications were not adopted as they implied substructures more than superstructures.

The post must be designed so as to span a 25-meter-wide ravine, cantilever from the side of a high cliff, and rise 25 meters high above ground level. This particular concept embodied both a bridge and a tower into a solution that allowed observation from two different positions. It also responded to both ravine and "high-rise" requirements by being a bridge and a tower with one structure.

PROJECT 2: A BRIDGE AS DWELLING

The immediate goal of this project is to develop a structure for spaces that question the conventional notion of a dwelling, as well as to illustrate how technical matters may influence and enable intangible matters. This process allows the student to oscillate between ideas conceived in aspects remote from structure, and ideas in consideration of structure.

The project is intended to be a study of a structure spanning over a ravine and the accompanying implications on the interior spaces of the dwelling. In this context, the spaces-suspended-in-space provide the opportunity for redefining the enclosures and the structure of the dwelling.

PROJECT 3: A SPACE FOR ROALD DAHL

This project exemplifies the "pendulum" approach, which swings between the intangible concept and the tangible structure. The spatial concept encapsulates the essence of Dahl's writing, which renders familiar the unfamiliar. Likewise, the spaces typified by the Singapore shophouse are transformed into unfamiliar ones by contrast and by inversion

Contrast. The old structure (masonry party wall) becomes a mere screen with a texture markedly opposite the proposed steel-framed roofs and their supports, expressed as separate entities. Although the shophouse outline is retained, the structural frame that forms itself into this familiar outline has no existing precedent. Old forms in new structures here give new spaces that become the unfamiliar.

Inversion. The roof form and entry space in the front half of the shophouse is inverted in the rear half of the house. The rear spaces and forms become inverted mirror expressions of those in the front. The entire roof structure is linked by a common lower beam, which is the only unifying element between familiarity and unfamiliarity.

The drawings documenting this project are exquisite!

It is important to stress the adroit handling of a range of inherently incongruent issues here, in effect to develop a happy state of irony..

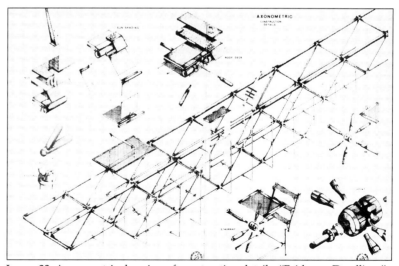

Image 33. Axonometric drawing of construction details, "Bridge as Dwelling."

tonic. TAXON THREE: Hermetic. Artifact. Individual. *Personal.* Social. *Edifice.* Monumental. Neighborhood. City. TAXON FOUR: No Scale. Ambiguous. Relative. *Referential.* Full. TAXON FIVE: Nonvisual. Electronic. Actualized. Expressive. *Descriptive.*

Serendipity: Accidental Discoveries and Sagacity!

Darla Lindberg-Berreth and Robert D. Hermanson
University of Utah
Salt Lake City, Utah

The procedure, from intuition to fact to text, is in many ways contrary to the norm, but has the advantage of being circular—closing on itself—rather than linear. For readers unfamiliar with the present connotation of "text," Professor Robert Mugerauer of University of Texas-Austin provides the following definitions. Text in literary terms: Autonomous sign-systems that refer only to each other. "Signs" are always signs of something else that is absent, and that cannot be thought of apart from the entire set of historical signs. Text in architectural terms: Architecture is a sign-system that communicates; specific presentations of forms—columns, stairs, seating—all denote their own use and connote or promote their ideology and mode of functioning.

Battling preconceptions is a commonly held goal among beginning design teachers; numerous examples employing various means can be found in this book. The use of objets trouvés works especially well in addressing this issue.

Another recurring theme is the "kit of parts" concept.

This three-part project, given in the first year of graduate studies, begins with the tale of The Three Princes of Serendip, who were sent out into the world by their father to experience the wonders of foreign lands. In their travels the three sons became known for their wise and insightful observations of the world. The heroes were "always making discoveries, by accidents and sagacity, of things they were not in quest of." The tale also suggests that sagacity did not happen through the gaining of external knowledge or the knowledge of others alone. The three sons' success and ultimate wisdom and fame came through the implementation of their own internal evidence.

PART 1: SERENDIPITY

By exploring an event or tale (a day's journey, a memory of an experience, etc.) through two- and three-dimensional "found" objects, the students revealed preconceived notions (mental "baggage") about the world observed around them. Color, repetition, datum, texture, two- and three-dimensional surface, etc., were discovered as architectural language systems used to communicate a personal experience. The first phase involved simply gathering found objects and arranging them intuitively in order to tell the tale. The second phase investigated and transformed the found material into architectonic expressions capable of communicating an individual experience to the collective.

PART 2: VISUAL THINKING AND THE LANGUAGE OF FORM

Continuing with the notion of the design process as a journey, the second project explored the language of architecture by using a kit of parts (architectonic elements as mental and spatial communication systems). Through two interrelated phases, students first explored knowing the elements (words and their meaning), and later transformed these concepts as words via syntactic relationships (analogous to the sentence) to create meaning. The kit of parts allowed students to experiment with principles such as solid/void, figure/ground, displaced space/implied space, etc., within the limits of a specified abstract territory (the universe in an 8" spatial cube). This resulted in a variety of investigations that suggested the role of play in the conceptual process.

A modest program and site (a ski pavilion) were introduced in the transformation phase to emphasize spatial relationships and their meanings, in addition to the perfunctory roles of function and context. A change of scale and a shift in emphasis encouraged the students to work directly with each other in orchestrating an overall site strategy, as well as developing their own individual designs.

PART 3: THE FINAL PROJECT

The class was divided into two expedition groups taking simultaneous journeys : (1) the haptic experiences of space centering on the body (The Spatiality of Movement), and (2) the contemplative inner reflections in contrast to the outer contextual experiences (The Tabula Rasa).

The first journey, titled "The Spatiality of Movement," was the design of an experimental dance studio and involved members of the Modern Dance Department as visiting critics. Following a series of movement exercises with the dancers, each student developed a study based on Rudolf Arnheim's commentary in differentiating the methodology of constructing a spatial container—namely that of the egg versus the burrow. The project, like many others within the studio, yielded a paradoxical condition: the duality that exists between man's mobility, a diachronic condition (especially in dance), versus architecture's synchronic constancy in attempting to transcend these changes.

The second of the simultaneous journeys was titled "The Tabula Rasa." Working with faculty in the University Writing Program, the project involved John Locke's assertion that all ideas come from experience, both external and internal. The program involved the design of gallery spaces for artistic works that would tell the stories of experiences and then challenge those works through writing. Following a site investigation, students began an exploration of the facade as a vertical poché, the dialog between inside and outside. Contextual images became part of the generating force informing the facade studies. These studies initiated a series of plaster tablets (81/2" x 11" x 1") recording carved images based on conceptual ordering principles derived from site and program, as well as formal ordering strategies. The tablets became texts—written impressions carved into the plaster surface. Into the plaster tablets students carved many layers of information that recorded the site and surroundings as context, as well as notions about the project—the text. Students differentiated margins where "notes" on materials, details, and proportioning systems were carved. The plaster carving became a conceptual sketch that was informed continuously through the act of making, revealing new relationships through the materials. Synthesizing these knowledge processes, the Tabula Rasa studio concluded with an investigation of the sectional properties of the various spaces. The architectural volumes were "read" as a series of incremental "pages" beginning with the cover—the facade.

Image 34. Axonometric drawing.

Kinesthetic activities focus attention on architecture as a fourth-dimensional phenomenon.

Avatars of the Tortoise

Bruce Lindsey and Paul Rosenblatt
Carnegie-Mellon University
Pittsburgh, Pennsylvania

The breadth of intentions in this project is admirable. The mechanism for achieving these ambitions is equally comprehensive.

Again, the nine-square exercise. This may well be a 27-square variant.

The change of scale, from referential to full, is too often omitted from design exercises in general.

The two parts of this first-semester project were preceded by a few simple two-dimensional design problems. The immediate goals of Part 1 are to foster an understanding of connection and detail, the concept of hierarchy, and construction as a group activity; for Part 2, resolution of the intersection of two different geometries, and the making and developing of projects using physical and computer models. The long-range goals of the entire project center on relationships of part to whole, of model to real, of designing to building; on the relationship between form and representation; and on the examination of the frame as spacemaker. In the opinion of the authors of the project, Part 1 proved a "very successful fusion of 'building something big,' design fundamentals, and computer modeling." Part 2 "resulted in effective integration of different physical and computer modeling strategies in the design process."

In Part 1, titled "9-Square: Cube Constructed," the student begins by constructing a 12" nine-square cube in two sizes of balsa wood. The completed cube reveals distinctions that were not anticipated: The center, the corner, and the edge are unique due to its geometry.

Next, a joint from the cube is studied at a larger scale. A family of situations—3-legs, 5-legs, 6-legs—is explored. Because of the new size, new possibilities for connection are provoked, and connections now deal with distinction as well as construction. At this point, groups of five students join forces and look for collective possibilities. They must construct a single three-foot cube with "an attitude," one which represents their collective wisdom.

The studio of six groups (30 students) chooses one of the three foot cubes to build "full scale," 9 feet to the side. Construction time is limited to one week, the budget is tight but reasonable, and they (the cubes) must be "extraordinary." The construction process becomes one of group therapy. In an act of refinement, the connections are studied full size. Finally, the completed cube joins two more from other studios in the great hall of the College of Fine Arts.

Part 2, known as "9-Square : Grid : Intersected," explores paired constructs in a way that reveals the implications, possibilities, and limitations of each. The first stage uses two drawn grids to explore the possibilities of ordered structures to produce "beautiful" relationships. The second stage takes this two-dimensional representation and provokes three-dimensional implications using visual transparency, overlap, and occlusion. These drawings are then taken into three dimensions; the implications become literal. The third stage gives the abstract three-dimensional grids a program—the definition of a dominant interior space and a secondary exterior space. The grids become loaded with architectural possibilities, and are constructed and drawn in axonometric view. The object is examined again, this time in three mutually limiting ways: first in the model, second through hand drawing, and third in a computer drawing. Next, the student places the object onto a site, which is meant to exhibit a reciprocal relationship with the spaces and the structure. The site is considered in a subtractive way, providing a contrast to the linear elements of the cube structure. Finally, each student presents his or her project both verbally and visually.

The computer exercises, as seen by this book's authors, play a critical role not readily indcated by the text of the project.

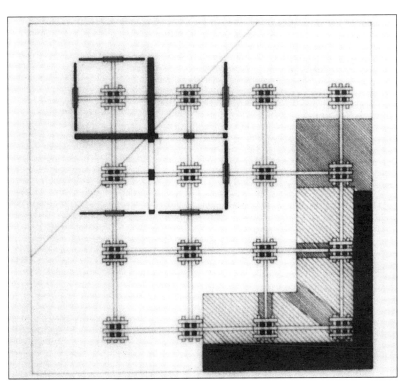

Image 35. Nine-cube plan view drawing.

Image 36. Nine-cube model.

The Promenade

Nicholas Charles Markovich
Louisiana State University
Baton Rouge, Louisiana

This project, like all others at LSU, is presented to the students verbally. The contention is that "this helps to assure verbal/visual understandings." Is there any research that proves this point? If so, the tradition of the written brief may need revision.

It would be interesting to see the predecessors ("design knowledge explored in previous two- and three-dimensional 'abstract' shape and form studies") of this project.

"The Promenade," a two-and-a-half week project, is the first project at LSU in which human and behavioral references, and the issue of site, are introduced. The students are asked to work within parameters of design knowledge explored in previous two- and three-dimensional "abstract" shape and form studies and reconsider them in anthropometric terms.

In this problem a park-like setting is selected as a site. The project is for the design of a promenade; that is, a place to walk, rest, view, meet, and engage in general social activities. Students are also provided with a set of "definers" regarding human behavior that must be represented in the promenade. The students are required to work with foam-core board and museum or Strathmore board, in white only. Removing the elements of materiality, tone, and color accentuates the play of light and shadow, thus allowing the finished construct to read more clearly. This generally gives the student a greater degree of accomplishment, as well as clarity in visual interpretation.

The immediate goals for the exercise include the integration of functional aspects of design into the design process, while providing the student with an initial understanding of site/design relationships. Emphasis is placed on the manipulation of form and path within a given context. Longer-range goals focus on a broader understanding of site/design relationships; attainment of visual, spatial, and connected behavioral understanding; and the realization of the link between aesthetic and visual vocabulary and the functional aspects of design.

The project's author notes, "The results of the project have exhibited a high degree of success in synthesizing 'abstract' notions of visual literacy and architectural form with the very 'real' concepts of site and behavior."

SYSTEMATICS TAXON ONE: Conceptual. Analytic. Nonobjective/Compositional. *Compositional/Architectonic.* Architectural. TAXON TWO: Poetic. Metaphoric. Literary. *Human Concerns. Environment.* Visual Vocabulary. Procedural. Programmatic. Tec-

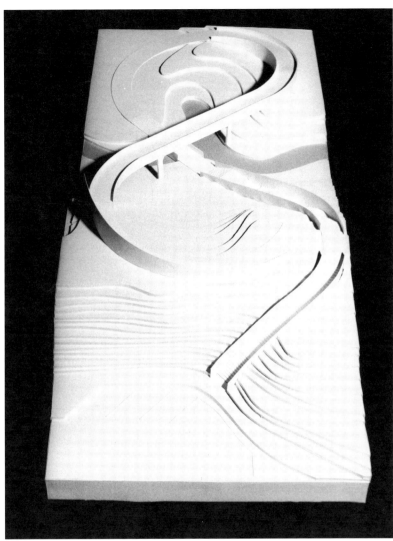

The methodology of moving from purely abstract, or nonobjective, projects into "real world" projects has a long history. An even-handed comparison between this approach and that of "instant architecture" is voiced in the closing essay of this book.

Image 37. The Promenade, model.

Thinking Hands

Lorna Anne McNeur
Cambridge University
Cambridge, England

The "thinking hands" concept is a powerful metaphor. What's more, it is also pure poetry.

This is one of several projects in this collection that derive at least a portion of their content from artistic sources. This one, however, is special in that it is concerned with the visible and literal space of the painting rather than some other issue—geometry, for instance— that is at least once removed from the true fabric of the painting.

Examining and contrasting perspective and Cubism, and the revolutionary artistic aspects of the Renaissance and the early part of this century, represents historicism at its best: a dialogue between the "hows" as opposed to the "whats" and "wheres."

This multiphase problem introduces the student to the numerous layers that contribute to the quality of inhabitation of place and space through design and the study of history, theory, philosophy, construction, structure, and meaning in architecture. The architect must be prepared to use a great deal of imagination—not only regarding design solutions, but also in the initial approach to design problems. The unconventional forms of the first six projects stretch the imaginative capabilities of the students. They are encouraged to discard some of their preconceptions about buildings, which can sometimes keep them from discovering more innovative solutions to previously unresolved problems in architecture.

Throughout the year the underlying assumption is that one thinks with one's hands, rather than predetermining a design in one's head. While the hands build, the eyes perceive and the mind learns, constructing more ideas for the hands to think about, while building. Thinking, making, perceiving, and learning occur simultaneously in the thinking hands, the precious gift of the architect.

The first project includes the analysis of a painting or print from the late medieval to early Renaissance period. Owing to this period's particular location in history, the student becomes familiar with some of the issues of symbolism and perspective, and their historical and theoretical relevance to the twentieth century. Through researching and then constructing a space that has been created by one of the masters, the student soon becomes familiar with such phenomena as qualities and sources of light, perceptual and symbolic weight of objects and space, materiality, and meaning of place. Through dwelling in a time substantially different from our own, the student begins to gain some insight into the state of contemporary architecture.

The second project, "Place," introduces the students to the process of design. After researching and discussing some of the twentieth-century art and architecture movements having to do with perspective and Cubism, they then proceed to design a significant space called "A Room of One's Own" (inspired by Virginia Woolf's work of the same name).

Two rooms now created, the third problem directs the student to design and construct a structure to house them. Whereas the two previous projects involved the use of materials to create a small-scale place that implied that it could actually be a full-scale room, the third project introduces the student to the use of materials on a scale closer to "one-to-one." The focus of his or her attention is primarily on the design of details, as well as the gesture and form of the structure.

SYSTEMATICS TAXON ONE: Conceptual. *Analytic.* Nonobjective/Compositional. Compositional/Architectonic. *Architectural.* TAXON TWO: *Poetic.* Metaphoric. Literary. *Human Concerns.* Environment. Visual Vocabulary. *Procedural. Programmatic.* Tec-

The fourth project is a study of the space of movement as a significant experiential condition. This project is intended to counteract the unconscious assumption that the space between rooms is less important than the rooms themselves, resulting in nonspaces called corridors. This particular project focuses on vertical circulation, employing the use of elements of intrigue and surprise, by designing an experiential path as the inhabitable space of transition between the realities of the "Medieval" and "Cubist" spaces that have been created thus far.

After completion of the architectonic building of two rooms, a path, and the structure, the fifth project calls for the construction of measured drawings of the building in plan and section. This project exclusively discusses and studies various kinds of drawings—measured drawings, historical sections, and perceptual drawings involving qualities of light, shadow, and texture. The concept of section is discussed relative to the structure of the human body and architecture, along with interiority and the inhabitation of space.

Returning to the structure for the sixth problem, the design of facade is discussed relative to its ability to reveal and conceal the structure, the spaces, and the qualities of the interior. Upon completing the design of facade, the student then constructs drawings of it.

Finally, after dwelling upon the phenomena of analysis, place, path, monument, section, and facade, and the numerous issues associated with them, the student is now prepared to design a building dealing with all of these issues simultaneously—as is the case in the design of architecture. The student is asked to choose an artist and to design a house and studio for him or her. This house is to be a retreat from the complications of city life, a place where the artist will be able to concentrate on his or her work in the quietude of a peaceful setting. The house should reflect the sensibilities of the artist chosen as well as be respectful of the context in which it is created. The considerations of the context include the history and character of the "place," and the dialog between the new building and the existing environs. Since this project is situated between the "city" and a pastoral view, it affords the opportunity to develop the design according to the theme inherent in the site—the transition from culture to nature. Therefore, the design can acknowledge this theme in some way appropriate to the artist chosen.

The accretive quality of this project isn't all that unusual. What is unique, however, is the literal usage of solutions from previous phases of the problem.

This multilayered and intensely thoughtful project is as rich in meaning as they get.

Image 38. Home for Fra Filippo Lippi, facade collage by Cressida Phillips.

A Pool

Leonard Newcomb
Rhode Island School of Design
Providence, Rhode Island

This and one other project in this series (LSU) address the landscape as a source for architectural design. In general, students of architecture should be made more aware of the potential for landscape to inform their decisions; projects of this type may point the way.

It is good to see the linkage between an apparently abstract—some might say melancholic—project and real—much less, significant—buildings.

The loaded metaphors, at times bordering on poesy, serve to enrich this project greatly.

"A Pool" is designed to establish and represent natural and man-made aspects of "site" as an objective fact; to explore the relation between social order, natural order, and built order; and to establish clear definitions of context and the public realm. Through a sequence of exercises in which basic modeling materials are employed in a kind of constructive play, choices are made among material and spatial connections. The goal is the definition of the internally driven—and spontaneous—motives of form-making, and their coherence with social meanings and cultural production observed in the real world. Through ideas about movement, space, connection, (such as approach, entry, and horizon) and scale—ideas that integrate sensuous and intellectual perceptions—virtual occupation and human presence are re-presented by the designer-as-observer.

A dialogue within the studio begins to shape the interaction between formal vocabulary, language, and critical discussion. At mid-semester an analysis problem is introduced in order to examine and clarify these critical relationships through study of and visits to buildings and their sites including, in recent years, those of Aalto, Gropius, Kahn, and Le Corbusier. Focusing on techniques and processes for abstracting formal themes, spatial and material components, and structure and construction, the analysis provides an effective framework for investigating and representing complex works at different scales and degrees of abstraction. Its position in the studio sequence serves to ground emerging themes and ideas in a broader cultural and historical context, and to initiate personal research.

"The Pool" is defined by human occupation; the project thus opens opportunities for insights into social attitudes. The pool is an embrace that separates, excludes, or permits events to enter. Presuppositions about public space and public nature are reexamined in a way consistent with the intuitive and rational development of the foregoing projects in the semester. In an attempt to move beyond the architectural project as an object—something the designer looks down upon on the desktop—the investigation of conditions and the means of representation reveal that the author was there, that she or he saw, touched, and recorded with the same degree of sureness with which the buildings were observed in the earlier exercise. The notion of public, then, is rooted in individual perceptions and self-awareness. The idea of public—including the communal as a special configuration of public—is what interests us as architects: how it manifests itself in our speech, writing, actions, artifacts, claims to space, and uses of the landscape.

The first week of the project is spent in constructing individual site models. No history is given of the settlement from which the users will come, nor of the site. The (hi)story is derived from the student's own sensibility and process. Constructing a landscape at the edge of the sea elicits laws of nature and its features and initiates tectonic speculations, or propositions, as if the underpinnings of gravitational force would illuminate the necessities of our own physical supports. The site model, then, is more than surface; it articulates both apparent and actual social structure.

Students show early preferences en route to the reconciliation of the built work and the landscape: Some choose local sites so that ideas can be tested in actual places; others "remember" sites and explore places of particular meaning in the past. An occasional urban site implies a preference for a landscape culturally transformed.

Precedents and other historical references are cited in antiquity, mythology, literature, in our contemporary media, and, of course, in our immediate buildings and landscapes. These are encouraged for consideration, inclusion, and transformation in the individual's substantive grounding of the project. This is considered to be the beginning of a personal research that may become more defined in the pursuit of the student's own field of interest or chosen discipline.

Derived from this "personal research," a statement of belief is driven by internal forces—spontaneous, accurate, powerful. Clear, incisive images are the medium of the artistic sensibility; to the extent that they endure, they are the key to architecture's vitality. To embody these images in the architectural work, we need a precise and articulate language. Precision in "seeing thought" is then possible only with testing the work on all levels, the passion to reexamine, to use one's particular discipline to strip down again to simple, unalterable truths.

Is any guidance given the students in ensuring a class-wide range of site types (e.g., seaside, landlocked, remote, urban, etc.), or is this catch as catch can? A guaranteed breadth of site typology could provoke some very telling comparisons.

The aspect of introspection, or "personal research," in this project is particularly compelling . . .

. . . and at least as compelling is the lovely, yet stunningly conflicting, metaphor of "precision in 'seeing thought.'"

55

Image 39. Pool project model by Eugene Walker, student of Javier Navarro, fall 1989.

The Otherside of Seaside

Judith Reno
Savannah College of Art & Design
Savannah, Georgia

Michael Kaplan
University of Tennessee
Knoxville, Tennessee

The collective project, here posed as "community," is employed by other contributors. In those projects, too, there is the dual sense of community.

The project authors contend that "no previous basic design study" preceded this multiphase project, yet depending on the parameters and intentions of the "collage models" noted in Project1, these could be viewed as a kind of "basic design" study divorced from purely architectural issues. Likewise, the "visual vocabulary developed in earlier exercises" notation in Project 3 could be similarly held.

"The Otherside of Seaside" consists of three interrelated and interconnected projects. It was preceded by two quarters of freehand and constructed drawing study, but no previous basic design study. The student is introduced to architectural design itself as a problem-solving procedure.

The project is concerned with the development of both the imagination, based on a belief in the possibility of teaching artistry by applying the principle of "reflection in action," and a sense of community, within and between individuals, that supports intrinsic motivation. Also of concern are the creation of artifacts representing the expression of self within the context of a community; examination of the issues of structure, space, and enclosure; and an exploration of the interplay between two and three dimensions, the compositional (abstract) and the utilitarian (physical), and convention and invention.

PROJECT 1: MODELING THE SALVAGE OF CONVENTIONS

The first exercise was a three-dimensional manipulation of conventional, familiar elements: plastic scale-model kits of autos, airplanes, boats, and rocket ships. The two kits selected by each student were to be of different color and scale in order to establish hierarchical relationships when combined. Elements selected from the kits were combined into a "collage model." In step 2, a selected piece of the collage model was enlarged using planar and linear materials, continuing the exploration of composition and hierarchy. Perspective drawings were constructed of this model in the third step, depicting movement around it to represent its volumetric form. In step 4, these drawings were overlaid and combined into a single collage drawing. As a final transformation, a carefully crafted balsa wood model was "extracted" from the last collage.

PROJECT 2: TRANSITIONS

A hypothetical community was created, located adjacent to Seaside, Florida. Like Seaside, it occupied 80 acres and was developed at the same density as its neighbor. The community's major built elements included a gridded central business district, commercial strip, boardwalk, and housing. The Boardwalk was the transitional element in the design of the community that provided a link between the lake and the sea, a bridge over the highway, and passage between the private domain of the house and the public domain of the beach. Codes were established to support a balance between individual expression and communal interaction. This new community was called "Otherside."

Teams of three students were asked to design a length of the Boardwalk that would derive its formal and structural language from the final collage models of Project 1 and appropriately connect to its neighbors at each end. Functional requirements for access, seating, viewing, and shading were to be satisfied. Each team developed a tower node that contained access from ground level (by stair and ramp) and a viewing platform. Vertical structure and circulation also were to be resolved.

PROJECT 3: HOUSE

The final project represented the conclusion of the design process: the ordering of an expression of self into house. Each student was asked to design a beach house for himself or herself using a rule system provided by the professors to guide the location and organization of the design, but not its formal outcome. The student was again required to summon prior knowledge: the visual vocabulary developed in earlier exercises. There was an intent to support the ideas of community and minimal impact on the natural landscape: The clusters of houses were compactly sited and lifted off the ground on poles.

The physical program was defined not by specific square-footage areas but by activities: eating, sleeping, living, working, and bathing. The enclosure provided natural light, ventilation, and view to the boardwalk, lake, and ocean. A carport was required, and one-third of the house had to be either a cabaña or a screened porch. Lot size and shape were determined geometrically. House was the culmination of a process enabling the beginning student to invent forms that would translate into detailed architecture through the initially intuitive, but ultimately conscious, development and application of a personal vocabulary.

Final presentation artifacts included complete schematic drawings, framing diagrams, and a highly detailed model. Work from two studios was exhibited together on a large base model that included the Boardwalk.

Image 40. House grouping, models from Reno studio.

This is an extremely rich and dynamic project!

Design and Build a Sky:
A Tensegrity Project

Alan Stacell
Texas A&M University
College Station, Texas

There are other projects in this collection that integrate studies of structure and design, but this is the only one that builds directly from a specific tectonic type. It is also the only one that phrases the problem in poetic rather than technical terms—no mean feat, given the topic.

This is a fine example of a project that breaks down the artificial conflict between idea, aesthetics, and structure. There are other examples of this intention among the projects in this book.

The tensegrity project is called "build a sky," or "design a sky," because the metaphor links architecture to structure. Tensegrity is a place to begin exploring what structure is all about, and the idea of a sky, or a shelter, is a place to begin pondering what architecture is all about.

Tensegrity is a physical and visual force diagram. Tensional integrity, from which the author of Synergetics, R. Buckminster Fuller, coined the term tensegrity, reveals force pathways and their dual nature—action and reaction, tension and compression. While tensegrity principles have been used in the study of structure at many schools for a number of years, they are normally addressed in a straightforward, pragmatic manner. This exercise, however, is conceived in poetic and metaphoric terms.

Tensegrity is somewhat like executing graphic statics in three dimensions. The force polygons, funicular polygons, and other familiar features of elementary vector mechanics are present and accounted for. There is no equivalent substitute for the formal study of statics, strength of materials, and structural theory with the precision of math, but what tensegrity models and other kindred tensile figures do for the design student is to demonstrate the principles behind equilibrium and stability. Tensegrity opens doors by closing the gap between what architectural school curricula typically deem separate—namely, statics and aesthetics. For the beginning design student, grasping the idea that abstract concept and sensory experience have common ground in the design of structures enables the integration of structural and design thinking in the tutorial studio.

The problem, as given to the students, calls for the design of a "sky," the formal equivalent of a dome that behaves like a balloon. It would be a more ideal balloon if it were a geodesic; i.e., if instead of meridians and hoops of differing diameter, it were made from circles of the same diameter. Meridians and hoops are not confined to circles or segments of circles, but are free to assume most of the great family of funicular shapes that cables naturally take under various distributed loads. The model has a shape somewhere between a parabola and a catenary. What the model does well is to employ cables and struts to their greatest structural advantage in enclosing a volume. The stress pathways created to transfer loads are all either axial tension or axial compression, and this remains the case if the loading shifts and redistributes stress. This system has a great capacity to deform without loss of efficiency. It can flex or not flex, because all joints in the superstructure will translate and rotate without developing secondary stresses.

SYSTEMATICS TAXON ONE: Conceptual. Analytic. Nonobjective/Compositional. Compositional/Architectonic. *Architectural.* TAXON TWO: *Poetic. Metaphoric.* Literary. Human Concerns. Environment. Visual Vocabulary. Procedural. Programmatic. *Tec-*

The structure twins, Concept and Image, are children of our perception. Elephants, bluejays, apples, and beans; arches, domes, vaults, and beams are their progeny. The diatom and the woodpecker share between them a thousand shadows. The dog's ear and the cistern gather rain. How many closets can a push broom have?

Professor Stacell is not only a fine architectural educator, but an inspired poet as well (not to mention a prolific painter). We need more poetry, and artistry, in the study of architecture.

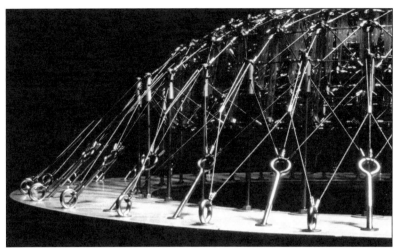

Image 41. Tensegrity model.

The Generic Possibilities of Artistic Pattern

Janez Suhadolc
University of Ljubljana
Ljubljana, Slovenia

The two dimensions to three dimensions explorations that form the heart of this project are quite common. The distinction is the particular cultural bent of the solutions.

It would be interesting to learn more about the instructor's role in this critical process of selection.

The exploration of fertile cultural traditions can be a powerful design determinant, one found to a greater or lesser extent in several projects within these pages.

This series of exercises, presented in seminar, is based on deductive rather than inductive methods of teaching, and stresses architecture as an eminently artistic, intuitive, creative act wherein aesthetic aspects dominate the secondary, utilitarian ones. The goal of this exercise is to have the student creatively convert a generic pattern into a meaningful architecture or design, and to document the stages of its transformation. The making of architecture is conceived as a less rational process guided primarily by its inherent aesthetic code, and only secondarily subject to utilitarian, functional, technical, and scientific standardization. In short, it seeks an architecture of socially relevant dimensions, with a goal of rescuing architecture from the world of techne to that of poesis.

In the Design Seminar classes, work begins with a pattern chosen arbitrarily, by either the instructor or the student. The task of the student is to develop compositions, flat or spatial, whose inherent characteristics invariably lead back to the basic design. Put differently, the student is asked to explore the "hidden" possibilities in an element or pattern, and thus to establish what the generic qualities of an artistic pattern are. The results of this work are diverse, and may include children's toys, objects of everyday use, furniture, residential houses, hotels, or model towns. The finalized works are generally represented in drawn form, but prototypes, models, and maquettes are equally common and welcome.

The results are always compared with previous student works, and with achievements in local and international architectural and design production. At times, students are given exercises that expressly demand the inclusion, either direct or paraphrased, of local cultural tradition. It would be naive to think that their solutions sprang entirely from their own imagination. A certain amount of information may, consciously or not, affect their creative potentials; however, the dilemma of the role of formal education and the forms of positive knowledge transmission remains open as to the essence of creative mechanisms. In any case, the works of the students are all made with great enthusiasm and often in quantity and quality that surpass all expectations.

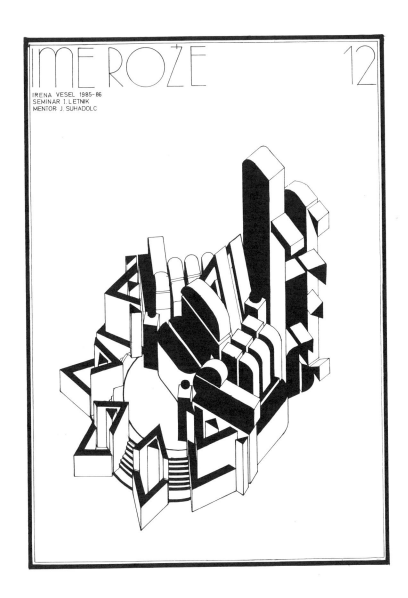

Images 42 and 43. "Ime Roze," two pattern permutations by Irena Vesel.

tonic. TAXON THREE: *Hermetic.* Artifact. Individual. Personal. Social. *Edifice.* Monumental. Neighborhood. City. TAXON FOUR: No Scale. Ambiguous. Relative. *Referential.* Full. TAXON FIVE: Nonvisual. Electronic. Actualized. Expressive. *Descriptive.*

Basic Design

Munehiko Taniguchi
Kogakuin University
Tokyo, Japan

The idea of projects connected to lectures rather than the reverse implies that the actual studio context is less important than is typically the case. Clearly these exercises are accomplished outside the university setting.

It seems that in many spheres, even the merest shred of Bauhausian issues—or the simple consideration of sheer beauty—has become passé. It is refreshing to find a teacher who not only is unafraid of the beautiful, but who even utters the word, repeatedly.

These projects enhance the students' familiarity with design fundamentals and architectural terminology, as well as their interest in and understanding of color—particularly the effects of color on design. The projects also increase their interest in architectural design and structures. The project series is preceded by a lengthy illustrated lecture series addressing issues of course structure, design principles and methods, color theory and application, and ideation. The lectures are accompanied by assignments designed to reinforce the lecture content.

EXERCISE 1: REPRODUCTION OF A SLIDE

A slide of a composition by a famous twentieth-century artist (such as Mondrian or Vasarely) is shown to the students, who are given about ten minutes to sketch the image and to take notes on the colors used by the artist. On the basis of their sketches, the students must reproduce the composition on a sheet of paper 120mm by 120mm. The compositions chosen as models have been carefully selected by the teacher. The main criteria for selection are that they must be based on a simple ratio (e.g., 1:2:3), and that the colors used must be readily understandable.

EXERCISE 2: PROGRESSIVE AND RHYTHMICAL COMPOSITION USING LINES

This exercise calls for the creation of a beautiful composition consisting of horizontal and vertical straight lines, including thoughtful engagement of the planes defined by these lines. As in Exercise 1, the picture area or field is 120mm by 120mm, and work is done in colored paper collage. To begin, a typical set of progressions, such as harmonic progression, geometric progression, Fibonacci series, or logarithmic progression, is shown as examples using a video/slide projector system. These progressions serve as an underpinning, or guide, for the exercises.

EXERCISE 3: TWO-DIMENSIONAL PATTERN USING SQUARES

The students design two beautiful yet systematic patterns using at least five squares as a design motif. The two patterns must be different in terms of the design principle and the color pattern used. Format is identical to the earlier requirements. Solutions that provoke rhythm and movement created by the employment of an appropriate system receive the highest evaluation.

EXERCISE 4: CUBIC EXPRESSION

In this study, designed to investigate cubic effects, students are encouraged to express their own ideas freely. To provide inspiration, several examples of cubic effects are shown. The most successful solutions include multiple cubic images that emphasize harmonious colors.

EXERCISE 5: HOW TO COME UP WITH IDEAS, PART 1

Students are to imagine what form an isometric solid with proportions of 1:2:3 would take if it is made of paper, metal, string, clay, wood, etc. They are then asked to draw as many images as possible in their sketchbook.

EXERCISE 6: HOW TO COME UP WITH IDEAS, Part 2

The students now work for the first time in three dimensions—here in low relief using pieces of slit and folded paper, 60mm by 60mm each in their original flat configuration. The goal is to create a range of relief forms of high visual interest by making the most imaginative use of the placements of the slits, which can be made anywhere on the sheet so long as they do not affect the sides, and of the cubic effect achieved by folding the paper.

EXERCISE 7: CUBIC IMAGINATION

This project is realized in a fully three-dimensional manner. Students are required to make two different undeformable three-dimensional forms using a square of paper 150mm by 150mm. They are allowed to cut and fold the paper, but no part of the original square may be removed. Pieces of colored paper may be attached to some parts of the forms in order to emphasize the configurations. Applications of architectural construction techniques—pin joint and truss-like structures—are introduced to prevent these three-dimensional constructs from deforming.

The origami aspects of this phase are irrepressible and delightful.

The introduction of structural issues seems almost gratuitous in this series, which otherwise is centered on the development of a visual vocabulary.

63

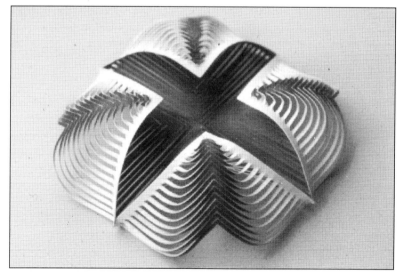

Image 44. Example of Exercise 7, Cubic Imagination model.

Vocabulary of Space
Kurula Varkey
Centre for Environmental Planning and Technology
Ahmedabad, India

Of the various "orders" mentioned, including "the order of symbols and meaning systems," how could the study of "social order" be introduced into this project?

This problem is typical of the point/line/plane genre.

In "the voice of the place" in the full-length version of this project in Annex 1, the author speaks of "the rediscovery in the past of the essence of India's ethos." What is there in this project that we can relate to such a statement?

In this project students are introduced to the basic elements of space-making—the wall and the column—and to the possibilities, through combinations of these elements, for the evolution of a variety of spatial types and varying degrees of enclosure and openness. Permutations and combinations of wall and column yield what may be termed "spatial words." As in language, words can be assembled so as to create different organizations—the equivalent of sentences—that carry distinct meanings. The laws or principles by which the words combine to create these sentences can be thought of as grammar, the architectural equivalent of which is order—spatial order, dimensional order, geometric order, material and structural order, proportional order, and the order of symbols and meaning systems. These orders establish both the relationships that unite parts into a totality and the character of the final solution.

Throughout the project reference is made to three basic principles of design: the theme or idea that unifies parts into a totality; order and discipline, by which they are related to each other; and variation and sensorial stimulus.

In the first part of the exercise students choose as basic elements one of the following groups (no more than nine elements are allowed in a group):
1. cubes of 2.5 M and 5.0 M sides,
2. cylinders of 2.5 M and 5.0 M diameter,
3. hexagonal or octagonal prisms of 2.5 M and 5.0 M sides.

In each case a maximum of three elements from another group can be included, creating potentially a working collection of twelve elements. Partial units that imply a whole may also be used. The addition of level changes and freestanding walls or columns to signify entrance, movement, direction, transition, foci, interval, and termination is encouraged. Using these elements plus the allowed additions as building blocks, the student explores issues of space and spatial order.

In the second part of the exercise, the design solution developed in Part 1 is modified to include roof forms. The relationships of mass and space alter substantially because of the introduction of these overhead elements, which have their own values of position and direction. In addition, the student is to introduce a water body of some appropriate shape and a tree in a suitable position. All work consists of three-dimensional models, subsequently made into drawings.

Image 45. Part 1, models.

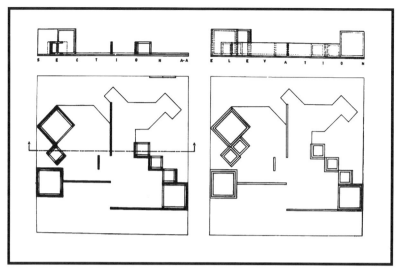

Image 46. Part 1, plan, section, and elevation drawings.

65

Studio and Dwelling for a Bookbinder

Betsy Williams
University of Michigan
Ann Arbor, Michigan

The author's honesty is refreshing in her frank admission of "tricking" the students, which, in reality, many of us do.

Field trips such as this greatly enrich a project.

There is in fact a rich tradition of relating diverse creative pursuits such as painting, sculpture, or literature to the study of design. There are other examples of that technique in this book; such an approach was central to the pedagogy of the Bauhaus, among others.

"Studio and Dwelling for a Bookbinder" is given in the first semester of the second year of undergraduate architectural studies. Prior course work includes one term each of construction, environmental technology, history, and design fundamentals, plus two drawing courses and two design studios. The author notes:

> *Students' design skills are not always commensurate with their technological and intellectual abilities. Studio projects tend to suffer if not structured in such a way as to offset this imbalance. I find it most successful when the problem scope is limited and defined, and introduced through abstracted architectural explorations.*

In the creation of this studio problem, an attempt was made to address the common student question of how to begin the design process. The ideal was a project type that would prove conducive to individual interpretation and the search for meaning. By starting with an abstract yet related project of making, the students would be encouraged to think about conceptual issues that could inform their architecture. In a way, they were "tricked" into thinking about architecture.

The project was an experiment of the author's invention, inspired by her personal interest in paper constructions. It was an attempt to assign a simple yet sophisticated project that could capitalize on both the knowledge and the naïveté of the students, who are asked to design the studio and dwelling place for a hand bookbinder on an urban site in Ann Arbor. The project begins with a tour of a local bindery, after which each student receives the problem statement in the form of small unbound sheets of paper, artfully wrapped by the teacher. The contents of the handout package include a miniaturized reproduction of "The Art of Bookbinding," from Bibliopecia by John Hannet. The pages are then assembled or bound in a manner that either explores or challenges the concept of "binding."

Through discussion following the initial exercise, common ground is found between the issues of the act of binding and the act of making architecture; students are asked to derive relationships between architecture and other creative pursuits, and are encouraged to think about conceptual issues that could inform their architectural solutions. They were also introduced to the relationship of craft and idea, while developing an understanding of and respect for the work of their proposed client.

SYSTEMATICS TAXON ONE: *Conceptual.* Analytic. Nonobjective/Compositional. Compositional/Architectonic. *Architectural* . TAXON TWO: Poetic. *Metaphoric.* Literary. Human Concerns. Environment. Visual Vocabulary. Procedural. *Programmatic.* Tec-

Phase 2 calls for translation of the ideas explored in the binding exercise to the design of a shop, studio, and dwelling for the bookbinder. For some, the ideas explored through binding became the generator for their building development. For others, the binding project served as a point of departure for the architectural project. In either case, the process of using a handcrafted object at artifact scale as a metaphor for a building proved an effective tool in breaking down stereotypes.

The more interesting solutions submitted were those most clearly and directly informed by the act of binding.

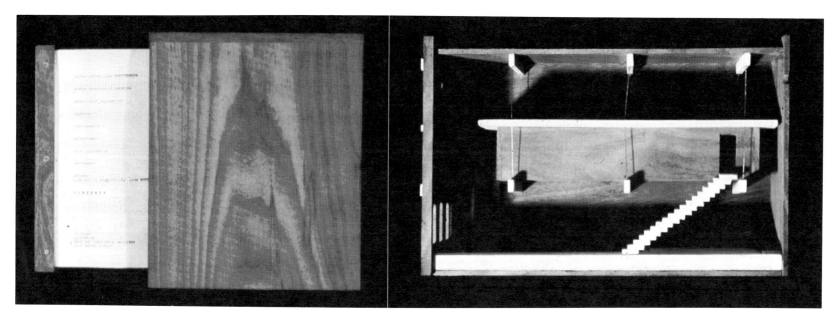

Image 47. Book designed by Ken Nye, and his model of the studio/dwelling for a bookbinder.

Understanding Structures Through Models

David T. Yeomans
University of Manchester
Manchester, England

Discussing structure as a crucial early learning design decision, as opposed to being a late—sometimes unwelcome—arrival brought in to "prop up" one's DEE-zine, is very healthy.

"Only with actual buildings..." is a bit dogmatic. See Professor Yeomans's own essay, which closes this book, for a more balanced and in-depth argument.

"Only with actual buildings..." is a bit dogmatic. See Professor Yeomans's own essay, which closes this book, for a more balanced and in-depth argument.

This project involves modeling the structure of existing buildings in order to explain, and thus understand, the structural actions involved. The intention is to introduce architecture students to the role of structures in buildings, and to give them an idea of the influence that the choice of structure might have on the resultant architectural form. The essence of the exercise is that students select a building from a list provided, make a model illustrating its structure, and use that model to explain this in a class seminar.

Only with actual buildings can we explore the relationship between architecture and structural form, and this can be developed further by looking at more than one structure of a similar type. Thus the list from which the students select has groups of similar structures, usually three, and while they create a model of just one of them, they are asked to compare its structure with the others in the same group. The study of real buildings has an element of fun because students select buildings that interest them. It is also enjoyable because students are being encouraged to think for themselves instead of simply following a set experimental route. Indeed, thinking for oneself is an important part of the exercise: Students will not be able to find the answers in a textbook.

The subjects on the list given to the students date from Roman times to the present day. If there is any weakness in it, it is the relative paucity of more recent buildings. This is not because they are not interesting, but rather because of the occasional difficulty of finding good structural information. Students are given a list of sources that have proved useful—books for the earlier buildings, and journals for the more recent ones. Not all the structures chosen will have simple explanations, and it is useful to include some examples of these to provoke discussion. It is also interesting to include structures that are not as they appear to be. The Sainsbury building at the University of East Anglia, for example, appears to be a portal frame but is in fact just trusses resting on large "columns."

It is worth noting that the exercise does not stand alone, but is associated with a series of lectures on historical structures, which runs in parallel with a complementary course on structural analysis. The lectures are presented as a brief history of structures, but the intention is as much structural as historic, demonstrating that it is possible to make approximate assessments of the forces and stresses in quite complex structures using very simple means.

The importance of the final seminar, when students explain their structures, cannot be overemphasized. While it does involve an element of assessment, this is of minor importance at this stage of the course. First, the seminar enables all students to see a range of structural types. Second, it is important to uncover any misconceptions that they may have about the behavior of structures. It is necessary to stress that it is not the quality of the model itself that is important, but rather the quality of the visual explanation. Thus it is critical to emphasize that this is not an exercise in fine model-making.

Stressing the use of "messy" models to communicate a diagrammatic point, without getting hung up in "craftiness," is good in this context

Image 48. Structural analysis model.

ANNEX 1
Project and Program Details

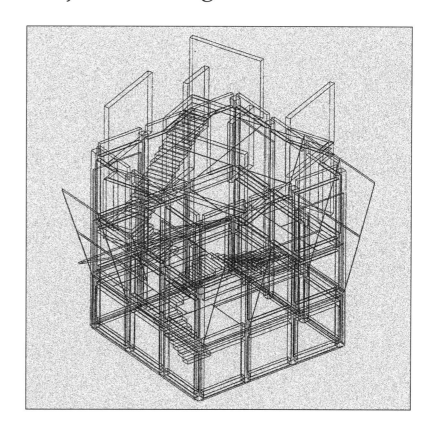

The Journey

John Andrews
Royal Melbourne Institute of Technology
Melbourne, Australia

SUPPLEMENTARY INFORMATION

THE VOICE OF THE PLACE

Interior Design has moved from being a specialist service in the void between decoration and architecture into a holistic profession addressing complex issues ranging from detailed, object-based problems to immense "interior cities." Because of this widening vision and scope, it is becoming difficult to observe where the mark of one previously autonomous discipline ends and another begins. By implication, we may be observing in the near future an increase in the number of total environmental practices, which include landscape design, interior design, architecture, industrial, furniture, and graphic design. The designer will be involved with a wide range of expressive media including performance, computer-assisted film-making, publication, and hands-on production. Social, political, and ecological concerns are also affecting the designer's program, potentially inspiring an entirely new aesthetic.

The Interior Design course at Royal Melbourne Institute of Technology is project-based, and its philosophy embraces a wide spectrum of design approaches and fields. These make possible the enrichment of traditional concerns with the imagining of space through engagement with theoretical discourse, objects, furniture, theater and film, and large-scale urban "interiors." The department is composed of layers: Design, Technical Studies, History, and Theory. Sometimes these interlink, and at other times they are autonomous. Together they form a complex network of interrelationships. In describing these components, a portrait emerges that reflects the current spirit and optimism of the school.

THE INTENT OF THE PROJECT

The primary concern is not isolated formal building blocks of design, but rather an accumulative "journey" of creative imagination that raises design issues in the course of its path. "The Journey" exists as an inquiry that moves inward into spaces that provoke students' creativity. It begins on the exterior—recording and observing existing environments—then guides students to start exploring within themselves, and within a building's fabric, ultimately to delve within an environment's form and structure to identify, explore, and create spatially.

THE DURATION OF THE PROJECT

The foundation program in design is a full-year subject, divided into two thirteen-week semesters. Only the first semester is outlined in detail in this book. It covers four areas of emphasis: Perception and Measured Drawing, Travel, Objectives, and Synthesis. Each area culminates in an exhibition. The second semester of the foundation year continues on, to invite students to investigate the cultural and poetic framing of notions of space. The semester begins with a History/Theory studio, and then approaches a set of interrelated and accretive projects. The first phase is a generation and study of urban mapping. The second demands a self-generated project that reflects the student's understanding of all the previous design projects, and their current perceptions of what interior design is. The third phase involves a synthesis of these explorations in the creation of an interior design project in that section of the city which the students have previously mapped.

THE RMIT CURRICULUM

The Bachelor of Arts in Interior Design is a four-year course, offered only on a full-time basis. The department has the following postgraduate degrees available: Master of Arts in Interior Design, Master of Architecture in Interior Design, and Master of Applied Science in Interior Design.

The place and level of platform courses

As has been noted previously, beginning design takes place in the first year of college study.

The pedigree of the project

This course of study is the invention of Professor Andrews, based on work he had done at the Architectural Association. He introduced it at RMIT upon becoming head of the interior design department there.

THE EVALUATION

"The Journey" has been given twice, in the first semester of 1991 and the first semester of 1992.

Having the benefits of a slight distance from the First Year program (apart from attending the many exhibitions, pin-up juries and one of the travel studios), I feel I am in a perfect position to offer a subjective evaluation of this new year.

The major impression or aura that stems from this particular year is one of raw energy, enthusiasm, and a genuine desire to learn. It is indicated clearly in all the interim presentations and finished work and also in the group activities such as workshops, seminars, openings, and trips. Whether this stems from the course structure, selection process, the lecturers (Ross McLeod, Roger Kemp, Andrea Mina, Robyn Lines, and Jean James), or purely from the individuals that make up this group I cannot say, but something is in the ether that surrounds them, and it is obviously most potent.

—John Andrews

THE PROJECT

PERCEPTION AND MEASURED DRAWINGS

This part of the program provides a framework for direct experience of existing city surroundings, and an introduction to the language and concerns of the built environment.

For the first semester of 1992, the specific environment chosen for exploration was a city intersection, where a 1914 Magistrates' Court

Image 49. Sketch of Magistrate's Court by Cassandra Fahey.

Building and a 1991 Commercial Office Building are located on a diagonal from each other.

The context of these buildings creates a visual dialogue that can be addressed, allowing issues of perception, understanding, and communication to be raised. Recognizing and questioning the context liberates each building from an isolated "object" status, and focuses on formal

Image 50. Sketch of office building by Taak Akrasanee.

Image 51. Earthwork model of "Gateway Project" at Coober Pedy.

qualities for analysis. This questioning also begins to make the student conscious of the filters through which each individual perceives the environment.

Through developing abilities to sketch, draw freehand perspectives, and work in different media, students begin to hone individual observations, and to move beyond attempts to make "exact" recordings. Yet at the same time, the formal qualities of the buildings are also explored with measured exactness. Conducting measured surveys and drawing plans, elevations, and details introduces students to the precision and the conventions of measured drawings, and establishes opportunities for conversation, through drawing, with related disciplines.

Regular critiques of the work are held, encouraging verbal presentation skills and establishing a forum for objective criticism. They provide opportunities for students to identify progression in their work, to learn from their contemporaries, and to finish and mount work to a standard suitable for public display.

TRAVEL

The exploration of "known" built environments now develops into an investigation and engagement with the landscape. The design pro-

Image 52. "Impressions" of mountains by Jasmine Wong.

and abstract, experiences and impressions in sketches and in built form. In addition, groups work toward a definition of their collective place in, and response to, the landscape.

Via sketches and maps students identify borders around the campsite, a process that begins to analyze and define the reality of the campsite area. Students map personal interpretations of the area, such as light, rock formations, sound, or atmosphere. Sketches often examine small details in the landscape as a version of the universe in micro. These reveal forms that can be examined, interpreted, and abstracted as a catalyst for design. Locating personal spaces, students respond to these spaces in poetry, and also built form, creating temporary sculptures as representations of themselves in the landscape.

An exploratory critique is held on return to school, where students can compare and confirm similar experiences, and work begins on an exhibition to realize the camp experience in a spatial sense.

OBJECTIVES

The study area "objectives" seeks to loosen up thinking, to question, explore and experiment with possibilities and to propose new forms and thoughts in respect to everyday objects. It extends ideas of designing via the landscape and personal reference, begun in the travel studio, to include other areas of reference such as history, culture, and function.

Focusing on the "object" is central to this study area, introducing creative exploration in three dimensions, and exposing students to formalized design tools, related disciplines, and the idea of visualizing nonreality.

The students' task is to design and produce an object to meet a set of parameters. A series of day *esquisses* support the development of the object by exploring the many levels beyond the functional one at which the objects most obviously exist.

Through the *esquisses* students are encouraged not only to research design precedent and to record existing forms, but also to work beyond these. They are asked to challenge their prejudices and to reveal the hidden possibilities that can generate and support their design.

This studio necessarily extends the students' understanding of related disciplines, and continues to develop their ability to communicate both orally and visually. "Objectives" also highlights a process of problem solving and develops awareness of the complex issues that

gram always includes a travel studio to allow students this opportunity. The first group traveled to the desert of Central Australia, including Uluru (Ayers Rock) and the underground town of Coober Pedy, where the Gateway project shown in Images 4, 8, and 51 is sited. The following year the students were divided into three groups, traveling to the ocean, the river, and the mountains. These trips provide an opportunity for students to meet each other and the lecturers in a relaxed atmosphere, and to move from being observers of an urban environment to consciously locating and positioning themselves within a landscape.

The "camp" exercises lead from developing a personal understanding and awareness of the environment to beginning to translate,

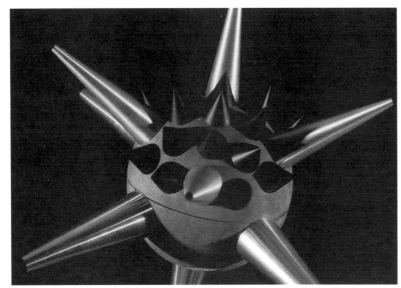

Image 53. "Object" by Jasmine Wong.

provide a generating impulse for work. The objects develop a "precious" status with the advent of a curated exhibition.

SYNTHESIS

"Synthesis" offers the opportunity to integrate understanding from the previous studios in the design of interior environments.

The studio works through a process leading from object to space in a series of conceptual shifts that work toward an unpredicted endpoint. The "solutions" to each of the projects are momentary resting points before journeying further.

The exercises transfer focus from personal expression to questioning the dynamics of the physical space our bodies occupy. Realizing the physical space of the body in drawing is the first approach, which becomes the basis for the construction of a maquette as an abstraction of the human body in a dynamic or static context.

Each student then begins to explore the space within their maquette, embarking upon a conceptual spatial journey. This journey is translated into sketches and models so that the imaginary space can be entered and traversed.

This exploration introduces conscious manipulation of interior

Image 54. "Maquettes": left, Ivan Li; right, Sioban Ashton.

space, allowing students to see beyond the model as object and engage with images in a spatial sense. The object-as-form loses importance, as form develops meaning as a conscious tool in spatial development.

The final exercise is a synthesis of these explorations, developing nine consecutive images of a creative and physical narrative within their imagined spaces. This process empowers the students as they translate their space in scale and medium, taking control of what is seen and the space that is viewed. The students create a narrative of vision and experience, and in maintaining control of "nonreality," they define themselves as designers.

EXHIBITIONS

The processes throughout the semester are paramount, but do not overshadow the results. Each of the four areas of emphasis—Percep-

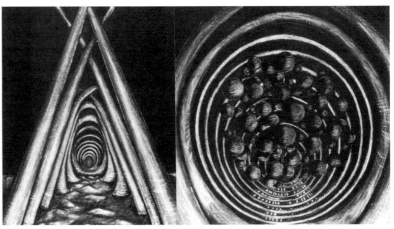

Image 55. "Narrative drawings" by Sandra Grulli.

Image 56. Exhibition from the Objects Studio.

tion and Measured Drawing, Travel, Objectives, and Synthesis—culminates in an exhibition. The progression in the style and approach to these exhibitions is in itself a set of accumulating stages in design exploration.

An exhibition of the Perception and Measured Drawing work is for the students filled with excitement and panic. It provides the group with its first experience of critiquing each other's work, and of displaying their own in public. It is a form of "coming out," revealing their experiences and learning to coordinate individual work so as to create a group expression.

The Travel studios exhibition is an event that encourages students to reinterpret, relocate, and re-scale the reality of their travels. The most recent exhibition existed as a "journey" through the three landscapes, with the students realizing their travel perceptions in a spatial sense for others to experience.

The Objectives studio exhibition, curated by the staff, creates a forum for vigorous critique, discussions about definitions of excellence, and the criteria for the selection of exhibited pieces.

The final exhibition displays the Synthesis projects and selected work from previous studios, with the students providing the motiva-

tion and design in a display of skills acquired during this formative journey. The organization, invitation, and exhibition of the fruits of their labors become an entirely self-motivated and executed exercise—the fullest expression of the individual as designer.

Nine-Square Matrix

James Bagnall, William Benedict and Laura Joines
California Polytechnic State University at San Luis Obispo
San Luis Obispo, California

SUPPLEMENTARY INFORMATION

THE VOICE OF THE PLACE

The objective of Cal Poly's professional program is to develop the design and technical skills necessary to pursue a career in the field of architecture. Architecture is concerned with man-made environments and the people who inhabit them. The architect is required to develop an understanding of, and sensitivity to, human needs, while developing a variety of technical skills. The program is broad in nature. With careful selection of elective work, areas of specialization may be included.

THE INTENT OF THE PROJECT

This project provides students with a formal format for exploring basic issues of architectural design related to simplicity and complexity, proportion and scale, and making sets of relationships between parts and the whole. The project is designed for a guaranteed level of success to encourage beginning students.

THE DURATION OF THE PROJECT

The project lasts for three weeks in a thirty-week sequence.

THE CAL POLY UNIVERSITY CURRICULUM

The curriculum is a five-year professional Bachelor of Architecture degree program.

THE PLACE AND LEVEL OF PLATFORM COURSES

Beginning design studios occur in the second year of university study. They are preceded in the first year by prerequisite graphic analysis and communications courses. The "Nine-Square Matrix" project is presented near the beginning of the second ten weeks. It sits as an architectonic project in the middle of an abstract-to-architectural continuum that begins with basic design principles and builds to encompass a broad range of architectural issues.

THE PEDIGREE OF THE PROJECT

We are unclear on the pedigree of all projects, and are more interested in their usefulness and efficacy to our particular needs rather than their history. The sources of inspiration are manifold, sometimes even obvious, but their application and how they evolve in their application is more interesting to us. We developed these projects without reference to precedents but with regard to our own educational needs in the studio. Any originality would be a happy offshoot of the process of designing these projects; it was not an ostensible goal.

THE EVALUATION

There are many factors that influence project design—the personality and interests of the teachers, the culture of the school, the curriculum, educational theories, architectural philosophies, etc. The "Nine-Square Matrix" project is the product of a group—The Foun-

dation Design Network—that is working to reshape the fundamentals of architectural design program at Cal Poly. The group's goal is to develop a three-quarter-long program with coherence and focus that would evolve over time through the unique contributions of each participant.

"The "Nine-Square" project shares objectives with the other fundamentals problems that address communication, process, and content goals. Specifically, the "Nine-Square" project supports communication objectives in the areas of model building, layout, and concept diagramming, and draws on general design principles previously introduced and explored. The project's theoretical focus is the definition of architectural space. Its key objectives include development of the ability to define a hypothesis or strategy for investigating complexity in spatial definition; being able to consciously manipulate the number, attributes and organization of architectural elements to create spatial compositions of relative complexity; and being able to communicate in words and diagrams the hypothesis investigated, concepts employed, and discoveries made in the investigation.

—*Jim Bagnall, Will Benedict and Laura Joines*

THE PROJECT

The student is to design and construct a three-dimensional composition of spaces for each combination of floors, walls, and roofs at each level of complexity identified in the investigation matrix—a total of nine compositions.

Each simple-to-complex continuum (1/2/3, 4/5/6, and 7/8/9) is to exhibit three clearly different and evenly spaced levels of complexity; they should present a smooth gradation from simple to complex. Each simple-to-complex continuum and/or the matrix as a whole is to test a defined hypothesis concerning the perception of spatial complexity. The models may be constructed only of white or colorless opaque, translucent, or transparent materials. The sites/bases may be nine individual, three horizontal, or one inclusive unit. The compositions may

Investigation Matrix

Level of complexity

	Simple		Complex
Floors	1	2	3
Floors & Walls	4	5	6
Floors, Walls & Roofs	7	8	9

Element Combinations

Image 57. Investigation matrix.

not extend horizontally past the boundaries of their individual sites and/or the base. Each composition must contain a minimum of three visually accessible, inhabitable spaces, each of which employs its assigned combination of floors, walls, and/or roofs. A minimum of one scale figure must be placed within one of the inhabitable spaces of each composition. An inhabitable space is any space with no dimension less than the height of the scale figure.

The models must be accompanied by a two-dimensional presentation that communicates in words and diagrams the complexity hypothesis; the specific concepts employed in its exploration; and observations on the successes, failures, and discoveries of the investigation.

FRAMEWORK ELEMENTS

The four essential elements of the framework include the matrix and continua, the elements of architecture, complexity, and a research orientation. Each of these elements is an important contributor tot he strength of the project.

Image 58. Nine Square Matrix model by Susana Chan, student of Laura Joines. Above: perspective view; below: top-plan view.

Matrix and Continua

The matrix and continua structure the project and give it unique educational value by placing the compositions into a relationship. This requires that each composition be evaluated in relationships to all others. Comparison becomes a source of information through which ideas and relationships can be clarified and strengthened. The continua require that extremes be defined that expand the student's awareness of the possibilities contained within an idea. Based on the extremes, middles are created—the grays or subtleties of an idea are confronted. The compositions' relative qualities must be examined and manipulated to create a smooth transition from one to the other, requiring that both independent factors be isolated and interactions observed.

The use of the matrix and continua ensures that the models—the externalization and representation of ideas—become sources of understanding and discovery. Design decisions are seen not as right or wrong but as appropriate given the context and goals. The interrelationships demand that the student consciously take control of the elements and thereby the compositions themselves. Finally, the overall effect of the matrix and continua is an increase in the thoughtfulness and depth of understanding achieved from the project.

Floors, Walls, and Roofs

One side of the matrix establishes the combinations of the basic architectural elements—floor, walls, and roof—to be investigated. By categorizing the space-defining elements in these terms the project takes on an explicitly architectural orientation, and books such as *Archetypes in Architecture* (Thiis-Evensen, 1987), *Architecture Form, Space and Order* (Ching, 1979), *Elements of Architecture* (von Meiss, 1990), and *Architectural Composition* (Krier, 1988), among others, become sources of theoretical enrichment for the problem.

Complexity

The foil for exploring the space—defining possibilities of floors, walls, and roofs is complexity—an issue of compositional and aesthetic concern that Robert Venturi's "gentle manifesto" in *Complexity and Contradiction in Architecture* reintroduced into architectural dialog. Complexity has the power to focus the full range of compositional concepts and issues. It can be presented as a neutral context within which stu-

dents can take a position, The simple question "Which is more complex?" has consistently elicited spirited discussion between students and drawn out a rich and comprehensive range of issues. It fosters examination of both the elements and the whole. In the simplest terms, complexity can be seen as a function of number, variety and relationship: the number of elements, attributes, and organizations; the variety of elements, attributes, and organizations, and the relationships between the elements, attributes, and organizations.

Research

The project is explicitly given a research or invetigation orientation. As such, the subject of the research must be defined by the student. The framework provides only a structure or context; the student must provide the agenda or value system that will bring it alive. The project's meaningfulness grows in direct proportion to the degree to which students invest themselves in some discovery.

As an investigation, the project requires the student consciously identify a set of factors to be investigated and explicitly communicate them to others. This process builds students' vocabulary and abilities in translating ideas into words and diagrams. It also aids in building an understanding of the difference between a concept and a specific manifestation of that concept.

The two-dimensional component of the presentation is an essential part of the research orientation of the project. Its role is to make explicit the hypothesis or positions that the investigation is exploring, identify the specific concepts being manipulated, and reflect on the exploration's discoveries. The process of making project-thinking explicit facilitates conscious decision making and meaningful learning.

FRAMEWORK INTERPRETATIONS

The framework provides a structure that supports several basic interpretations or strategies. A teacher or student can choose to emphasize one or more depending on the issues he or she is interested in exploring. The most fundamentals interpretations relate to the choice of elements and the relationships between the nine compositions. The choice of elements can range from nine unique sets of elements to one single element used throughout. A middle position might be that the elements are common to each set of three compositions. For example, the same elements are use dint he simple-to-complex continuum

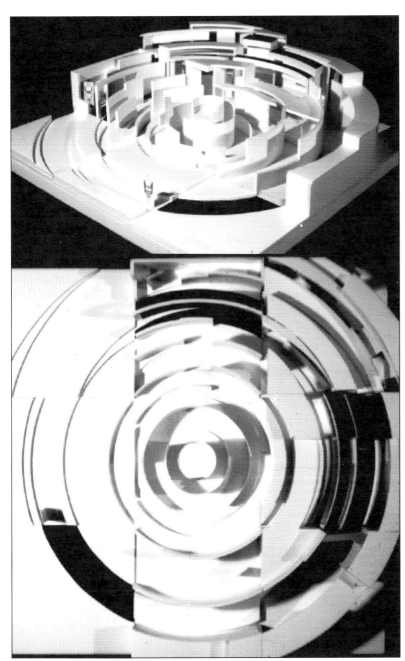

Image 59. Nine Square Matrix model by Jae Lee, student of Laura Joines. Above: perspective view; below: top-plan view.

for floors. Another strategy would be for the floors designed in the "floors" continuum to be carried on as a basis for the floors and walls continuum, etc.

The relationships between the compositions can range from nine independent and autonomous objects to one composition of nine parts—the compositions can be physically independent and unrelated, physically independent but related, or physically connected and related. A middle interpretation might be for the elements and/or compositions to produce a sequential relationship through a gradation and/or transformation.

Finally, when addressing the elements and relationships, the students' strategy could be to run nine independent experiments, three simple-to-complex experiments, or one inclusive experiment.

ENRICHMENT ADDENDA

The framework is like the frame for a picture—it provides the overall focus for the specific projects within it. The framework is the vessel for the evolution of the meaning, history, and enrichment of its inscribed projects. The enrichment addenda are the layers of meaning, like the deposited layers of an oyster shell, layers that address permutations and demands. The enrichment addenda add alternative interpretations to the framework dialog, giving the resultant pearls their unique qualities.

Adding layers to the project frame allows a "network" of instructors to use the frame as a basic project approach and overlay it with supplemental issues and agendas. Layering allows for individual interests and concerns based on the educational philosophies of the instructor to inform the project frame. The layers serve to adapt the skeletal frame to fit the particular needs of a studio situation. They adjust the educational level and intent of the project to the local context and conditions of the school, location, or students, and allow for a particular architectural focus or attitude toward a project.

The enrichments can be built into the original problem statement or introduced through a series of focused explorations. They are able to deal with a fusion of parts not ordinarily associated, fusions whose speculations and combinations are allowed to obey an altogether different rule of order, yet whose layers of enrichment fit into a larger composition. It might be seen as a linked progression of experiments composing a formal sequence. This approach allows each individual student to find his or her unique direction within the frame.

The layered-enrichments approach responds to current conditions in the profession that indicate that the role of the architect is becoming less defined as a maker of prime objects, irreducible in their nature, and changing to one of making combinations between spaces, relationships, and things. As architects we spend more time revising, replicating, and recombining then we do creating new and irreversible truths.

The method of overlaying a frame with enrichment layers addresses this evolving role of architects. It encourages students to see a project as composed of many information bits and legible units. Through their interaction and association, both the structural frame and the layers of content become greater in their overall meaning than they would be as singular investigations. Overlaying and integrating information and ideas enriches the process and the eventual products.

There are many ways to enrich the basic framework, and each issue can be built into the frame or introduced as overlays. The following are enrichments that have been explored by teachers in the network: explorations of a variety of spatial types; variations of surface, in color and/or texture; reinforcement of the role of proportion in the interpretation of simplicity and complexity, and in the definition of spaces; infusion of expression and meaning; the introduction of human scale; and an intense requestioning: "What is a floor, a wall, or a roof?"

SOURCES

Thiis-Evensen. *Archetypes in Architecture.* Oxford: Oxford University Press, 1987, 1989.

Zevi, Bruno. *Architecture as Space*; how to look at architecturre. New York: Horizon Press, 1957; revised, 1974.

Ching, Frank. *Interior Design Illustrated.* New York: Van Nostrand Reinhold{??}, 1987.

Ching, Francis D. K. Architecture, *From Form to Space and Order*. New York, Van Nostrand Reinhold, 1979.

Summerson, John Newenham, Sir. *The Classical Language of Architecture.* Cambridge: MIT Press, 1966, c. 1963.

Licklider. *Architectural Scale.* London Architectural Press, 1965.

Bachelard, Gaston. *The Poetics of Space.* New York: Orion Press, 1964.

Mapping Tools

Peter Beard
Architectural Association
London, UK

SUPPLEMENTARY INFORMATION

THE VOICE OF THE PLACE

The AA has a slightly maverick course structure developed principally by the late Alvin Boyarsky. It operates as the only independent architecture school in the United Kingdom, outside conventional university models and course structures, and hence defies immediate description.

THE INTENT OF THE PROJECT

What perceptions do architects possess? This is a study in considering how our perception is framed by the instruments and methodologies we adopt for looking, and then considering the distance and relation between the means of representation that architects use to develop proposals and the real, lived-in space of buildings and places. At the same time, it is about mastering techniques of making and craft, tested in the construction of a working instrument of measurement, representing qualities of a place (site) in a drawing (map), and relating a built artifact (the instrument) to a site and to a set of conceptual intentions.

THE DURATION OF THE PROJECT

The project lasts one full term.

THE ARCHITECTURAL ASSOCIATION CURRICULUM

The five-year AA Diploma consists of a 1 + 2 + 2 model. Completion of the three-term first year permits entry into the two-year Inter mediate School. After completing Intermediate School, the student enters the two-year Diploma. The AA has no credit system, and no grading.

THE PLACE AND LEVEL OF PLATFORM COURSES

Candidates for first-year design studios may or may not have followed a one-year foundation course at the school prior to entering the program. The "Mapping Tools" project is given in the first term of the first-year design studio.

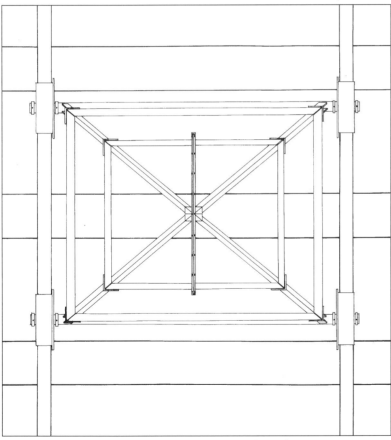

Image 60. Top-plan view of mapping device by Helena Thomas.

THE PEDIGREE OF THE PROJECT

The "Mapping Tools" project is the original invention of Professor Beard.

THE EVALUATION

This project is conducted by Peter Beard as Unit Master, with the assistance of co-tutors Mark Brearley, Liza Fior, David Racz, and Mike Weinstock. It has been given once, in 1990.

> *The project was originally seen as the starting point for a building proposition on the site, but eventually took over as the primary center of attention. Building the instruments was a very time-consuming process. The level of detail and craft was much greater than had originally been envisaged—the depth and success of these investigations prompted us to extend the program for this part of the project.*

> *Main criticisms centered on the introspective quality of the pieces and their hermeticism. The sense of relation between the tools and the space of the site was lost in the world of the workshop and machine tools. The project has been reformulated for the year 1990–91."*

—*Peter Beard*

THE PROJECT

From the original project brief given to the students: "Primary tools of your own devising will be used to make and measure land—staking out and scratching the earth's surface, then mapping and recording using the techniques of the archaeologist, surgeon, surveyor, draftsman, navigator, physicist, tailor, and geographer. . . ."

The project considers the relationship of perceived reality and its representation, the correspondence between paper and land, between

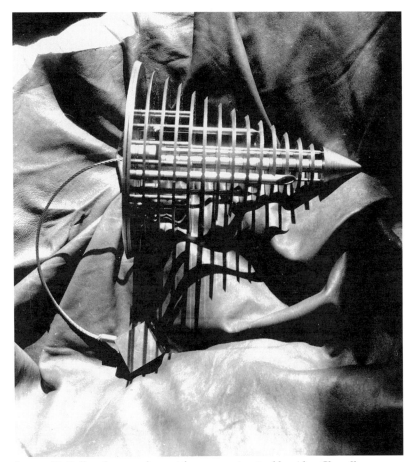

Image 61. Full-scale cone element from mapping tool by Alan Chandler.

a map and real space.

Central to the project was the making of a tool with which to effect this correspondence. This involved detailed issues of working with materials, jointing and construction, dimension and scale, all of these being considered in relation to the operation and use of the tool. The tool acts as a mediator between the body of the surveyor and the site. It frames the surveyor's perception and actions and in so doing uncovers a hidden text; it simultaneously blinds and speaks.

The project was originally seen as the starting point for a building proposition on the chosen site, a piece of wasteland at Canning Town, East London. The act of mapping the site in this direct and individual

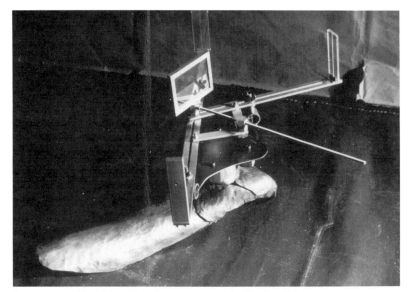

Image 62. Full-scale model of mapping tool by Taylor Galyean.

form was seen as a way to a singular and detailed perception of that place. This could then be exploited as a theme for the building proposition. What was originally seen as preparatory work became a project in itself, and the building proposition was abandoned.

SPECIFIC FOCUS

The specific focus was threefold:
1. mastering techniques of making and craft, tested in the construction of a working instrument of measurement;
2. representing qualities of a place (site) in a drawing (map); and
3. relating a built artifact (the instrument) to a site and a set of conceptual intentions.

BROAD THEMES

There were two broad themes:
1. consideration of how our perception is framed by the instruments and methodologies we adopt for looking; what perceptions do architects privilege?
2. consideration of the distance and relation between the means of

representation that architects use to develop proposals and the real "lived-in" space of buildings and places.

OUTLINE

The project was introduced to the students with a visit to the Whipple Museum of the History of Science in Cambridge, England, which has an extensive collection of surveying devices dating from the eighteenth century and earlier. These surveying devices suggested a range of approaches to the idea of measurement, and provoked a consideration of the way such tools frame a perception of space. The project brief did not ask for the re-creation of such tools, nor did it ask for a measurement of the site in the same terms, i.e., spatial dimension. The tools that were constructed challenged the land surveyor's perception of space. The proposition is that many things in a place contribute to its qualities and conditions; thus, every reading of a site is subjective. What is to be measured is open to question.

The notion of "tool" carries with it an idea of an intimacy of scale and a close relationship between the body of the user and the tool as an artifact. The tool must be attuned to the space of the body of the user, and this condition provokes a close consideration of the body itself. How is the tool to be held? What is its scale and weight? What senses of the body can it extend or address?

The traditional surveyor's tool acts as a kind of intermediary. It extends the space of the surveyor's body into the site through its ability to register or record. In its registration of conditions of the site—for example, the measurement of position through the use of a sighting device and the measurement of its alignment with a graduated scale—and in the process, the tool itself is changed. It adapts its own form in response to the site, and that response is recorded in that revised form. In this sense there is a relationship set up between the internal space of the tool and the external space of the site.

What maps do conventionally is to extend this correspondence of tool and site into a more tangible form. Information is built up through a series of incidental correspondences and fixed, traditionally, in two-dimensional graphic representation. These records of places then subsequently act as the documents for our own speculations about those places. We trust the mapmaker not only for dimensional accuracy, but in the ultimate validity of what he or she has chosen to record.

The tool, as the students were asked to devise it, is a highly condensed architectural piece. A specific site was chosen to focus attention on an actual rather than an imagined situation. The tools become specific to an individualized rather than a generalized perception. It is important that the earth of the site be touched; the state of the wasteland site was such that digging, marking, and other forms of intervention could be made freely.

The secondary program of the project relates to the development of an understanding of processes of making, and the translation of conceptual intention into material fact.

The process of accurate fabrication naturally demands a parallel document of drawings and notes. Firsthand experience reinforces awareness of the necessity of these documents in the construction process. The relatively small-scale nature of the pieces enabled working drawings for the most part to be made at a 1:1 scale, and with this, the relation of artifact to a simple set of working drawings is clearly made.

In a similar way, knowledge of materials is developed through direct experience. The use of steel or brass demands a visit to the supplier for the purpose of seeing possible raw materials at first hand. Once having selected materials, their properties are explored through their working. Test pieces were made prior to fabrication of the final piece to enable the refinement of construction techniques.

The building of the instruments was an extended process. The

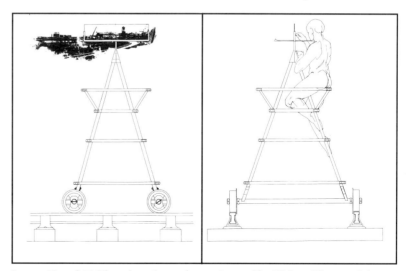

Image 63 and 64. Elevation views of mapping tool by Helena Thomas. left: dynamic elevation; right: "occupied" elevation, or tool in use.

Image 65. Full-scale model of mapping tool by Helena Thomas.

level of detail and craft in the actual construction was much higher than had originally been envisioned. The depth and success of these investigations led to the extension of this part of the program.

TOOL DESCRIPTIONS

Alan Chandler

A cone constructed with a steel and copper skeleton and copper skin is dropped successively at points around the site. A laminated timber beam is used to drop the cone from a height of 3 meters. As the cone hits the ground, both cone and earth are scarred. The damaged copper skin becomes the map, eventually being peeled off and laid out flat to be read. The steel discs that form the structure of the cone are turned on a metal lathe to develop fine cutting edges that bite into the skin as it hits the ground. Their delicacy also makes them vulnerable to further trace damage as the mapping progresses. Dimensions: cone, 200 mm by 250 mm; beam 3500 mm by100 mm.

Taylor Galyean

The tool is a device to map a drawing from a metal plate onto the site using the principle of a sextant. The map becomes a measure of the difference between the mapped figure and the real topography of the site. A beaten copper sheath cradles the user's arm, and a series of split mirrors and registers hinged together allows the sighting of markers found on the site. An idealized figure contained on the etching plate clamped beneath the device acts as a framework for interpretation. Materials: brass, glass, mirror, beaten copper. Dimensions: 500 mm x 300 mm x 200 mm.

Laurence Liauw

The tool consists of a storage-and-pulley system that requires the user to collect fragments of the site using wax imprints of the ground, and to store them in a series of compartments ordered by events of a chosen text. A physical map locating the found imprints on site is inscribed on the brass container and relates to the wax stamps stored inside. The device itself becomes a kind of archive, and the site can be traversed in the imagination by a review of its contents. Materials: mild steel, brass, aluminum, casting wax, bicycle chain. Dimensions: 620 mm x 200 mm x 1300 mm. (see Image 16).

Helena Thomas

A viewing frame moves along the site on existing railway tracks, mapping the skyline outside the site to either side. The frame holds a glass sheet on which the viewer scribes a record of the horizon. The tracking and orientation of the device are determined by the line and orientation of the disused tracks. Materials: timber, mild steel, glass. Dimensions: 1800 mm x 2000 mm x 2000 mm (see Image 16).

A Commemorative Pavilion for Joseph Cornell

Owen Cappleman
University of Texas at Austin
Austin, Texas

SUPPLEMENTARY INFORMATION

THE VOICE OF THE PLACE

At the time of this writing, the School of Architecture at the University of Texas at Austin is in an exciting state of flux. Several older faculty are retiring; the dean of some sixteen years has stepped down, and a new dean has been chosen after an intensive search process; and a number of new, young faculty with fresh ideas have recently signed on. In spite of the many uncertainties that are unavoidable in such a salutary period of transition, there are nonetheless certain constants that either remain—relatively intact—or else gradually evolve over time. As the flagship institution in the University of Texas system, UT-Austin has consistently attracted the cream of the state's student population. This situation has only improved in the years since higher admission standards first decreased student enrollment, then finally capped it. Lately, the infusion of greater numbers of out-of-state, minority, and foreign students has further enriched the student ranks. Add to all this an unusually diverse faculty, and two refurbished and expanded buildings of historical significance providing facilities that are nonpareil, and one sees a rosy picture indeed. In sum, the voice of

the School of Architecture at the University of Texas at Austin is a proud one, a voice that speaks of diversity, talent, and healthy change.

THE INTENT OF THE PROJECT

The Joseph Cornell project has multiple intentions, with three goals that are most pronounced: (1) broadening the student's horizons through the demolition of stereotypes and clichés; (2) learning not to be precious with one's work; and (3) developing the habit of seeking the unexpected. Amid all this, the not-so-hidden agenda addresses the learning of a visual, formal, and spatial vocabulary; skills attainment in drawing and crafting; accommodation of human needs; and response to the site in a specific climate and terrain.

THE DURATION OF THE PROJECT

The project lasts for one full five-week summer semester. The students meet five hours a day, five days a week, in a combined beginning design/visual communication studio.

THE UNIVERSITY OF TEXAS AT AUSTIN CURRICULUM

The School of Architecture has a wide array of curricula from which to choose. At the undergraduate level, there are four degree programs: (1) the "standard" five-year Bachelor of Architecture, the school's largest single program; (2) a four-year nonprofessional Bachelor of Science in Architectural Studies; (3) a six-year professional dual-degree program in Architecture and Architectural Engineering; and, (4) another dual-degree program in Architecture and Liberal Arts Plan II Honors, a more holistic and inclusive education that results in a degree in Liberal Arts and a professional B.Arch degree. The graduate offerings include a first-professional Master of Architecture degree, a Master of Science in Architectural Studies degree, postprofessional degrees (including one travel-based program directed by Dr. Charles Moore), and a Master of Science in Community and Regional Planning.

THE PLACE AND LEVEL OF PLATFORM COURSES

In the new curricular model first implemented in 1991–92, the foundation course is given in the first semester of the first year in a nine-semester design sequence. This first-semester design studio (along with those in the second and third semesters) has a companion course in Visual Communication.

THE PEDIGREE OF THE PROJECT

The idea of working with Joseph Cornell as a subject focus, up to the creation of the shadowbox, was a team effort shared by Professor Cappleman and Professor Michael Jordan, who has since moved to the University of Oklahoma. The remainder of the project, including the purposeful destruction of the shadowbox and all the subsequent sequence described below, is wholly the original creation of Cappleman's.

THE EVALUATION

The project in its current form has been given twice, both times in the summers of 1990 and 1991.

The Cornell project, more than any other of countless ones given in a quarter-century-career in architectural education, has proven the most successful. Perhaps the linchpin of its success is that not only do the strongest students soar with it (as they should with any decent project), but unlike many projects, it seems to cause the weaker students to overachieve in a manner they never dreamt possible. If I am ever shed of my current administrative duties and returned to the first-year studio, I'll definitely "do" Cornell again."

—*Owen Cappleman*

Image 66. Face-on view of the "Cornellesque" shadowbox (intact) by Diana Huang.

THE PROJECT

Holding to this author's long-held philosophy regarding cognitive early learning in architectural studies, the students were not told until the last part of the semester that they were designing a pavilion. In this particular methodology, each step along a seemingly jerky path is an apparent end in itself. Only over time does the student come to realize that the steps are accretive, building toward a kind of gestalt further down the line; the kinks straighten out, and over their shoulders the path becomes clear and apparent. This process allows learning, in all its magic and joy, to become like a game, with serendipity at every turning. Along the path, clichés are shed like discarded clothing, the imagination is let loose, the unexpected becomes the norm.

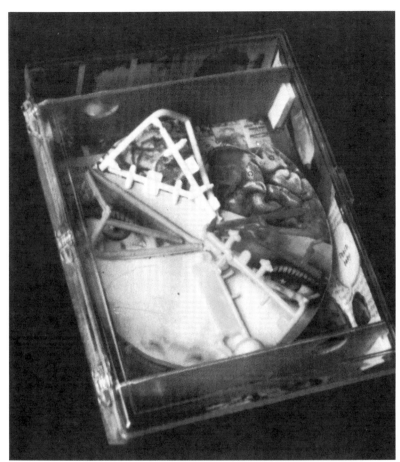

Image 67. Perspective view of the "Cornellesque" shadowbox (intact) by Diana Huang.

Although the work of Joseph Cornell was introduced in the second week of class, and was clearly the focus at the outset, the working title of the project made no reference to Cornell at all, so as to maintain the benign deceit inherent in this method. The project was called "Spare Parts." In fact, the whole notion of parts was punned almost (some would say wholly) to death, and thus some indulgence is asked of the reader. First, the project had five major parts, each of which had one or more subparts. And the whole thing began with a kit of parts . . .

Image 68. View into shadowbox after saw cut by Diana Huang.

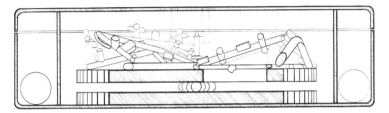

Image 69. Section drawing of cut shadowbox by Diana Huang.

89

1. PARTS IS PARTS: DECONSTRUCT

Students begin with model kits (cars, airplanes, etc.) costing $10 or less. The kits are disassembled and "recognizable" parts are discarded. All remaining pieces, including connectors, are dumped unceremoniously on a large table to create a "bank" of parts. The students then circle the table, selecting parts one at a time based on their compellingness, their formal interest, or their own simple intuition. They are encouraged to pick between twenty and thirty pieces that exhibit range and variety, with emphasis placed on having "way too many" to allow for informed editing as the project proceeds. Students also know that the bank remains open for later withdrawals or exchanges.

2. PARTS AIN'T JUST PARTS: ABSTRACT (ANALYSIS 1)

This section focuses on figure/ground relationships, tonality, color harmonies, and geometric analysis in two dimensions. Following a lecture illustrated with slides of paintings that establishes a typology of six basic figure/ground conditions (vignette, field-dominant, figure-dominant, interactive, ambiguous, and pattern), the students create black-and-white collages illustrating each condition. This is done by

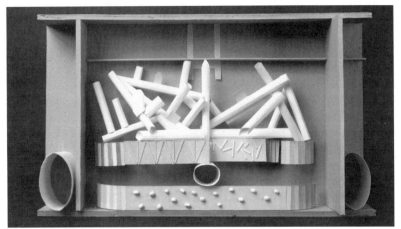

Image 70. Permutation One, "Dimensional Transformation with Tints" by Diana Huang.

using an overhead projector to cast a silhouette of arrangements of selected parts onto either square or rectangular fields (8" by 8" or 8" by 10", respectively), seeking a significant level of abstraction (unrecognizability of the inherent object-ness of each component).

The next step provides the students' first foray into "seeking the unexpected," when they are asked to create figure/ground reversals. This is simply the process of making everything that is white be black, and everything black, white. New tools, techniques, and materials are introduced here; instead of black construction paper on white board, the reversals are done in India ink on tracing vellum. The reversals show the students how much the visual character and emphasis of an image can be dramatically changed (or not, in some cases) by merely altering a single aspect of it.

In the two steps that follow, the students first translate the black-and-white images into a range of tonalities, and from these, into three studies in color harmony: pseudo-monochromatic with split-dyad accents; tertiary triads; and broad, analogous colors. For both exercises, found papers are used as collage materials on rigid boards.

The last step in this phase is the "hinge" into the next phase of the project. Each student selects three of his or her figure/ground studies and subjects them to rigorous geometric analysis using drafting instruments and yards of yellow trace. After numerous distillations and simplification processes, the final analysis is committed to tracing vellum as a hard-line drawing in ink.

3. . . . GREATER THAN THE SUM OF THE PARTS: RECONSTRUCT

After engaging in the abstract exercises used to begin to build a basic visual vocabulary in Part 2, the student returns to the material reality of the parts themselves, seeking an even deeper, or enhanced, reality. As preparation, first the life and work of artist Joseph Cornell are discussed, and slides are shown of his haunting shadowboxes. Then the student receives a fortune cookie inside of which is a literary squib ranging from a few words to a short paragraph, from the whimsical to the macabre to the poignant to the baffling. From the squib they develop a thoughtful metaphor. The final preparatory act begins with an exhibition of all the previously done geometrical analyses. Each student selects one geometry not his or her own that best matches the student's metaphor, photocopies it, and returns the original to the owner.

Now the student is fitted with all the matériel needed to proceed: materials (the original parts, liberally supplemented by other two- and three-dimensional "stuff"); an idea (the literary metaphor); and a map (the selected geometry, to be used as a compositional guide). Armed with this matériel, the student proceeds to create a Cornellesque shadowbox.

Image 71. Scale model of Joseph Cornell Commemorative Pavilion by Diana Huang.

4. PARTS IS TOO PARTS!: CONCRETE (ANALYSIS 2)

This phase involves several acts of "exploratory surgery," divided into two sections: examination and permutation.

After reviewing and photographing the shadowboxes, students take the first step in the examination process: making the incision. The students assemble in the shop, identify a major axis in their constructs, and then run the shadowboxes through the bandsaw along that axis. The first lesson of this brutal exercise is dual: that destruction is often a part of creation, and that one must never become precious with one's work.

The second lesson is the revisitation, in a much more powerful way, to the concept of seeking the unexpected. The student peers into one half or the other of the divided box, seeing it for the first time from a wholly unanticipated point of view. This view is immediately recorded in ink on vellum, not only teaching in an unambiguous way the concept of the architectural section (complete with poché) and the correct drawing convention thereof, but providing now a new "map" to begin the permutations phase.

Here the students create a series of four low reliefs, using any materials they can get their hands on. The first relief is a direct translation of the section drawing, colored in full-chroma hues in a color harmony of the student's choosing based on earlier color studies. The second relief is the first of the three permutations, each of which changes dramatically the formal and color characteristics of the original according to very clear, but undaunting, sets of rules. In the first permutation, a dimensional transformation occurs along the long axis, which can be either elongated or compressed ("stretch/squish"). The color transformation here is the tinting of all but at least one—but no more than three—of the new incarnations of the original elements in the first relief ("lighten up").

The second permutation is additive and subtractive: at least two elements must be added to the composition, and at least two taken away. The color change in this step is called "get dark," in which all original elements appear as shades of the original hues (except for the "preserved" one to three parts that continue to retain their full chroma). The third and final permutation involves "shear," or an axial shift along a previously identified datum line, even as all but the one to three pure colors "gray out," or toned, by the admixture of a neutral gray.

5. PARTS AND PARTÍ: SYNTHESIS

Now the students are told that they will design a commemorative pavilion for Joseph Cornell. This revelation occurs at the site where the pavilion is to be "built," the promontory at Laguna Gloria Art Museum. This wooded and craggy and meadowed spit of land stretches west of a crumbling old stuccoed villa long ago transformed into a museum of twentieth-century art, and forms a divide between Lake Austin and the "glorious lagoon" after which the museum is named.

First the students stalk the site, making photographs, sketches, and notes and identifying the location of major trees. Upon return to the studio, they superimpose this material on measured drawings of the site in a series of site analyses relating specifically to sun angles, prevailing winds, and views both into and from the site. During this process, the four or five most desirable specific potential building sites are chosen, and a class site model of the promontory is constructed.

Next, each student writes a brief paper that contains a rewrite or paraphrase of the literary squib that somehow relates to the qualitative properties of a pavilion. At the same time, the paper must make broad references to the grounds of the art museum, the promontory, and the

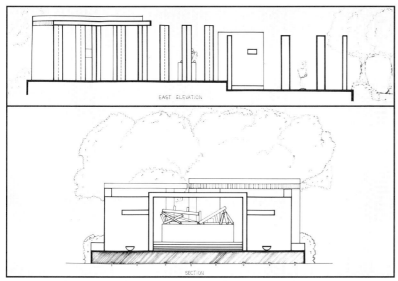

Image 72. Elevation and section drawings of Joseph Cornell Commemorative Pavilion by Diana Huang.

lagoon, and specific references to the actual building site. Also included in the paper is a description of the experience of the Joseph Cornell Pavilion in terms of sequence (drawn from the simple program provided), specifically addressing issues of space, light, and materiality.

The program states that "the Pavilion's purpose is for general public gathering and enjoyment, culminating in the celebration of and reverence for specific icons/relics of Joseph Cornell, viz: (1) a mural of the original shadowbox from which the permutations were derived; (2) a glassed-in display of faithful replicas of three or more original Cornells; and (3) the exhibition of one or more of the original 'parts,' now treated as a large-scale sculptural event. The 'experience' sequence of the Pavilion should be as follows: (1) an open plaza area (with seating?); (2) a congregation area (covered); and (3) the exhibition area (possibly, but not necessarily, chapel-like)."

The major formal resource for the Pavilion is one or two of the permutations. One permutation is used as a "slice" of the finished pavilion in one of the following manners: a floor plan, a high horizontal section, a roof plan, a vertical edge, or a vertical section. Colors and surfaces used in the design of the Pavilion could be derived from the same permutation, or from a different one, but had to relate to existing building materials that were exhibited on a "materials board" during the final review of the project. Other presentation requirements included an "archaeological history" of selected projects done earlier that led up to the final design; a model of the Pavilion that "plugged in" to the class site model; orthographic drawings (site plan, elevations, and sections); and some method of communicating the experiential aspect of the Pavilion, such as walk-through vignette sketches, carefully done montages, or shoebox dioramas.

As an added touch of "legitimacy," the director of Laguna Gloria Art Museum was invited to the final review. Everyone was amazed—not least the students themselves—at how much had been accomplished in only five weeks.

The Novel and Architecture

Elizabeth Patterson Church
(formerly of Mississippi State University)
Vermont College Of Norwich University
Montpelier, Vermont

SUPPLEMENTARY INFORMATION

THE VOICE OF THE PLACE

The School of Architecture at Mississippi State University (where the project was given) believes that architectural education can best be accomplished in an environment that stimulates a creative search for ideas by both faculty and students. The size of the school and its small-town setting make possible a highly personal, yet intense academic experience. This intimate atmosphere also promotes the importance that MSU places on the student's personal exploration, investigation, and discovery about the intentionality of ideas as they relate to space, form, order, and craft. The aspirations that motivate all activities, whether academic or nonacademic, classroom or studio, are those of excellence and maximum creative effort.

THE INTENT OF THE PROJECT

"The Novel and Architecture" project was designed to address beginning design students' need for critical thinking by challenging their preconceptions about what a building should be. The vehicle of literature was chosen because it was anticipated that these former high school honor students had already been exposed to a process of critical thinking within the framework of high school and college English courses. The students' familiarity with the concepts of metaphor/symbolism/abstraction, the interpretation of information on a variety of levels, and the juggling of simultaneous pieces of information would have been available to them in the context of an English class. The novel was used to build a cognitive bridge from critical thinking in the written word to critical thinking in the design studio.

THE DURATION/ OF THE PROJECT

The project lasted one and one-half weeks.

THE MISSISSIPPI STATE CURRICULUM

The curriculum is a five-year Bachelor of Architecture program.

THE PLACE AND LEVEL OF PLATFORM COURSES

Platform-level courses are at the first- and second-year levels. First-year architecture courses include Introduction to Design, Freehand Drawing, and Introduction to Architecture. This project was given in the first semester of the first year, following studies in figure/ground, proportioning systems, and geometry in two- and three-dimensional compositions. The students had also been introduced to a number of ordering methodologies: order through geometry and proportion, order through climatic concerns, and order through solid/void relationships.

THE PEDIGREE OF THE PROJECT

"The Novel and Architecture" is an original invention of Professor Church's.

THE EVALUATION

This project was first given in November 1990; it has been issued just once. Using the novel as a point of departure yielded three categories of projects that can be loosely related to the breakdown of modes of perception of text:

1. Projects that were simply illustrations of the novel. The students could not get beyond either what the author described, or what their own preconceptions were dictating to them. These can be referred to as the concrete reading.
2. Projects evolved from what is best described as diagrams: diagrams of relationships and diagrams of narratives. The solution has gone beyond a surface reading of the text, and the use of the diagram has been employed to form new associations and relationships carried out in three dimensions. Both the diagrams of relationships and the diagrams of narratives fall into the category of conceptual reading. The project illustrated in this book is an example of the diagram solution.
3. Projects authored by students who appeared to have had the most experience with the process of critical thought. This process of critical thinking, either conscious or unconscious, had been a part of the students' lives either in an educational setting or in their homes. These students were the ones who leaped away from the notion of house immediately and struck out away from the "known" and into the realm of metaphorical.

THE PROJECT

Preconception is a bane to all design studios, but perhaps most in the first-year design studio. Students clutch their preformed images and ideas of what forms should be, what drawings should look like, what projects they expect to work on in the design studio. They cling to these "should be" images for protection because they may be insecure in this new environment called college; they may anticipate judgment from authority figures; or they may fear being wrong in front of an audience, in a jury where nothing is hidden, in the grade book or the private conference.

But in fact, the defensive posture that relies on the "should be" images, the "should be" ideas, does no service to the student. That posture is a barrier, a thick, impenetrable wall that prevents movement forward, prevents seeing beyond, and blocks all original thought, ultimately holding the student back from venturing into the unknown territory that design requires.

Preconceptions are fed and developed from a wide range of sources: family, religion, education, peers, media, and personal experiences. Similarly, the preconceptions reach deep down to the bedrock of the student's developing personality. The roots are deep initially because the source of experience may be tied to value systems, ethical reasoning, or sentimental associations. With time, the preconceptions have become part of the young person's survival gear. The memories, attitudes, ways of thinking, ways of seeing, ways of ordering one's own environment are as basic and instinctual as knowing how to feed, clothe, and shelter oneself.

Granted, it is this gathering and sorting of information that is a part of what enables the young person to move forward. But somewhere along the way, the student learns that speed in formulating an answer is crucial, that appearing to have all the answers is what's important, that asking questions or following a path that meanders is a waste of time. And so, the young person discards the inefficient, time-consuming processes that were so much a part of early childhood—processes such as exploration and discovery, examination without judgment, creating relationships via association, and solving problems without consideration of the preconceived "shoulds" and the predetermined end product.

This studio design project, entitled "The Novel and Architecture," was designed to address the notion of breaking down these boundaries of preconception. Second, the project was to be an assimilation of the entire semester's explorations—figure/ground, proportion, geometry, two-dimensional composition, use of drawing and model material, and, last but not least, formulating a convincing response to the given program. Third, the project sought to promote reading, writing, and critical thinking in the context of the design studio. The fourth goal of the project was to introduce a new ordering methodology. A number of ordering methodologies had already been introduced: order through geometry and proportion, order through climatic concerns, order through solid/void relationships. This project was to introduce order through an abstract idea.

In recognition that this project might be the first departure from the "known" for many students, a familiar vehicle was selected—the reading of a novel. The novel seemed a particularly good point of departure because it is a crafted form composed of abstract ideas discussed in a high school environment, and so might be an area in which the students had already begun to employ the process of critical thinking.

By the end of the Thanksgiving break, the students were to have read a novel:*To Kill a Mockingbird, The Great Gatsby*, or a selection of their choice with approval from their critic. They were then asked to select three passages that best exemplified the development of a character, and to write a short essay about each of their choices. This segment of the process was intended to push the students into making explicit their implicit selection of the passages, thus taking the abstraction of the project's "program" further away from a superficial reading of the text.

Finally, the students developed a three-dimensional spatial response to all three passages. The response had to distinguish between the three spaces, but be united within one structure. Further-

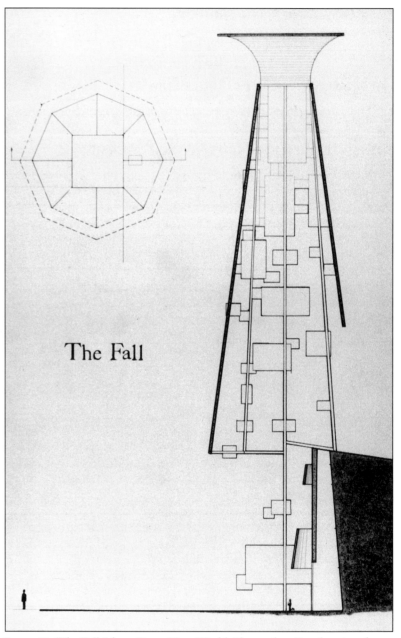

Image 73. "The Fall," from Brave New World. Plan and section drawings by Muse Davis.

Image 74. "The Fall," from Brave New World. Model by Muse Davis.

more, the response was to be generated primarily via a study model that used only linear and planar components of a certain size. Drawings were done after the design had reached a level of completion using just the study model. The entire project took a week and a half, and culminated in the customary end-of-semester juries.

Most of the students who experienced frustration and disequilibrium had gotten through their lives, and into architectural school, with problem-solving skills that were just now proving to be on the verge of obsolescence. The concrete preconceptions that they had so long ago developed were not sufficient in this arena. They were given a clear set of alternatives: expand their thinking abilities; suspend their judgment of the process; and begin to explore, experiment, play, and create new ways of making relationships happen in the development of a solution. They were being given the opportunity to take on those long-forsaken characteristics of childhood.

The project chosen to illustrate this studio is from an alternative novel, Aldous Huxley's *Brave New World*. The layering of space, the movement and rhythm of planes and linear elements, the breakdown of form and a clear sequence of events are prominent characteristics of Huxley's writing.

The line "John travels his straight and narrow path to pitfall" is illustrated in plan, section, and model, images 73 and 74.

The pitfall becomes a *real* fall in the elevation drawing, image 19.

The student, Muse Davis, has created a tower with a singular approach and a singular experience, much like the persona and activities of the main character he chose to explore. The success of this project lies in the fact that the student was able to take a particular stance toward the novel and develop that stance into an intention about a design project. It is not illustrative of the novel in a literal sense, but it does embody the essence of what this student has selected as a major thematic development.

The vehicle of literature brought a unique dimension to the problem. The novel has the quality of already being one step into abstraction. A novel of any caliber has several levels of meaning, complexity in plot and character relationships, and imagery that can have metaphor and/or symbolism embodied in it right from the start. So, in fact, the manner in which the "program" was presented created opportunity for design outcomes that had a head start in terms of their ability to become complex and layered with meaning.

An ancillary benefit that arises out of using the vehicle of literature in a design problem is the promotion of reading and writing skills for the beginning design student. Certainly the phrase "to think is to draw" is apt for a design student, but so is "to write is to think." Encouraging students to use reading and writing in the design studio can only assist in fostering critical thinking skills.

Spatial Apotheosis for Apollo and Dionysus: A Study in the Dichotomy of Order and Disorder

Alan R. Cook
Auburn University
Auburn, Alabama

SUPPLEMENTARY INFORMATION

THE VOICE OF THE PLACE

The School of Architecture at Auburn University is dedicated to a pluralistic overview of issues and theories pertinent to the architectural design continuum. The school includes the departments of building science, industrial design, and architecture. The Department of Architecture has programs in interior design, architecture, and landscape architecture, all sharing the same design studio sequence for the first five quarters of each curriculum.

THE INTENT OF THE PROJECT

The famous quote from Louis Kahn, "Order is," gives tribute to the presence of order and begs the question as to its nature. The intent of this exercise is to focus attention on this question, i.e., the nature of order. Particularly the question is framed to force inquiry into the attributes of what we call order and what may differentiate these attributes into a continuum polarized by simplicity and complexity. It is hoped that the students come to realize the importance of context and relativity when comparing the level of complexity and/or simplicity of a pattern. Also, they should come to understand the value of thematics as a device for establishing a datum of reference for relativistic evaluations. The issue of syntax is given priority over that of semantics in an attempt to increase focus on the role of basic design as a universal, non–culturally limited system for evaluating order.

The immediate goals of the project are the following:
1. to enhance understanding of basic design principles and patterns and their expressive implications;
2. to introduce principles of information theory (i.e., uncertainty, redundancy, periodicity, noise, etc., and relationships to entropy and thermodynamics), serial vision and spatial sequence (information serialized by installments, controlled by apertures and entry thresholds), and the roles these theories play in the development of architectural messages such as defining arrival and a sense of place;
3. to further develop and improve model-building skills;
4. to investigate the issues of simplicity (homogeneity, integration) versus complexity (heterogeneity, differentiation), and the relative nature of perceiving order, i.e., the role of a context in the perception and understanding of information; and
5. to introduce the use of a (symbolic) theme as a design issue, i.e., the Greek mythological gods Apollo and Dionysus.

The long-range and integrated goals of the project are the following:
1. It is important for beginning students to increase their awareness of abstract expression (physiognomy) as an unavoidable design issue and of its potential value in the realization of design intentions. The issues involving information theory, serial vision, and gestalt closure can be very useful in relating to the idea of choreographing a design movement sequence and anticipating the probable perceptual sequence. The issue of simplicity transforming to complexity provides that equivocal middle ground which is pregnant with possibilities, involving perceptual tension reduction as an aesthetic device.
2. The studio experience for this project is structured with a quasi-comprehensive Design Pattern Checklist (see below) to provide an analytical methodology for evaluating basic design principles and patterns early in the architectural design process. It is suggested that the students employ this simple evaluative procedure on future design projects to make the issues of abstract syntactical expression a more conscious part of their overall design process, thus obviating unintended expression. It must be made clear that the synergy of combining several patterns or qualities may produce expressive contradictions relative to the proclivities of some solo patterns. This last point, concerning contradiction, usually involves a change of scale (or relative magnitude) of patterns.
3. The students are expected to develop conceptual abilities in the expression of "sense of place," the identifiable domains of distinct character. This includes issues ranging from evaluating ambient

contextual influences, such as enclosure and thematics, to understanding the implications of path systems and their effects on the perceptions of users who are oriented and constrained by them.

THE DURATION OF THE PROJECT

The project lasted for one week.

THE AUBURN UNIVERSITY CURRICULUM

In addition to the five-year Bachelor of Architecture and Bachelor of Landscape Architecture degrees, there are four-year bachelor degrees in building construction, interior design, and industrial design. Also, there are two master's degree programs, one in industrial design, the other in regional planning. The B. Arch degree is of the 4+1 model.

THE PLACE AND LEVEL OF PLATFORM COURSES

Beginning design starts immediately in the first quarter of the first year. This project is for first-term beginning students. It requires no mature graphic skills since it is presented completely in three-dimensional model form. Typically this exercise is preceded by some simple two-dimensional abstract compositional studies involving gestalt figure/ground and grouping principles, and a three-dimensional construct involving similar principles. There are handout materials for this project, and a slide-lecture presentation pertaining to serial vision and information theory.

THE PEDIGREE OF THE PROJECT

The main idea of conjoining opposites has ancient roots visible in the duality of the vertical and horizontal bars of the cross, the superimposition of oppositely oriented triangles in the star of David, and in the complementary aspects of the yin-yang symbol. However, in each of these pairs of opposites the levels of complexity are the same. In this project, however, the duality of the levels of complexity forms the implicit opposition. As a beginning teacher at North Dakota State University's Department of Architecture, I was introduced to architectural historian Ronald Ramsey's notion of the Apollonian and Dionysian pendulum, which he observed seemed to swing his

torically back and forth between the stylistic tendencies of (noble) simplicity and (frenzied) complexity.

I synthesized these ideas with serial vision exercises I had devised as transformations of my studio experiences with Tim McGinty, whom I had in my second year of architecture at the University of Nebraska. It was then that I was introduced to Gordon Cullen's timeless book Townscape, which elaborates on the concepts of here and there, anticipation and arrival, and other serial vision devices. This was further augmented by my later find of Rudolf Arnheim's book Entropy and Art, which contrasts the catabolic destruction of entropy with the anabolic tendency of a structural theme.

THE EVALUATION

"Spatial Apotheosis" was given seven times between 1979 and 1984, and again in 1986.

The better students generally succeed in using a syntactical theme to establish the sense-of-place identities fairly well. The Dionysian domain is more difficult to resolve spatially as a place. The serial vision aspect needs reinforcement, since the students tend to get more involved in observing the sculptural form as an object from without than as an environment from within."

—Alan R. Cook

THE PROJECT

Each student is required to study and present two places in model form: one for the Greek god Apollo, the other for the Greek god Dionysus. For our purposes these gods symbolize order and disorder, respectively. As noted in the problem statement handout, the Dionysian domain is frenzied, wild, agitated, and disordered; the Apollonian domain is harmonious, measured, balanced, and ordered.

These two places are designed without representational imagery—that is, with abstract elements only (line, direction, shape, tone, texture, and size)—and they are to have one interconnecting path that forms a transition of anticipation and arrival to each domain. Other logistical constraints include a designated scale of 1/4" = 1'0", an overall 10" x 10" x 20" volumetric limit on the model size, orientation as desired, and an achromatic tonal palette. The last two times this project was assigned, the additional constraint of requiring one domain to be dominantly additive geometry and the other to be dominantly subtractive geometry was incorporated, with positive effect.

The studio meets for two hours each weekday morning, usually beginning with a discussion of developments and concerns common to the entire class. The remaining time then consists of individual student desk critiques addressing specific project design issues. Informational handouts dealing with issues of related theory are distributed and discussed in class, with non–project specific examples being presented and related in the context of the material on theory. These issues of theory are presented early in the assignment. The Design Pattern Checklist, shown following, is distributed on the first day and the students are asked to make inferences about how appropriate they think each basic design pattern is for each domain, based on past experience with these patterns on previous projects.

DESIGN PATTERN CHECKLIST

A design pattern checklist may be used as a generic, preliminary methodology for generating likely starting points in a design process that involves the meaningful use of abstract design patterns. It is also useful later in the design process as a check against unintended expression, i.e., the avoidance of inappropriate patterns for a given type of design identity or programmatic use. The patterns and elements on this list could be expanded or modified for application to a greater variety of problem types, with the listed items being more problem-specific. The intent of this working document is to involve the designer in an analytical approach to design process in which the general fitness and appropriateness of the items for application to a directed design expression are tested, without direct comparison to any specific grouping or associative combination of elements. In this manner, preconceptions may be avoided at the outset of a problem, and the probability of fresh insight and new awareness will be nurtured.

Note that this is only one of many methodologies that may be used to begin a problem-solving process. This approach relies on one's correct understanding of the expressive potentials of each listed item, especially as they operate in isolation from other patterns. Of course,

several patterns will have to be employed in arriving at the appropriate design solution, and these will constitute a gestalt that will have expressive properties not always predictable from an evaluation of the parts. The ultimate goal is the improvement of the designer's intuitive fluency with visual ordering and expression.

In the list that follows, each item can be ranked from 1 through 5, with 1 representing a strong fitness for the Apollonian character, 5 a strong fitness for the Dionysian character, and 3 being the most neutral range. The appropriate number for each list item is circled, corresponding to a careful evaluation of its expressive fitness.

List Items

gradation	1	2	3	4	5
organic hierarchy	1	2	3	4	5
statistical hierarchy	1	2	3	4	5
shape anomaly	1	2	3	4	5
position anomaly	1	2	3	4	5
direction anomaly	1	2	3	4	5
linear datum/axis	1	2	3	4	5
area datum	1	2	3	4	5
mass datum	1	2	3	4	5
volume/space datum	1	2	3	4	5
radiation/focalization	1	2	3	4	5
axial symmetry (mirror, folding, biaxial, etc.)	1	2	3	4	5
point/rotational symmetry	1	2	3	4	5
rhythm/alternation/repetition	1	2	3	4	5
counterpoint rhythm	1	2	3	4	5
positive/negative symmetry	1	2	3	4	5
dynamic symmetry/proportional harmony	1	2	3	4	5
informal balance/asymmetry	1	2	3	4	5
imbalance/asymmetry	1	2	3	4	5
chaos	1	2	3	4	5
rectilinear/orthogonal/perpendicular	1	2	3	4	5
curvilinear	1	2	3	4	5
diagonal	1	2	3	4	5
bright/light	1	2	3	4	5
dim/dark	1	2	3	4	5
matte finish	1	2	3	4	5
gloss finish	1	2	3	4	5

Since "Spatial Apotheosis" is a one-week project, the schedule works best when the projects are due on a Monday. This gives ample weekend time for the students to focus on the final craft work, with less distraction from their other courses, while providing a maximum of instructor feedback during the earlier developmental stages. This project is conducted near the end of the first quarter of study, or sometimes near the beginning of the second quarter of design studio.

ILLUSTRATIONS

Image 75

The student made a clear insight into the issue of orientation—he positioned the project such that the Apollonian domain was at the central zenith point. He used scale well in that access is by climbing on a series of rectangular prisms that in general make a helical ascent. This is developed with appropriate gradations of stepping height and horizontality of tread; i.e., the most fitting conditions are polarized toward the top, Apollonian domain. Near the bottom the prisms are scaled such that walking would require a full involvement of all the user's limbs and attention, thus being polarized toward the consciousness of the body. The regularity near the top allows freedom of attention for the more lofty occupation of the rational mind. The prisms at the bottom are most irregular in tone, proportion, size, orientation, and potential use as elements of the path. Some of the bottom prisms serve multiple functions, such as support for the higher construction, spatial enclosure, and surface for the path. Near the top all the elements are regularized in tone (white), proportion, size, and orientation, and are of the path. The exception is the unique last one in the sequence, which is a much taller and perfectly vertical black prism with a symmetrically placed white vertical void vignetted on the arrival approach side. The anomalies converging here give the effect of making the viewer clear about the intention of dominance, and they provide the strongest focus and poignancy on the idea that the object of veneration here is light in space. At the bottom, the domain of Dionysus has enclosure but no clear focus; the viewer's attention is diffuse, but still there is a sense of place. The strongest part of this design scheme is a perceptually accessible and principled system of order, which provides a datum about which thoughtfully considered deviations from the norm may become expressive.

Image 75.

99

Image 76.

Image 76

Though this solution lacks any obvious overriding device for unity, it most clearly exhibits the contrast of order and disorder. Where one is open, focalized, axially symmetrical, and rhythmic,the other is closed, diffuse, knottedly asymmetrical, and arrhythmic. The Apollonian domain is spatially clear and well focused with some subtlety regarding the expression of light in a void. The Dionysian domain is most engaging in its labyrinthine character and diverse tonal and formal quirks. The element of the path is significant and expressive in both of these domains, and works well in transition to communicate a sense of anticipation and arrival. The magnitude and symmetry of the Apollonian domain is sufficient to act as a datum element that assimilates the smaller and axially juxtaposed Dionysian domain.

Working with Piranesi

David Covo and Derek Drummond
McGill University
Montreal, Quebec, Canada

SUPPLEMENTARY INFORMATION

THE VOICE OF THE PLACE

"If there is a single 'ism' that represents the 'voice of the place' at McGill, it is *pluralism.*"

THE INTENT OF THE PROJECT

This project is formulated to develop design skills by confronting students with the power of drawing. Perspective is presented as both a medium for the exploration of ideas and a process in which images of places that exist and places that do not are generated with equal enthusiasm and conviction.

THE DURATION OF THE PROJECT

The project typically lasts seven to ten days. "This is not a great deal of time, but we are usually able to schedule the project so that this period includes at least two—and often three—full studio days."

THE McGILL CURRICULUM

McGill's undergraduate program follows two years of postsecondary study in science and engineering, and is divided into two parts. The first part is a three-year program (six semesters) that leads to a nonprofessional Bachelor of Science in Architecture. The second part requires a minimum of one year of study (two semesters) to receive a professional Bachelor of Architecture degree, which is recognized by Canada's licensing bodies. "The clear majority of our students go on to the B. Arch degree, picking up the B.Sc (Arch) 'along the way'."

THE PLACE AND LEVEL OF PLATFORM COURSES

Design starts in the first semester of the first year. This project is assigned at the end of the second semester as the final assignment of the first-year design studio program. At that time, students are also completing their second required freehand drawing course. This two-semester freehand sequence develops skills in life drawing in various media, including charcoal, conté crayon, pen and ink, and ink wash. The platform studios are the first two of eight required design studios leading to the Bachelor of Architecture degree.

THE PEDIGREE OF THE PROJECT

The project in its present form was introduced for the first time by Professors Covo and Drummond in the course "Architectural Graphics and Elements of Design," which is the required design studio in the second semester of the first year. An earlier version of a related project, in which Piranesi's *Carceri* were analyzed but not expanded, was one assignment in a four-credit summer studio called "Design Sketching," taught by Covo and Professor Howard Davies in April 1988. Other instructors involved in the development of the project over the years are Gavin Affleck, Terrance Galvin, and Lea Zeppetelli. It is in some ways analogous to the "in the manner of" design exercises developed by John Meunier and Gordon Simmons at the University of Cincinnati in the late 1970s.

THE EVALUATION

Feedback from students and colleagues has been extremely positive.

—*David Covo and Derek Drummond*

THE PROJECT

The first-year curriculum at McGill University's School of Architecture incorporates perspective drawing and sketching within the design studio program. Typically, following a series of lectures in which they are introduced to the theory and techniques of perspective projection, students are asked to produce a number of perspective views of one of their own projects. They are often further challenged to consider the assignment as a stage in the development of their schemes, and they are encouraged to make design changes in the actual perspective drawings. In this way, they are told, design judgment—as well as basic skills in drawing and visualization—are developed at the same time as their design proposal matures.

In many instances, however, the emerging perspective provides inescapable evidence of deficiencies in the design, and students soon find themselves developing images of schemes that are now confirmed as weak or even unsuccessful. When this occurs, students may respond in one of two ways: Some become preoccupied with redesign and virtually abandon the perspective, while others proceed—albeit somewhat mechanically—with the preparation of drawings of projects that no longer stimulate or engage them. The opportunity to explore perspective as a strategy in design is lost and students may, in the worst case, begin to think of perspective as appropriate only in presentation drawing, providing realistic but, from a design point of view, inert images.

The mechanics of perspective are still introduced in a traditional way, but in the spring of 1989 a follow-up exercise was added that illustrates much more dramatically the importance and potential of perspective drawing in the design process. The exercise is based on the series of sixteen etchings by Giovanni Battista Piranesi in the second edition of his *Carceri*, published in 1761, and calls for the design of an expansion of the space described in any single plate.

After a lecture in which they are introduced to Piranesi and the *Carceri* etchings, students are provided with 11" by 15" photocopies of the sixteen plates (the original plates measure approximately 16" by 22"). Each student selects a plate, analyzes it, formulates a strategy for expansion of the space, and then prepares a larger 24" by 36" perspective drawing of the expanded space, incorporating within this new drawing the original plate at 11" by 15". Working entirely within the perspective framework and in Piranesi's graphic language, students draw the new expanded space by simply extending the original image.

All pretensions to, and preconceptions about, technique and personal style are laid aside as they lose themselves in the apparently resolved world of the selected plate.

Work is executed in soft pencil, conté, or charcoal on white card, and is completed in one week. The results are visually stunning. Drawings are large and bold, vigorous and highly imaginative. When forty-five students draw at this size, the studio resonates with the sound of cross-hatching. The act of drawing is seen and heard and, as drafting tables rock on characteristically uneven legs, even felt. Energy in the room is palpable and infectious.

Students experiment with a variety of strategies in their first attempts to understand Piranesi's visions. Some use color to separate and identify major compositional forms and structural elements; many construct schematic plans based on horizontal sections taken at different elevations in the original plate (inspired by the analytical diagrams of Ulya Vogt-Göknil). Almost everyone at some point lays a large sheet of tracing paper over the plate in order to isolate and extend the governing perspective lines, and many students find their first cues for the expansion of Piranesi's space in the forgiving wire-frame world of these perspective grids.

The results of these and other investigations are invariably surprising. Vanishing points that ought to coincide do not; they seem to drift, sometimes along the horizon, sometimes above or below it. The horizon line itself is often low, near the bottom of some plates and even outside the bottom edge of others. The temptation to treat the original plates as fragments of larger visions becomes irresistible, transforming the exercise for some individuals into a special kind of searching for clues to this larger image. One student even wondered if groups of the plates could be related to each other, and tried to develop his expanded image as a kind of pictorial bridge between different plates. Others explored the notion of reflection, using water to add or distort information, and one resolved the problem of a particularly challenging plate by treating part of it as an actual mirror, reflecting elements beside, above, and beyond the viewer.

Great shafts of sunlight and dramatic shadows animate many of the plates, suggesting detail outside the cone of vision and possible relationships with the outside world, but openings in walls that ought to provide glimpses of gardens or the sky reveal instead "vistas onto further stairs, bridges, and multiple ranges of arches" (Robison). This multiple layering of space recalls images published by the Bibienas and others in the mid-eighteenth century (Robison), and the resulting

self-similarity, found in so many of the plates as portions are enlarged, gives many of the etchings a tantalizing, fractal-like quality. For many students, the layering and self-similarity form part of drawing and design strategies that become extremely important in their drawings of the expanded space.

Students quickly learn that valuable sources of ideas and inspiration are, in fact, other plates in the series, from which they freely "borrow" props for addition to their own drawings. These props include objects like hanging lanterns, bollards, a fall of rope or chain, and mysterious bits of machinery, and they invariably add a certain narrative content to the images. During this process student Bruce Eckfeldt made an impromptu lighthearted gesture by creating his "analog decision dial," also known as the "random Piranesi palette selector" (see Image 77). Rendering techniques adopted during this phase are in many cases based on Piranesi's own handling in the original plates of material, light, and shade.

Imaginations are further stimulated with the introduction of other models—in particular, Hugh Ferriss and Umberto Eco. In the extraordinary drawings of Hugh Ferriss, who has been more than once compared to Piranesi, students explore visions of a world where "modern" architecture is rendered with the same "dignity, strength, movement, mystery, power" (Goldberger) that characterize the world of the Carceri. And in Umberto Eco's The Name of the Rose and Jean-Jacques Annaud's 1986 film of that novel, which is shown to the class, students find in the descriptions of the library dramatic interpretations, in words and images, of spaces that might have been inspired, if not conceived, by Piranesi himself.

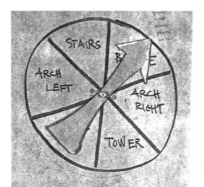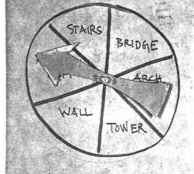

Image 77. Random Piranesi palette selector by Bruce Eckfeldt.

Image 78. "Continuous Cities," one of Calvino's Invisible Cities, conté and wash, 23" x 35", by Lucie Bégin, 1990.

In a number of the etchings, notably Plate IV, the Grand Piazza, and Plate XVI, the Pier with Chains (titles by Robison), students identify visual traps that use shade and shadow, similarity of form, and coincidence of line to deliberately subvert assumptions made about scale and space. The monument in the foreground of Plate XVI, for example, reads as a solid object, despite the transparency at the base, but also as a special kind of window, rendered like the arches beyond, into another space. Elsewhere in Plate XVI and in Plate VI, enormous bollards have been disguised as sinister cowled figures, moving alone and in groups, their backs turned to the viewer. The bollards could also be symbols of power (MacDonald). Baffling spatial ambiguities and impossible—or, at the very least, improbable—constructions are evident in a number of other etchings; for example, in Plate VII, the Drawbridge, and in Plate XIV, the Gothic Arch. How can structures so spectacularly unbuildable be rendered so convincingly?

Discoveries made as plates are analyzed, especially when earlier and later versions of the same plate are compared, generate lively discussion and considerable speculation regarding Piranesi's intentions. For two centuries, artists and other scholars have wondered about the ideas in and behind the etchings. Numerous theories have been proposed to explain everything from the prison theme to the puzzling and apparently intentional spatial ambiguities present in so many of the plates. Robison, among others, has suggested that the choice of subject matter represented for Piranesi a kind of liberation, allowing him to focus his "interest and creativity in the portrayal of architectural space, scale, and mass, and in the visual composition of basic structural forms." This liberation—from constraints implicit in design methodologies that start with the floor plan—remains one of the most compelling arguments in favor of the exercise.

There is another, equally compelling argument, related to the question of Piranesi's motivation in the initial publishing and subsequent reworking of the plates. From the outset, students understand that they are expected to identify and resolve design problems encountered in the representation of form, space, scale, and light. But in the very early stages of the exercise, their curiosity is aroused and they soon find themselves developing the new drawings with the same pleasure, mischievous sense of humor, and pure delight in invention that must surely have motivated Piranesi himself. For many, the discovery that the act of drawing can be like this is a revelation.

In attempts to capitalize on the momentum generated in this assignment, on two occasions the *Carceri* exercise was followed with a second, week-long design assignment requiring similar 24" x 36" perspective drawings. The first version of this follow-up called for another "imaginary view," this time based on a construction site, an image of

Image 79. "Zenobia," another of Calvino's Invisible Cities, pen and ink, 23" x 35", by Olivier Ménard, 1990.

architecture in the making. Drawings were extremely competent from a technical point of view but also extremely literal and, in comparison with the *Carceri* drawings, a little disappointing. The second version was based on Italo Calvino's *Invisible Cities* and required students to develop a perspective image, also 24" x 36", of a place in one of the cities described in that wonderful book. The idea of using Calvino as a

source was first suggested by Professor David Kepron, whose students have made models, as well as drawings, of Calvino's invisible cities.

The Venetian connection proved intriguing, and it was felt that Calvino would inspire images with the power of the *Carceri* drawings. Once again, it was found that most students tended to take Calvino's text literally, and the drawings, although in almost every instance quite well done, were considerably less engaging than the expanded views of the *Carceri* plates.

In both the latter cases—the unfinished building and the invisible city—drawings lacked the spatial intuition and spirit of adventure found in the *Carceri* expansions. This may be explained, at least in part, by the missing catalyst—the original plate—which functions so well in the first exercise as program, partí and palette, and also by the fact that most of the students seem to be more comfortable working with the complex interior perspective of the *Carceri* than with the more static exterior views commonly generated in the second assignment. Images that grow from one edge—of the original plate—are easily "pushed" to another edge—of the 24" by 36" sheet—filling the entire space of the drawing and drawing the entire space. And drawings that are already expansions of smaller images can themselves be read as parts of larger visions in which spatial relationships are clarified and the point of view of the observer both challenged and redefined.

The exercise with Piranesi's *Carceri* does not seem to require a follow-up assignment; it develops skills in drawing and design and, more important, the beginnings of a true understanding of the relationship between the two. It engages the student in a process of exploration and discovery and reveals in a most constructive way the importance and the power of perspective drawing in the consideration of architectural ideas.

SOURCES

Harvey, Miranda. Piranesi: The Imaginary Views. New York: Harmony Books, 1979.

Hofer, Philip. The Prisons (Le Carceri) by Giovanni Battista Piranesi. New York: Dover Publications, 1973.

Leich, Jean Ferriss. *Architectural Visions—The Drawings of Hugh Ferriss.* New York: Whitney Library of Design, an imprint of Watson-Guptill Publications, 1980.

MacDonald, William L. *Piranesi's Carceri: Sources of Invention.* Northampton, Mass.: Smith College, 1979.

Robison, Andrew. *Piranesi: Early Architectural Fantasies.* Washington: The National Gallery of Art; Chicago: The University of Chicago Press, 1986.

Vogt-Göknil, Ulya. *Giovanni Battista Piranesi: Carceri.* Zurich: Origo Verlag, 1958.

Exhibition Area at Cappadocia

Zafer Ertürk, Ph.D.
Karadeniz Technical University
Trabzon, Turkey

SUPPLEMENTARY INFORMATION

THE INTENT OF THE PROJECT

The project has several goals: the development of a sense of spatial dynamism, rather than creating defined volumes in a stiff manner; the search for a sensible approach for more confident and sound use, interpretation, and realization of the value of environmental data; the development of a proficiency in combining the possibilities of contemporary technology with cultural and social patterns; and the development of an ethos of aesthetics that makes use of the harmony of contrasts within similarities, while trying to ensure integration with the context of the surroundings.

THE DURATION OF THE PROJECT

The project lasted one month (four weeks).

THE KARADENIZ TECHNICAL UNIVERSITY CURRICULUM

The curriculum consists of four years' study toward a Bachelor of Architecture degree. There are two terms in each academic year plus seven weeks of summer school. An additional fourteen weeks of practical work is required: seven weeks of site and construction work, and seven weeks of office practice.

THE PLACE AND LEVEL OF PLATFORM COURSES

Design studios begin in the first year. This project is given in Design III, the first term (fall semester) of the second year, which consists of four hours of lecture and four hours of studio work per week.

THE PEDIGREE OF THE PROJECT

This project is the unique invention of Dr. Ertürk, born of his extensive work and study of—and passion for—the region of Cappadocia.

THE EVALUATION

The problem was studied over the last three years. Student solutions and their approach to the problem were found to be generally successful. Ninety percent of the students received a passing mark, and five percent of them deserved the highest mark.

THE PROJECT

INTRODUCTION TO THE SITE

The location of the site of this project is the Göreme Valley in the Cappadocia region of Turkey. Cappadocia lies in central Anatolia within the boundaries of the towns of 8Kayseri, Kirsehir, and Nigde. Geologically, Cappadocia is renowned as a region of unique landscape: Nowhere else in the world can its geological elements be found. Surrounded by volcanic structures, and in recent geologic time prone to volcanic convulsions, Cappadocia's atmospheric conditions have caused the formation of compact and complicated geologic patterns of which the isolated pinnacles, called "fairy chimneys," are the most predominant and memorable feature. These "fairy chimneys," which rise to a height of 40 to 45 meters, can be seen nowhere else in the world.

It is not known by whom or exactly when it began to be used, but the local stone—"tufa," which is porous and easily worked—provided settlers in Cappadocia with a convenient building material from which to hollow out dwellings. Today we can see the two- and three-story houses, churches, mosques, underground cities, and cold-storage depots that have been hollowed out over the last thousand years, at least.

The present-day region of Cappadocia is more or less congruent with the fluctuating borders of an area that has been known by the same name since at least the time of Herodotus, for it is the "father of history" himself who first uses the word "Cappadocia." That this should be so is apt, for it is virtually impossible to exaggerate the historical richness of this region. It is part of one of the three coeval Mediterranean "cradles of civilization"—the Hittite civilization, which flourished between 3000 and 1000 bc, along with the neighboring Minoan and Egyptian civilizations. A Hittite text circa 2300 bc contains the earliest reference to an urban settlement in the Cappadocian region. From that time onward Cappadocia was to exist under the hegemony of the Assyrian Empire, the Medo-Babylonian Realms, the Persian Empire, Alexander the Great, the Roman Empire, the Eastern (Byzantine) Roman Empire, the Seljuk Turks, and the Ottoman Empire until it became part of the Republic of Turkey in 1923. In looking at the succession of empires in Anatolia one can imagine the extent of the migrations of its populations and the foreign influences that trade, particularly the trade of an empire, would bring. Artifacts from Anatolia reveal a broad diversity of influence reflecting the cultures of the Hittite, Greek, Hellenistic, Roman, and Byzantine empires, as well as that from cultures based on shamanism, Manichaeanism, Buddhism, and, of course, Islam and Christianity.

To the west, the region of Cappadocia is perhaps better known as the eastern Roman province whose capital Caesarea (Kayseri) was so bound up with the early history of Christianity. By ad 185, there was a Christian community in Cappadocia, which is mentioned in the First Epistle of St. Peter. The site of this project, Göreme, hitherto Korama, was a main area of religious settlement. In the Göreme valley, there are more than thirty of the thousand or so original churches still extant in Cappadocia. The rock, so easily hollowed, allowed a great degree of complexity in architectural design, which itself reflects a great diversity of Christian cultural influence.

For the Turkish people the region of Cappadocia embodies the geographical and historical heartland of their rich cultural history: Their unique history here is actualized in its unique natural environment.

THE PROGRAM

The immediate goals of the project were to design a series of open and/or semi-open and/or enclosed exhibition spaces as a part of one of the open-air museums of Cappadocia, using a formal vocabulary that would be harmonious with the natural silhouette as a contemporary architectural piece within the historical site. This project was given in the first month of a four-month semester to a group of twenty-four

106

Image 80. Views of the haunting landscape of Cappadocia.

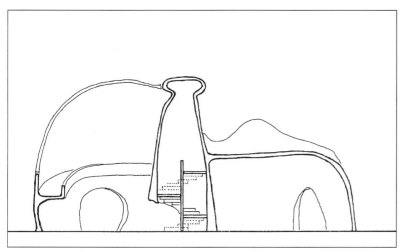

Image 81. Exhibition area, section drawing.

students. Meetings were scheduled as four-hour lectures and evaluations two days a week. Lectures were designed for the provision of visual information and discussion. Proposals of solutions were studied and developed in three-dimensional models of various materials, and evaluated by concentrating on the general concepts and fundamental principles of architecture. Great pains were taken to ensure that students fulfilled their creative potential, both during studio evaluations and at the presentation stage.

THE PROJECTS

The site of one project (Images 23 and 24) is a flat "platform" area in the Göreme Valley. Its scheme incorporates two colonnades that run adjacent to one another, forming an asymmetrical triangular space in which three half-shell structures interlock to form a circular space. The outer surfaces of these shell-like structures are covered with mirror-like, reflecting material. The colonnades rise up to a height of 18 meters and are of concrete covered with plaster, of a color matching the predominant tones of the natural environment. They are monolithic in character and are influenced by Anitkabir, the Monument of Atatürk (the founder of the Republic of Turkey) in Ankara. Within this vertically imposing space the three half-shell structures comprise a high-tech semi-covered exhibition area for display of local handicrafts and historical artifacts.

For the visitor the colonnades form a monumental, and perhaps even truculent, space in which to feel the weight of Anatolian civilization and react with the exhibition area and exhibits. They also provide a focus for the ever-changing reflections and striking color combinations of the natural environment that run across the convex surfaces of the exhibition area both in the course of the day and from the constantly changing perspective of the viewer. In one part of the site, behind one of the colonnades, a recreational area, has been made to allow a view of the exhibition through the pillars. The reflected image of the environment is superimposed on that of the colonnades that surround it. Thus, a vital synthesis of the environment and the rich history of Anatolian civilizations is figured in the superimposed reflection of the Göreme Valley, with the monumental columnar structures, on the high-tech surfaces of the exhibition hall. The overall effect is one of harmony and continuity between man, technology, and nature.

Regarding the siting of another project (Images 81, 82, and 83), it is important to note that the historical significance of Cappadocia does not begin with the Hittite civilization. In the last thirty years excavations and research in Anatolia have revolutionized archaeologists' understanding of its prehistory. In rural Cappadocia the largest Neolithic (late Stone Age) settlement discovered in the world was excavated. When the site was closed to digging, virgin soil had not yet been reached, but twelve different habitation levels dating between 6500 and 5500 bc were revealed. Although only one-thirtieth of the site had been uncovered, it was estimated that the population of the site was at least 5,000, a significant urbanization for the time.

Here we again explore the themes of man, technology, and the environment. Clearly, the Göreme Valley in Cappadocia is an ideal site for such a project. Not only does its rich history make this theme expeditious, but also, as research indicates, the present aspect of Cappadocia has not significantly changed since its prehistory. In Cappadocia, timelessness is a cardinal feature of the environment.

Thus, this project places on a flat "platform" area of earth a sloping wall, made of concrete and covered with dried clay from the site's locale, which forms a crescent embracing the literal representational model of a "fairy chimney" of the same material. The materials give an adobe-like effect and are in agreement with the predominant tones of the environment. The shapes at this site are organic and freeform, and imitate the prevailing softness of the morphological features formed in the process of erosional activity in the Göreme Valley, as well as the wide variety of shapes, so formed, whose echo can be seen in the hol-

Image 82. Exhibition area, model.

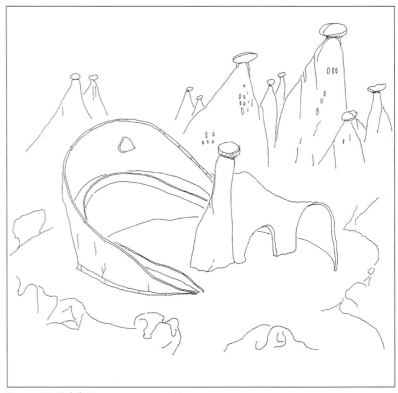

Image 83. Exhibition area, perspective.

lowed out dwellings that surround the project site. The main building is the imitative reconstruction of a "fairy chimney". The door and window spaces in the building reflect those found in the hollowed-out dwellings and churches, and in other architectural features in the valley. The wall also contains such referential door and window spaces. Along the inside of the wall a ramp follows the gently sloping curve of the wall and allows the visitor to view the "fairy chimney" from above and from various angles, while providing extra exhibition space along the interior surface of the wall. The "fairy chimney" itself houses historical artifacts in an imitation of their natural setting, while allowing the visitor to interact with the adobe-like material of the construction.

The echo of the geological forms in the area of the hollowed-out dwellings of the settlers, and the conscious echo of both in the design of the site and the use of imitations of primitive construction materi-

als, creates a quaint paradox—an engaging intimation of man, technology, and nature as figured in the history of architecture, not least of some of the considerations current in postmodern architecture. Again, the overall effect sought is one of resolution, continuity, and harmony.

Harmony

Jonathan Block Friedman
New York Institute of Technology
Old Westbury, New York

SUPPLEMENTARY INFORMATION

THE VOICE OF THE PLACE

New York Institute of Technology is an unusual phenomenon. Because it is an open-admission school, anyone with a high school diploma can walk in off the street and begin to take college courses. Thus there are all-comers in the Design Fundamentals program; as many as 700 students in almost forty sections take this one course in a single semester. On the other hand, NYIT offers a fully accredited NAAB five-year professional B. Arch degree, which graduates about seventy design thesis students per year. So in one case, it is the most egalitarian of places, while in the other it is one of the most elite. The program at the highest levels makes no compromises—indeed, deans of nearby architectural schools consider the NYIT program "world class." However, teaching the elite, as all in beginning studios know quite well, is the easiest of tasks. It is the foundation level that is the most challenging in the sense of truly understanding *the roots* of a study. This is no less true in learning or teaching architecture.

NYIT studios are temporary (hot studios), contact hours are brief (seven hours per week for up to 18 students), and the results are often dispersed to the point of invisibility (three campuses, six different session groups per week)—but New York is New York, whether in the bucolic setting of the Old Westbury country estate with its reconverted thoroughbred stable, the renovated veterans' mental institution in even more rural Islip, or the modified office building in Manhattan. Students learn to concentrate, get to work, and produce a lot, all the while managing heavy part-time jobs or even full-time jobs and family-raising. The serious ones learn to buckle down, produce what's required, and not shrink from increasing excellence in the work.

In both of the first two foundation years, the design problems are deliberately couched in terms of a human program while avoiding easily recognizable stereotyped building "types." Students don't "do"

houses, or meditation spaces, or office buildings, or the like. They work instead with projects that have a program of very definable spaces, with specific materials, circulation demands, etc., while avoiding any easy references to other buildings that students might dig up to copy. It is the belief that architecture comes from the inside out that fuels the continuous development of problems that virtually force the students to experience that revelation.

THE INTENT OF THE PROJECT

"Harmony" is intended to demonstrate to the student who has already mastered the essentials of organizing void through the placement of mass (the basic lesson of *Creation in Space, Volume 1: Architectonics*) that there is another aspect of spatial design that cannot be understood simply through the juxtaposition of solid blocks. The common Boolean operations of union and intersection reveal the architectural possibilities of shared spaces, zones that belong to more than one other volume. Thus the design issues in the "Harmony" project are stated simply: two 16' cubes on a 24' cube site, which forces their intersection at an 8' cube to achieve maximum deployment on the site. The Bag of Tricks is the available supply of construction materials. Their combinations and connections become an important substudy—as do the possibilities of vertical and horizontal circulation. The students are encouraged to explore ways to contrast the two major cubes as much as possible, through material, orientation, light/dark, etc. The question of joint, from smallest constructional to largest architectural scales, is also a major consideration. The students learn to model space through a perforated topology, in which light is modulated rather than completely excluded or contained. Students learn the interaction of concerns about structure, material, construction, circulation, and program in developing and resolving a problem of volumetric requirements. The program has been reduced to an essential relationship between two given volumes, and how these may generate additional spaces.

THE DURATION OF THE PROJECT

The project lasts about four weeks following a sequence of one week for understanding the basic partí issues, one week for developing alternatives at the preliminary design level (paper models of surface and volume continuities), one week for developing a preferred partí, and one week for refining general partí considerations, circulation patterns, material choices, joint details, etc. The last weekend of the month is devoted to full documentation of the model and design in ink on paper, although preliminary scale pencil studies have been developed throughout the project.

THE NYIT CURRICULUM

There are two undergraduate degree programs: a four-year program, which confers a Bachelor of Science in Architectural Technology degree, and a five-year professional Bachelor of Architecture program.

THE PLACE AND LEVEL OF PLATFORM COURSES

The courses are given in the first and second semesters of the first year. "Harmony" is one of four major studies given in the second semester of a beginning design studio course for architectural majors. Most students are still entering freshmen, about eighteen years old, and this project typically comes in the early-middle of the spring semester (late February to early March). An increasing number of students are returning adults; they usually catch on to the intent of a project such as "Harmony" faster than their younger classmates, but often they are more frustrated by their inability to solve it, to make something "nice," to "make it work out."

THE PEDIGREE OF THE PROJECT

While the most direct origin for the whole sequence of studies based on the Kit of Parts used in *Creation in Space, Volume 1: Architectonics* is Cooper Union's Nine-Square Problem—developed by Robert Slutzky, John Hejduk, and Lee Hirsche—other factors have entered into the generation of the modeling medium called the Bag of Tricks for this second part of Design Fundamentals, the Dynamics course. This whole program began in what appeared to be a simple extension of the Architectonics program and Kit of Parts set. Students in the second course were asked to find—from favorite buildings, current magazines, and even Sweet's Catalog—selections of five different stair types, five different window types, five different doors, walls, etc., and to make models of these at a scale of 1/2" = 1' 0" . The result was a disaster. Students made models of things that sometimes looked like buildings, but never worked like buildings. Subsequent attempts to correct these misperceptions focused on structural concerns, yielding works

that too often were object-oriented rather than space- or field-oriented. The results were interesting essays in sculpture, but often missed the point of necessary pursuit of the unique phenomenon of architecture. After some ten years of tinkering with both the modeling elements and the project statements, a set of design exercises has evolved that focuses on the primary issues of modeling habitable volumes with a given set of elements that are available in standard-interval dimensions. There have been many sources of inspiration along the way, including the grids in old-fashioned triode vacuum tubes, relativistic frames of reference in geometrodynamic gravitational fields, the fabric of Wright's later Usonian Houses (*La Miniatura*, etc.), Schindler's interiors, Meier's panel buildings at the Bronx Development Center and the Giovanitti House, and of course Gropius's studies of standard housing elements as well as Le Corbusier's extensions of the Maison Dom-Ino concept. "Perhaps the greatest step in resolving the pedagogical links between Dynamics and Architectonics was achieved by one of our students, who showed the rest of us how to use the Kit of Parts to study partí variations in the design project that follows '*Harmony*' in the Fundamentals Two sequence."

THE EVALUATION

This has been a fairly successful design exercise. The major drawback has been the much longer time it takes to seriously modify a three-dimensional model, compared with the rubber-cemented models of Design Fundamentals 1. This leads to a tendency to talk more in desk crits about "What if you might try this...?" rather than "Let's move this over here, and see how this is clearer!" One means for resolving this problem is to have students to make two complete sets of Bag of Tricks parts, and then work with a current model as well as begin a newly revised version without losing the references of the current study. We imagine that within a decade or so these concerns will be rather moot, as multimedia and 3D computerized documentation (even in direct model form!) will become commonplace. The positive outcomes of this project include a marked increase in students' ability to visualize plastic solutions through a continuity of interior and exterior volumes; a clearer understanding of the relationship between illumination, circulation, and space-making; and an insight into the unique property of architecture to make a volume "read" as part of more than one spatial order. As these areas are emphasized, some students are also able to grasp the way detailing of joints and material relationships can enhance a project, while other students find that they begin to lose control of their earlier simple and clear partí notions through the detailing. One of the best tests the instructor can make is to simply push the model sideways. If the joints have been well thought out and executed, then the work stays rigid or elastically returns to its original configuration. On the other hand, if the connections are sloppy and/or incorrect, the whole project can tumble into a shapeless heap. This is one instance of "My model fell apart in the car" as an indictment rather than simply a mishap.

—*Jonathan Friedman*

THE PROJECT

This project comes in a specific position of a general sequence that makes up the two-semester design studio course in Fundamentals of Architecture. "Harmony" is the first project to make major use of the second-semester set of design elements called the *Bag of Tricks* to organize specific spaces to an architectural program. The program is deliberately simple—the definition and organization of two similar volumes within a site that forces their intersection, creating a third volume. The pragmatic characteristics and uses of these spaces suggest architectural implications.

The first course, Architectonics, is documented and elaborated on in the author's textbook, *Creation in Space, Volume 1: Architectonics.* The premise of this study is that the innate childhood ability to arrange blocks in three dimensions is the shared (pre)experience of architecture that young and older adults bring to college-level studies in architecture. Generally, their sophistication in language, numbers, history, etc., is not matched by an equally sophisticated training in "block arranging." Thus the beginning course in Design Fundamentals picks up where the five-year-old block builder leaves off. The emphasis of this program is to enable the student to match previsions of space with the actual plastic results achieved in three dimensions. Thus model-making is seen as primary, while technical drafting documenting through planimetric, axonometrics, and other projections is secondary to the essentially spatial idea of the organization and arrangement of masses.

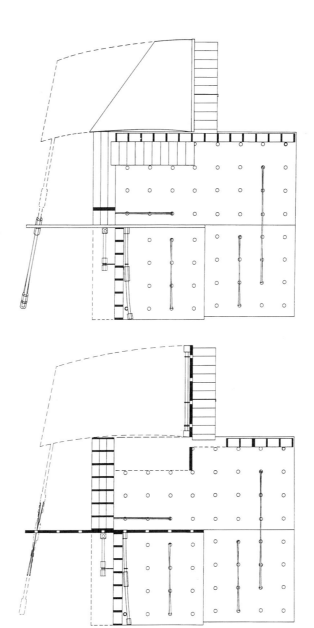

Image 84 and 85. Plan views of model by William C. Reyman, student of Jonathan Friedman.

This is what *architectonics* means. Simple, concrete projects, such as "make two spaces in dialog," focus on how essentially plastic ideas may be developed, differentiated, and improved. Rubber cement is the sole means of connecting the Kit of Parts, which encourages the continuous rearrangement of the composition. This generates both courage in experimentation and an increasingly discerning critical faculty through comparison of early configurations with later ones. Since all students use the same site and set of elements for their projects, creativity is revealed as independent of the content of the elements and essentially dependent on the relationships between them. This condition mirrors the common experience in architectural practice, in which the client's demands for so many bedrooms, baths, etc., is the given *content* of the design. (As Le Corbusier wrote, "Thus an architect learns to dance in his fetters.")

The Kit of Parts is composed of simple geometric forms—cubes and rods, first, as they are easiest to draw when learning how to make an axonometric projection! Pyramids, cylinders, and vaults follow. Stair and ramp elements are added for Timepiece, the last exercise in the sequence, and bring specifically human scale to the architectonic compositions. Common programs such as "bus shelter" or "meditation space" are deliberately avoided so that students will not resort to the clichéd images of "De-zine" that infest the investigative portions of their brains. Certainly this program meets with opposition from students in the beginning, especially from those who most want to get on with designing "real buildings." But by the end of the semester, most come to realize that the specific medium of architecture is space, and that what distinguishes architecture from shelter is the intentional relationship of elements to reveal ideas through the medium of space. The basic argument is that architectonic studies of arranging blocks are exactly what "real" architects do, but with fewer rules like budget, codes, etc., interfering with the essentially architectural issues.

The second course, DYNAMICS, recognizes one subtle oversimplification of the immediately previous sentence. Carpenters and masons are the ones who actually arrange the material blocks of our buildings in space. The task of the architect is to organize and arrange the *immaterial* blocks of humanly scaled habitable volume that make up the rooms, porches, vestibules, stair shafts, etc., which are the elements of architectural space. It is important to note that the basic geometric definition of "solid" does not distinguish between empty or filled three-dimensional figures. Thus a glass is a cylinder, whether empty or full of liquid. On this basis, both kinds of solids are impor-

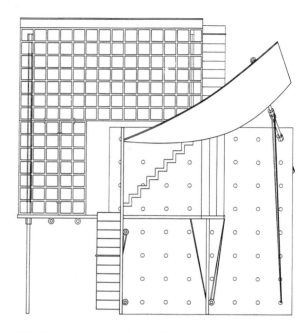

Image 86 and 87. Elevation views of model by William C. Reyman, student of Jonathan Friedman.

tant to the architect—the "cube" which is a brick and the "cube" which is a bedroom; the "rod" which is a two-by-four and the "rod" which is a corridor or elevator shaft. We may go further and say that if architectonics is the creation of space by the arrangement of masses to give meaning to the voids between them, then dynamics is the creation of space through the arrangement of masses *and* voids. We then can define a volume as any combination of mass and void that identifies a geometric solid. Simply put, mass + void = volume. Thus a typical room is essentially a cubic (actually, right rectangular parallelipiped) volume. The boundaries of such a volume may be implied as well as actually defined.

There is an essential difference between the filled and empty volumes of brick and room. If one adds a trellis to a flat roof, the mostly empty cubic volume likely will not crush the living room below it. But if the same volume on the roof were defined by filling it with bricks, concrete, or even cotton, it would most likely fall through the ceiling of the living room below it. In force fields such as gravity and wind, what keeps the masses of ceilings and walls in position around the voids of

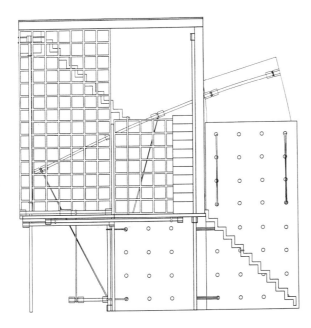

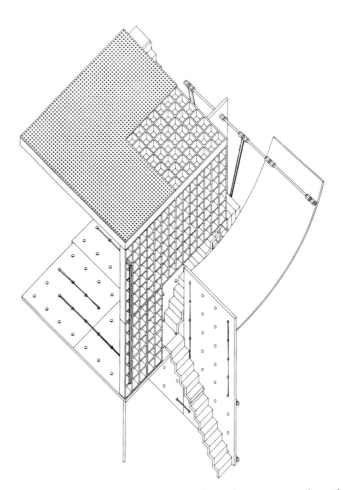

rooms? The precise combination of material qualities, shapes, and positions to resist such forces is what creates architectural volume.

The choice of the name Dynamics for the course requires a brief explanation. Like the Euclidean drawing of a triangle, a typical axonometric view of an architectonic study (of an arrangement of masses) seems to be perfectly immutable, weightless, beyond the everyday cares of rust, wind, or sag—in short, timeless. This conception in the Architectonics course is reinforced by making two assumptions: first, that all elements are made of the same magic constant material; second, that all connections of elements with rubber cement are sufficiently strong and permanent to withstand all foreseeable loads. Of course, in the real world such assumptions are rarely true. A one-inch white cube of alabaster sitting on a one-inch white cube of urethane foam will crush it, whereas reversing the cubes makes deformation imperceptible. Any volume in the real world is subject to forces that act to distort its form and dimensions over time. The distortions of filled solids like beams and columns become the subject of engineering courses for architects.

Are there equivalent force or load interactions between empty solids? Consider that a simply supported beam will deflect under a concentrated load. Maximum shear develops where the beam sup-

Image 88. Axonometric drawing of model by William C. Reyman, student of Jonathan Friedman.

ports restrict bending. If a room next to a corridor is an equivalent volumetric configuration to a block on a beam, then are there not planning forces equivalent to structural forces at work? Most architects commonly critique design work, whether in an academic studio or over their own drawing boards, through an elaborate set of articles, grunts, and gestures, which if tape-recorded as audio alone would sound virtually inarticulate. "Look, if this goes here, and you move this over there, and that allows this to open up enough to shift that over here . . . " is typical of this kind of communication. What is such design really about? It can be argued that it is the recognizing of the mutual interactions between related volumes. In Architectonics, the assumption is that masses—well behaved, respectful, and independent of each other—stand peaceably in proximity, making generally static if not stationary residual voids, and that together the voids and masses generate patterns of organized space. However, in Dynamics, the assumption may be stated as follows: Each and every element, mass or void, tends to react to the forces of nearby masses and voids in fields of forces. In effect, this means that volumes generate and react to fields of influence around them. As an example of this, consider a single room that opens into the middle of a long corridor. Whether the rationale is circulation, light, or plastic relationships, it can be suspected that most architects would find this simple configuration mute, dumb, and ultimately unsatisfactory unless some spatial gesture recognizes the unique intersection of the two volumes of corridor and room. Perhaps a Louis Kahn would pull the room away from the corridor to develop an intermediate zone for casual meetings (as he did at Erdman Hall); perhaps an Alvar Aalto would distort a wall of the corridor to make it "bulge" enough to accommodate the imposition of this unique volume along its length (something evident in the plans of the Lucerne Flats Tower (1965–68); perhaps a Frank Lloyd Wright or a Le Corbusier would emphasize the pressure on the corridor by popping the zone opposite the entry into a projecting balcony (as at Villa Stein, Garches) or into an extended bowered arcade (as at D. D. Martin House). Whatever the plastic response, the important point here is that the effect of one volume on another is to generate a spatial "force" between them that demands some kind of interactive plastic Dynamic response. Isn't this understanding of space as a fluid (hydraulic?) medium one of the essential secrets of successful architectural design?

House to Street

Charles P. Graves, Jr.
Kent State University
Kent, Ohio

SUPPLEMENTARY INFORMATION

THE VOICE OF THE PLACE

The School of Architecture at Kent State was created with a focus on technology. Today, even though it is balanced with a strong design program, there are still five faculty members who teach structures. Pluralism within a framework of clear constraints is the intended "style" of the school. Four of the five years of design studios are run with a set program wherein all studios at any but the third-year level work with the same problem, with individual professors manipulating the project toward their own theories. With each professor having a different background, the school offers a healthy mix of theories in design.

THE INTENT OF THE PROJECT

Current architectural discourse, in both the media and academia, continues to promote the concept of buildings as autonomous objects often responsive solely to the concepts that generate them. As a counterpoint, a first year exercise was devised that re-employs the street as primary spatial definer. This exercise introduces the student to an elemental method for investigating solid and void in an immediate way. It is implemented on a computer with the understanding that whether originated by traditional design concepts or originated by means of the congenial technology of the computer, the work of architecture will inevitably occupy and create space.

THE DURATION OF THE PROJECT

The project lasts for four weeks.

THE KENT STATE CURRICULUM

Kent State has a 4+1+1 curriculum. After four years the student receives a Bachelor of Science degree, with the option of one more year's study to earn a Bachelor of Architecture degree or enrollment in the graduate program for a two-year course of study leading to a first professional Master of Architecture degree.

THE PLACE AND LEVEL OF PLATFORM COURSES

Studios begin in the first year of college study. First- and second-year courses are referred to as "theory studios," those in the next five semesters as "design studios." The final semester is devoted to a thesis. "House to Street" is given at the beginning of the second semester of the first year. It has been preceded by a series of accretive projects that begin in the Bauhausian tradition and proceed to move into more inclusive architectural issues.

THE PEDIGREE OF THE PROJECT

The single housing unit is patterned after a first-year exercise created by Professor Herbert E. Kramel at the Eidgenoessische Technische Hochschule (ETH) in Zurich, Switzerland. Other sources include David Grahame Shane's "The Revival of the Street," *24th Lotus International*, Milan, 1979; and Joan Gadol's "Leon Battista Alberti, Universal Man of the Early Renaissance," *The New Visual Geometry*, Chicago, 1969.

THE EVALUATION

"House to Street" was given for the first time in the spring semester of 1991, in one studio. The results were given very high reviews by both the students and faculty.

THE PROJECT

The structure of this project is designed to introduce students to (1) the capabilities of the computer to facilitate the conceptualization and

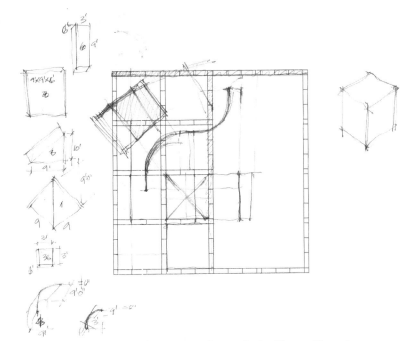

Image 89. Process drawing (computer print marked with pencil) used to develop three-dimensional tartan grid.

design of three-dimensional forms and spaces; (2) the design of a single-form housing unit; and (3) basic street typologies. The exercises are devised to give the student a quick understanding of the CAD software (MacArchitrion) and hardware (Macintosh SE30). As the students progress through each exercise they are exposed to more complex traits of the software and hardware, and thus advance in gradual but expedient stages.

FIRST EXERCISE

The first exercise teaches basic computer efficiency and shows how the computer can facilitate the conceptualization and design of three-dimensional space. For an introduction to the modeling software, all students are required to construct a gridded rectangle on the computer. This gridded rectangle has the outside dimensions of 21' wide by 31' deep by 21' high, and is subdivided into twelve cubes of 10' by10' by 10'. The architecture of the cubes is founded on the application of a tartan grid.

Prior to the introduction of a three-dimensional tartan grid within this computer exercise, students appeared to have a difficult time visu-

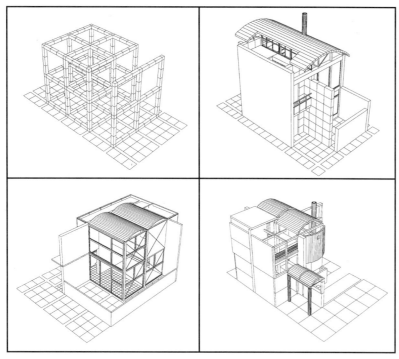

Images 90 through 93. Computer images of house prototypes.

alizing the placement of forms in space. Rendering images using the CAD program, MacArchitrion, occurs within a field of gridded dots that are used as both a compositional and a constructive device, but only while working in plan. In perspective the program does not offer a horizon line or a gridded field to allow the viewer to establish his or her position with respect to objects viewed. Designs had a tendency to "float" when being studied in perspective, appearing to have no cohesion and to exist in a field of chaos.

When the computer model is viewed in perspective, a base tartan grid adds depth and scale such as that described by Alberti and used by his contemporaries during the Renaissance. With the invention of perspective, the grid was used as a means of anchoring and locating a building in a two-dimensional simulation of three-dimensional space. An example of this use of the grid as an anchoring device may be seen in Serlio's three stage settings of street scenes: the *Satyric Drama*, the *Comedy,* and the *Tragedy*.

The tartan grid allows great freedom in design while serving two important functions. First, it helps students make a quick start by serving as both a compositional and a constructive device to control the abstract space of a design in a rudimentary but meaningful way. It aids the students in locating themselves in space. Second, it acts as a safety net, preventing a student from falling beyond the grid into utterly unstructured chaos.

The computer is sympathetic to this design program. It is structured to abstract real space in terms of x, y, and z coordinates, and thus replicates accurately the general architectural project of subdividing real space in those dimensions. The computer facilitates the strategic transfer of a student's attention by allowing him or her to zoom in and out on various details, moving from the far to the close while viewing the space both inside and outside from multiple angles. The grid thus offers both a tool for ordering and a sense of place. This grid may be discerned either as a constructive device—concrete, real, and architectonic—or as an abstract, mathematical, or dimensionless one of purely compositional value.

SECOND EXERCISE

The second exercise requires the student to design a single housing unit with respect to the gridded rectangle previously loaded into the computer. The square footage for one unit falls within the boundaries of the twelve 10' x 10' x 10' cubes, with the program for the single unit as follows: (a) a double-height living space; (b) one 5' x 10' x 10' cooking area; (c) a dining area; (d) a staircase; (e) one 2' x 4' x 15' fireplace and flue; (f) a study area; (g) a sleeping area; (h) one 5' x 10' x 10' shower room; (i) a garden space.

No particular site is given for the design of the single housing unit, allowing the student to view the object from any direction. This exercise may be seen then as endorsing the presence of "object fixation." However, by recalling Alberti's statement that the house is a small city and the city is a large house, the object-house may be viewed as a microcosm of solid-to-void relationships, and thus a prelude to the street.

THIRD EXERCISE

The third exercise, a basic introduction to a street setting, asks the student to investigate possible multiple configurations of the single unit in groups of twelve, creating three basic prototypical street settings. They are labeled, for purposes of classification, "Main Street,"

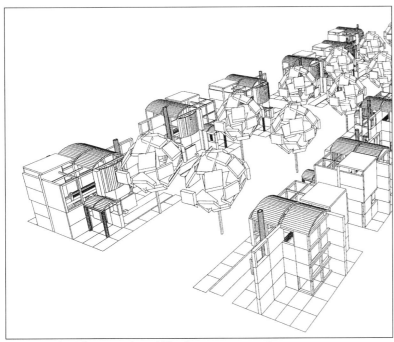

Image 94. Aerial perspective of Elm Street; computer image.

"Elm Street," and "The Strip."

Main Street is defined as a dense urban fabric with buildings sharing party walls that create a solid facade. On Elm Street there exists a balance between solid and void. The structures are separated by the minimal distance needed to signify individuality, yet they tend to share repetitive guidelines of setbacks and porch sizes. What the buildings fail to do to define the street edge is made up for by the repetitive spacing of trees set close to the street boundary. The final setting, The Strip, presents images of buildings that occur as objects randomly placed in space. With virtually no controlling rules, the buildings are located to call maximum attention to themselves as individuals. Any sense of street is defined only by repetitive two-dimensional surfaces and level changes denoted by the curb.

PARALLELING THE EXERCISES

Throughout the four-week program a number of basic urban issues are addressed in lectures. Parallel with the first exercise—the

Image 95. Ground level perspective of Elm Street; Computer image.

construction of a gridded rectangle on the computer—the history of the grid as either a construction device or an abstract, mathematical tool is presented. During the second exercise—the single housing unit—the lecture covers precedents for buildings seen as objects. Their internal-to-external relationship, public and private spaces, solid and void, and issues of context are compared. In the final lecture, the history of the street is presented, with discussions on the relationship and proportion of the following items to each other: the building height, the width of the street, the building set-back from the street, the spacing of the buildings, and the use of repetitive elements.

In the course of the exercises, critiques take place directly at the work station, while looking at the screen or at laser-printed hard copies. This situation allows the instructor and student to redesign during the critique, instead of having the student work on the changes after the fact and presenting the results at the next class. Once the process of manipulating the projects occurs on the computer, a user may move virtually through and around the design, thus gaining a better understanding of its three-dimensionality and spatial qualities.

CONCLUSION

The continued dissemination of commercial CAD modeling software will no doubt serve to expand the realms of architectural investigation. The possibilities of creating a "self-generative" architecture originating from the technological capabilities of the computer are indeed exciting, yet often result in the creation of autonomous objects that deny any real sense of physical context. Designers, however, must ultimately confront gravity if their designs are to translate into architecture. The exercises described above begin to establish basic guidelines for the transformation of single-form objects into urban space. By the very nature of inputting commands into the computer, the user becomes cognizant of a process of design through which the *how* of design is revealed. Ultimately, however, designers must face *what* has been created on the computer and consider the phenomenal implications of their designs in the built environment.

A Nomadic Shelter

Mary Hardin
Arizona State University
Tempe, Arizona

SUPPLEMENTARY INFORMATION

THE VOICE OF THE PLACE

Educational programs in architecture should aspire to the enhancement of knowledge necessary to link understanding to experience, theory to practice, and art to science in ways that respond directly to human needs, aspirations, and sensibilities. They should be responsive to an ever-changing consensus of what it is that architects do, will do, and are ethically and morally obligated to do.

THE INTENT OF THE PROJECT

Students are asked to join forces to conduct research, create the design, and ultimately construct a portable dwelling. "A Nomadic Shelter" was conceived as a way of introducing to students the issues of anthropometrics as generators of a building's form, size, and spatial layout. It also had to perform as a bridge between a series of two-dimensional graphic design exercises that characterize the first semester of a design fundamentals course, and a subsequent series of three-dimensional architectonic projects that make up the second semester of studio. These straightforward goals were, however, merely the beginning of a project that led to some unforeseen and controversial press coverage centered on shelter for the homeless.

THE DURATION OF THE PROJECT

The project lasts for four studio periods, comprising two calendar weeks.

THE ARIZONA STATE UNIVERSITY CURRICULUM

The curriculum is a 2+2+2 program, with the first two years consisting of lower division general studies. The middle two years are devoted to an upper-division preprofessional program, completion of which earns the student a nonprofessional Bachelor of Science degree in Design. In the final two years the student engages in graduate studies to earn a first-professional Master of Architecture degree.

THE PLACE AND LEVEL OF PLATFORM COURSES

Beginning Design occurs in the second year of college study following one year of general studies courses. It is the first semester of basic design as well as the first design studio course the student takes. Three required drawing studios may be taken before, concurrent with, or after this initial design studio. The drawing studios include hardline drawing conventions, freehand drawing exercises, and freehand perspective techniques.

THE PEDIGREE OF THE PROJECT

There is no known specific history of this project, although it may have derived unconsciously from "snippets of countless 'Instant City' projects witnessed in the early 1970s," when, incidentally, the author was an undergraduate student.

THE EVALUATION

At the final review, students discussed other issues that had arisen in addition to the obvious problems at hand. Besides struggling to meet the functional criteria the project presented, some designers discovered that creativity can actually be enhanced by rules and limitations. For some, the restrictions on the materials and the insistence on portability had led them down serendipitous paths that ended well. For other participants, the value of research was underscored. Inspiration drawn from examples of precedent was invaluable in their personal search for unique design solutions. Team members expressed both frustration and delight at having worked with and depended on others. Personal communication skills, reliability and punctuality were seen as attributes of potential architects who would most likely spend their careers working in project teams. Finally, associations were drawn between the experience of spending the night in an ephemeral shelter and the daily lives of transient dwellers. Some students developed empathy for the practical necessities of people seeking shelter, and realized that cardboard boxes did not provide for the essential needs of security, privacy, comfort or hygiene.

It was this latter point that accounted for the media attention and controversy that developed around a project innocently conceived. The gathering of students spending the night in their "tent city" on the lawn of the Architecture annex attracted the notice of the university press and then the local television news media. A short newspaper article and TV spot focused on the aspect of the shelters as transient dwellings, and students were coaxed into discussing their views of the national problem of homelessness. Quotes that were abbreviated or taken out of context then made their way to a national student news magazine, and provoked a good deal of editorial mail.

Some respondents praised the students for taking on a sensitive social issue, while others wrote scathing critiques of architects' naiveté at promoting such a superficial solution to a serious economic problem. A few students were caught up in the excitement of the moment and resolved to give their shelters to some members of the urban transient population around the campus, but grew despondent after investigating their living conditions and realizing how little impact the gesture would have. After the media attention waned, most of the projects were blithely relegated to the recycling bin.

—Mary Hardin

THE PROJECT

The requirements for a satisfactory portable dwelling were given as follows:

1. It had to house one adult of ordinary size;
2. It had to be movable (through disassembly or in its entirety);
3. It had to allow for at least the postures of sleeping and sitting up;
4. It had to be fashioned from cardboard and string *only*;
5. It had to provide shelter from sun, moderate breezes, and light rain.

Students began by researching other human "containers" designed for a tight fit, such as space capsules, tents, sleeping bags, coffins, and cockpits. They searched for architectural precedent as well, and discovered a legacy of huts, teepees, and lean-to structures that had served as portable shelters for nomadic populations throughout

Image 96. left to right: shelter parts; shelter under construction; complete exterior; "moving in"; shelter dismantled and packed; packed shelter carried by shoulder strap.

history. Additionally, student teams measured their own physical dimensions through a range of activities and compared their findings with the averages stated on anthropometric data charts. The differences between an individual's dimensions and those of the "composite man" were suddenly perceived as the root cause of discomfort in the world of standardized vehicles, furniture, and appliances.

Students remained in teams to develop schematic design ideas for shelters through sketches and study models. Several different alternative schemes were required for interim pin-up reviews, and the multiple options were gradually hybridized to form one scheme that embodied the best characteristics of the group effort.

Measurement and accommodation of the human body were the aspects of the problem that were most easily solved. Human dimensions, reach, and posture characteristics were the primary determinants of the shelter's scale, proportion, and form. The requirement of portability, however, proved to be the sticking point. Ideas that seemed like sure winners on paper were disastrous when translated into cardboard. Even the teams that experimented with small-scale models made of index cards were disappointed to find that rigidity was not a property that translated from one material and scale to another. A second cycle of design and testing was necessary to ensure that the full-scale structures would not buckle or crease under the weight of the cardboard over a given span, or that string connections and hinges would not tear through cardboard after several manipulations. Structural reinforcements and all manner of ingenious tabs, flaps, and interlocking devices were developed in the home stretch. As a final project requirement, the design teams were asked to transport their shelters a short distance by foot, assemble them in a secure area, and spend the night within them.

Results of the "Nomadic Shelter" project were quite diverse; structures resembling everything from solar yurts to Dymaxion race car bodies were in evidence. Some rolled up into compact backpacks for transport, while others could never be assembled a second time after breakdown (even by the designers). A few disintegrated during the night, either from exposure to the elements or as a consequence of the camaraderie that developed between the students as they passed the evening together.

Between Tradition and Modernity
Desmond Hui and Lye Kum Chew
University of Hong Kong

SUPPLEMENTARY INFORMATION

THE VOICE OF THE PLACE

The role of the architect in an urban setting such as Hong Kong has become one of manipulator and manager of the physical environment, with the objectives of enhancing the lifestyle of the individual and the improvement of the collective functioning of society as a whole. Increasingly concerned with the quality of social needs, education and the environment, young people tend to turn ideologically rather than vocationally to a career in architecture. Hong Kong's political future with China after 1997 is a factor of increasing importance to both its social and economic progress. In the past the Department of Architecture has been committed to developing well-motivated, creative professionals, conscious of their responsibility to society and to that meeting of East and West of which their city is a unique and outstanding paradigm. But now new questions arise as to the form the education of the architect should take to ensure that the graduating architect moves out with a new sense of purpose into the city and its newly enhanced national context and environs.

THE INTENT OF THE PROJECT

The immediate intention is to develop students' sensitivity toward the physical and social environment of their cultural origin, and to solve an architectural design problem based on the development of this sensitivity. The long-term goal is to investigate the problems arising from the confrontation and integration between tradition and modernity, and to formulate an approach through the direct and experiential interaction of fresh and ideologically unbiased beginning design students.

THE DURATION OF THE PROJECT

The project consists of a one-week field trip to China and two months of studio work.

THE UNIVERSITY OF HONG KONG CURRICULUM

The University offers a three-year Bachelor of Arts degree in Architectural Studies and a two-year Bachelor of Architecture degree. The students are permitted an optional year out between attainment of the B.A. and the completion of the B.Arch.

THE PLACE AND LEVEL OF PLATFORM COURSES

The first-year studio course covers three terms. The course is split between six units of architectural studies and six units of visual studies. Prior to beginning "Between Tradition and Modernity," the students had fifteen weeks of studio work, which included short exercises on architectonics, ergonomics, color, and geometric studies, plus projects that introduced architectural concepts dealing with site and program issues. They also learned sketching, both Chinese and Western painting, and Chinese calligraphy, as well as other visual and graphic techniques. Concurrent courses included Chinese and Western history of architecture, structure, construction, and environmental science. The field trip took place in the tenth week of these preliminary studies.

THE PEDIGREE OF THE PROJECT

No precedent is immediately known. "We are probably the pioneers of this kind of project."

THE EVALUATION

The project was given once, in 1990–91.

The results were satisfactory. Students were able to respond positively to the environment and adapt elements from their observation in their own designs that were novel and refreshingly different from the mere imitation of fashionable styles advertised in architectural magazines. To quote the words from one visiting critic to the final jury of the project: "All in all, it was exciting to see the diversity of

designs and the imaginative effort brought forth by what must have been a most wonderfully edifying trip. The students came upon their roots and obviously became aware that materials and shapes formed part of the living environment. They sensed that there were reasons for these to be what they are and that the living environment is, even in so remote a village, a part of a cultural link and that it could continue to be consciously designed by those who are sensitive to it. I believe the students have responded very well to this, their first challenge in architectural design."

—Desmond Hui

THE PROJECT

This is the major project for first-year students in the Department of Architecture at the University of Hong Kong. The students and teachers carried out a field trip for one week to the Shantou and Chaozhou area of Canton in mid-November 1990. They visited the traditional houses and examined their architecture for an understanding of the context and heritage in terms of building forms and techniques. Then they selected a typical Chaozhou village settlement still intact in terms of the building fabric and immune to the domination of modern technology. A survey was conducted for two days to understand the history and development of the village, *feng shui* (Chinese geomancy) and siting, social hierarchy, and conformity of design techniques and vocabularies with the general tradition established in the neighboring regions. Students were divided into groups and each measured a typical house and documented the history of its particular household. In the end, a specific site was chosen for redevelopment, from which students gathered the necessary data, details, and field measurements.

Studio work on the project was divided into phases. The first phase was assembling the data and information from the field trip into a report consisting of sections on history and culture, techniques of construction, structure, and environmental studies. Measured drawings were prepared and a 1:200 scaled site model was made. Owing to the university's organization of terms, the design program was handed out in the second term after another short project on the design of a

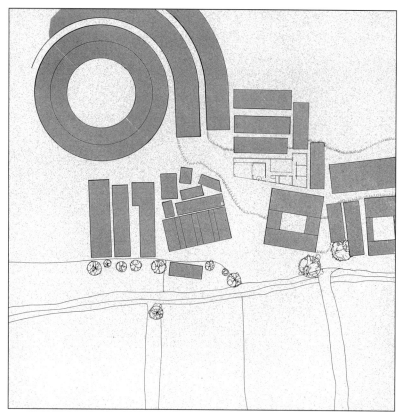

Image 97. Shophouse site plan by William Kong.

dwelling unit, which served as an introduction to the more comprehensive exercise of a house design. The program was a shophouse in the village, which in reality normally occupies about ten percent of the total gross floor area (GFA) of the house on the ground. It was specified that the GFA of the shophouse was not to exceed 200 square meters, and the height generally not more than two stories with no basement; a roof terrace was optional. As conditions exist in the village, there is a public water supply from pipes, but wells may also be provided for water not used for drinking. Electricity and propane gas are also available. However, waste water and sewage have to be taken care of by traditional methods, which means they are either taken away regularly as fertilizers for farming, or decomposed in individual septic tanks built within the house. Construction was assumed to be in

concrete or concrete block load-bearing walls and/or framed structure and roofs as concrete slab or timber frame with roofing tiles. Climate control would be by passive means.

Students were free to compose their own scenario for the project; i.e., the type of shop (a variety of which they all had the opportunity to observe during their trip), the ownership of shop and house, the size and nature of the family living and working there, the characteristics of the occupants, and the spatial/physical requirements of the rooms and areas. They were also free to choose, with qualifications and negotiations, one of the twelve selected sites in the village. In developing their design concept, they were required to observe the importance of the idea of "environment," which has been chosen as a philosophical theme for the design approach of the whole Department of Architecture. The following four categories of environment were identified:

1. *natural environment*: how a design relates to the natural forces, such as sun, rain, wind, view, vegetation, animals, *feng shui*, etc.

2. *technical environment*: how a design relates to the existing technical systems, i.e., construction practices apart from the above prescriptions, use of materials, and the "techne" of living, such as the provision (or not) of television, stereo, modern furnishings, etc.

3. *built environment*: how a design relates to the existing village context, i.e., the problem of fabric, texture, form, and scale.

4. *cultural environment*: how a design relates to the Chinese cultural context, i.e., the style of living, family and social concept, dining and cooking habits, appreciation of the arts, taste, etc.

The students' response to the above would help formulate their ideas in relating tradition to modernity in their architectural design.

Requirements of studio work consisted of a program brief and site analyses to cover the following: sun and wind direction with seasonal changes, rainfall, temperature, solar time, topography, vegetation, water sources, view, village structure, living patterns, "urban" or communal spaces, figure/ground relationship, etc. Students developed preliminary design alternatives based on the above in a scale of 1:100; eventually they created a final design in 1:20 scale with plans, sections, elevations, models, and sketches. They were also required to do technical studies of

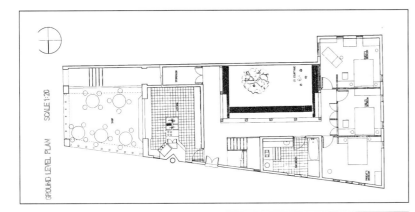

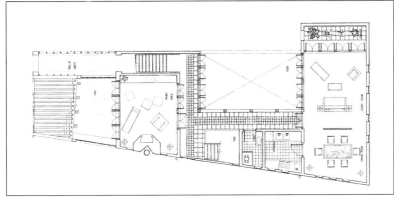

Images 98 and 99. Floor plans of shophouse by William Kong. Above: ground-level plan; below: second-story plan.

their designs for the structure, construction drawings showing the framing plan, a detailed wall section, and the drainage services.

Perhaps the rationale and significance of this project could best be summarized in the words of the French philosopher Paul Ricoeur, who urges one to go back to one's own origins so as to be worthy participants in the great debate of culture. Ricoeur points out that mankind on the whole is approaching a single world civilization, which represents on one hand gigantic progress for everyone and on the other hand an impending threat of swallowing up individual heritage. This world civilization, characterized by the scientific spirit and the development of technics, with the existence of a rational politics and universal economy, and the unfolding of an equally universal way

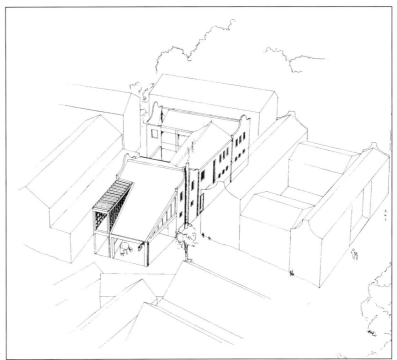

Image 100. Axonometric drawing showing shophouse in context, by William Kong.

of living, doubtless gives rise to many good things: the awareness of a single humanity, the availability of elementary possessions and access to certain values of dignity and autonomy for everyone, and the attainment past the threshold of a first rudimentary culture of mankind within the culture of consumption.

Many corresponding evils have also resulted from this universalization, however, constituting a subtle destruction of different cultures. This is evidenced by the spreading of a mediocre civilization as a counterpart of the elementary culture. The paradox of how to cope with modernity and at the same time return to sources is a phenomenon common among developing nations. It also manifests itself as a challenge for the highly industrialized Western societies to meet other traditional cultures. The inevitability of cultural encounter in human civilization leads Ricoeur to conclude that we must return to our origins to understand the ethico-mythical nucleus of our culture: "In order to confront a self other than one's own self, one must first have a self."

Translating Ricoeur's ideas in architectural terms, this project is an attempt to discover an architecture that relates to the cultural origins of the Chinese, yet partakes at the same time of the positive offerings of the modern universal civilization. This twofold participation is perhaps one step beyond what Kenneth Frampton (who was also inspired by reading Ricoeur) proposes as Critical Regionalism in that it is a commitment not only to place but also to space, or, in Heideggerian terms, a commitment to both the nearness of *raum* and the distance of *spatium*.

SOURCES
Ricoeur, Paul. *"Universal Civilization and National Cultures,"* in *History and Truth.* Translated by Charles A. Kelby. Evanston, Ill.: Northwestern University Press, 1965.
Frampton, Kenneth. *"Modern Architecture and Critical Regionalism."* RIBA Annual Dis course, December 7, 1982.

The Metaphysical City
Michael Jordan
University of Oklahoma
Norman, Oklahoma

SUPPLEMENTARY INFORMATION

THE VOICE OF THE PLACE

This exercise has been given at two universities in recent history, and the "voice" of each has colored the work. In its present context, the University of Oklahoma, the College of Architecture's curriculum is traditional and professional to the core. This conservative position is in direct contrast to its underpinnings. The memory of Bruce Goff, if not his method, continues to color both internal and external perceptions of the place. This legacy of vision and willingness to experiment, coupled with the existing well-defined attitudes regarding professionalism, can point the way to an exciting future.

THE INTENT OF THE PROJECT

At its base, the project is intended as an exploration of the relationships that exist, or might exist, between architecture and painting as a means to broaden the students' horizons. Its numerous phases delve into a wealth of issues, including an understanding of the work of a specific artist, color theory and application, the solving of both architectural and architectonic problems, the integration of graphic and modeling skills, and to no small extent the development of interpersonal skills as part of a group.

THE DURATION OF THE PROJECT

The version described below was eight weeks long. Other versions, incorporating additional phases, have lasted an entire fifteen-week semester. It is worth noting that there seems to be a critical mass of students necessary for successful completion of the project, and it is typically conducted by combining at least two studios (over fifty students) with the faculty team-teaching. The version illustrated here was executed in collaboration with Professor Dortha Killian during the spring semester of 1992.

THE UNIVERSITY OF OKLAHOMA CURRICULUM

A traditional five-year, ten-semester, ten-studio curriculum leads to a Bachelor of Architecture. The beginning studios also include students from other curricula within the college, specifically interior design and landscape architecture, as well as the occasional graduate student.

THE PLACE AND LEVEL OF PLATFORM COURSES

Studio begins on the first day of the first year. There are three consecutive studios required of all beginning design students in the college. The third semester is accompanied by a lecture series structured to support the studio work. This project is typically given during the second semester, i.e., during the last half of the freshman year.

THE PEDIGREE OF THE PROJECT

In truth this project evolved on the back of an envelope, as a reaction to several hours spent poring over a wonderful book on

Giorgio de Chirico. I felt a need to "see" the town he carried in his head, to understand it in something other than fragments. This connected with my long-standing conviction that students need to be aware of the history of visual pursuits beyond architecture, and to explore the connections, either real or potential, between them and architecture. I am in no way unique in this concern, and follow in the footsteps of others—John Hejduk and his adaptations of Mondrian, for example—who have passed this way ahead of me.

THE EVALUATION

As happens in the design of any process, this project has evolved from tentative and somewhat unsuccessful beginnings into one in which I have a great deal of faith. It has been favorably reviewed by both colleagues and external jurors. The bottom line, however, is that students truly enjoy the work, are proud of the product, and grow through the process of solving the problem.

—Michael Jordan

THE PROJECT

This project consists of numerous accretive phases connected both thematically, through study of the work of Giorgio de Chirico, and by a vision of the ultimate goal, the realization and habitation of his Metaphysical City. In contrast to the author's usual working method—revealing one phase of a project at a time, much like peeling an onion—students are enlightened about both the process and the final product at the beginning of the semester. Being informed focuses attention on the ties between the issues at hand and the larger context.

ANALYSIS OF PAINTED PRECEDENT

The exercise begins with the selection of a single painting by de Chirico from the period between 1910 and 1919. The only restriction regarding selection is that the painting must describe de Chirico's city. There are more than seventy such paintings, allowing for no duplication within the class. Discussion preceding the selection focuses on de Chirico as a painter, and on his place in the general art history of the time and in Surrealism in particular.

Each painting is subjected to a three-part analysis. First, the painting is reduced to a line drawing describing its essential geometry. Particular attention is given to the role of perspective in these images, and to how and why de Chirico distorted the rules of perspective.

Next, the color structure of the painting is analyzed. The product is a diagram of essential color interactions, relative proportions of colors, and their spatial implications. Finally, the painting is studied for its spatial cues, which often contradict those found in the color study. The product of this effort is a bas-relief, in white only, illustrating the physical facts of the space of the painting.

In two iterations of this exercise a "lost" de Chirico was discovered in an elderly woman's attic at this point in the project. Each student was assigned the task of imagining what that painting might be like, and then producing the painting. The result, beyond the physical act of painting, was the production of a wonderful collection of faux de Chiricos.

ANALYSIS OF BUILT PRECEDENT

The second phase centers on the study of an existing Italian piazza. The initial work involves library research and the collection of documentation on a specific piazza. Again, there is no duplication of subject within the class. Each piazza is dissected through diagrams to reveal its underlying geometry and partí in a manner similar to the analysis of the painting. Kevin Lynch's Image of the City, particularly his discussion of paths, edges, districts, nodes, and landmarks, serves as the source for further analysis. Finally, the piazza is studied in model.

RETURN WITH US NOW TO THE PAINTING

The source painting is again scrutinized, this time for literal architectural elements. Each student produces a set of scaled orthographic drawings—plan and related elevations—of her or his fragment of the city. They are instructed to use their knowledge of a real piazza to imagine the portions of the fragment hidden from view. For instance, when a facade turns a corner out of view, what might its length and architectural character be? How large, and what shape, is the piazza associated with that facade? Where in the piazza, and how tall, is the sculpture seen only in shadow?

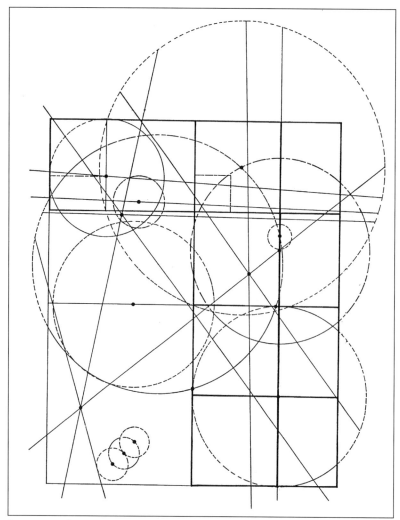

Image 101. Geometric study of "The Inconsistencies of the Thinker" by Chris Nguyen.

REALIZATION OF THE TOWN

In a frenzy of group activity, the orthographic fragments drawn above are collaged into a plan of the town. This is not an altogether ad hoc event, although there is certainly the element of invention. Each painting contains clues to its position in the town: The train track is a

Image 102. Spatial study; bas-relief of "The Inconsistencies of the Thinker" by Chris Nguyen.

virtual constant; sculptures and buildings are frequently seen more than once from different vantage points; the sea plays a role, as do the mountains beyond the town; finally, cardinal directions are known from the direction of shadows (time is determined by the numerous clocks).

Once completed (generally in a single class period), the plan is subdivided and each student is assigned the task of constructing mod-

Image 103. Charrette: assembly of the plan collage.

Image 104. Detail view of model.

els of the buildings in one segment. The building elevations drawn earlier, most often by another student, serve as guides. There is also a base-building team, and a team assigned the task of developing a final plan drawing of the town. The efforts of all focus on making the city "real" and documenting that reality.

THE CENTENNIAL

In the final phase of the project each student is assigned a piazza or open space within the Metaphysical City. The objective is the design of an architectonic event celebrating de Chirico's birth, a sort of surreal fair pavilion. At a minimum it is to contain three spaces, one each for Enigma, Melancholy, and "the lyric significance behind the surface appearance of mundane objects." The structure must respond to the space in which it is placed, the buildings that surround it, and, if applicable, the efforts of other students in the same space. The final product is built to scale in full, de Chirico-esque color and inserted into the city model. In addition, it is documented with a standard set of architectural drawings, including a "walkthrough" of perspective vignettes. Finally, the plan drawing of each individual pavilion is added to the drawing of the entire town.

SHOW AND TELL

Final evaluation of this project normally takes the form of an "open house." Critics are invited to discuss the results, and it is the students' responsibility to take them by the sleeve and ask pointed questions about their contribution to the whole. The best part, however, is that friends, lovers, and family are also invited. It is one of the rare occasions when those outside the studio get to see the results of many sleepless nights in anything like a real situation.

127

Teaching Structures for Architectural Application

Joseph Lim
National University of Singapore

SUPPLEMENTARY INFORMATION

THE VOICE OF THE PLACE

The School of Architecture is responsible for training competent graduate assistants for local practice, and as such its educational objectives are pragmatic and practice-oriented. This preoccupation is reflected in the nature of third-year and final-year design projects, which attempt to integrate technical and practical considerations in a rigorous fashion. The school aims to provide students with a good grounding in the practical aspects of architectural education, together with a varied exposure to fine arts, architectural theory, and computer-aided architectural design.

THE INTENT OF THE PROJECT

The divisions between the design approaches of the architect and the engineer are rooted in historical circumstances related to the existing divisions between art and technology. These divisions will be perpetuated in the teaching of succeeding generations of architects and engineers unless steps are taken to prevent this from happening. The sum of these three interrelated and sequential student projects focuses on the use of structure in architecture as a response to the gaps between the intangible ideas in architecture and the craft of object-making in translating these ideas into usable reality. There is thus the oscillation between the ideas related to culture, and those of construction and the resisting of gravitational forces in nature. The design process encourages the generating of several possibilities without attempting to prescribe from purely technical points of view. In the design process, students are encouraged to develop an understanding of structures in architecture, far beyond the technical realm, in order to break the existing divisions between art and technology, and to allow for architectural ideas that determine technological application.

THE DURATION OF THE PROJECT

Three interrelated and sequential projects are of fourteen weeks' total duration: Project 1, four weeks; Project 2, five weeks; Project 3, five weeks.

THE NATIONAL UNIVERSITY OF SINGAPORE CURRICULUM

The curriculum is a 3 + 2 program, with a required year in local architectural practice after the third year. Two degrees are offered: a three-year Bachelor of Arts in Architectural Studies degree, and a professional Bachelor of Architecture degree following the year in practice and two more years of study. There is currently one School of Architecture in Singapore, which produces forty graduates a year with professional degrees and seventy with the B.A. degree.

THE PLACE AND LEVEL OF PLATFORM COURSES

The platform courses take place in the second year of the B.A. degree program. This set of projects is offered in the second studio semester of that year. It is preceded by an initial two weeks given to the development of the design brief and usage specification—including seminars on design process, structural types, and applications—and case studies and their relationship to architectural form, space, and use. The seminars relate structural behavior to structural form, and illustrate how variations in the character and scale of interior and exterior spaces may determine structural configuration. The studio input relates structural thinking to architectural meaning. Since these design projects are of a kind in which there is little or no precedent, the students may more easily avoid preconceptions.

THE PEDIGREE OF THE PROJECT

Since the learning process oscillates between technical reality and intangible concept, the resulting schemes do not become *either* purely technical in nature and devoid of architectural meaning *or* purely visual manifestations of ideas where constructional reality is not central to the philosophical argument. Although these are not uncommon goals, the methodology employed is unique, and thus without known precedent.

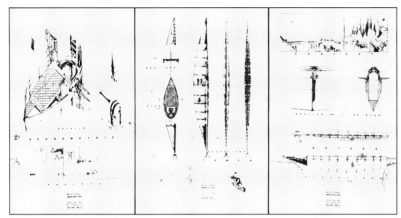

Image 105. Three military outposts.

THE EVALUATION

These projects were given three times since 1990, resulting in a high percentage of good grades.

THE PROJECT

This studio approach focuses on the application of structural theory in architectural concepts. It is a response to the gap which lies between structural analysis and structural concepts in architectural form-finding and planning.

Very often, the first aspect of teaching structures may be easy to incorporate in the *general* curriculum, but difficult for the student to apply in the *design* studio. This approach tends to focus on the analysis and the verification of *one* set of conditions. It usually has little to do with the generating of a variety of conditions.

The integrated studio approach, however, provides the kind of information most sought after by design students, but is more difficult to teach because it involves the understanding of both architectural and structural theories, and two modes of thinking: convergent (or linear) and lateral thinking. Here numerical analysis has marginal play in the design process of generating configurational possibilities in a structural problem.

This integrated approach involves the generating of many architectural proposals based on structural consideration. In one sense, it is best seen in the light of one definition of structural "play" as the art of conceiving elements in space so that they may direct forces to the ground in a stable manner. There are no *rules* that dictate how these elements may be arranged; instead, there are considerations with which the designer may generate endless possibilities, limited only by his or her imagination. However, the starting point of this process is not very often in the structure itself, for architecture cannot be determined by technology alone; there are social, cultural, and utilitarian considerations, for example, that are essential to architecture.

This approach to teaching encourages the development of structural understanding beyond the technical. It attempts to break the existing divisions between art and technology.

PROJECT 1: A MILITARY OBSERVATION POST

The immediate goal of this project is to relate the structural aspects of design to architectural forms and spaces. The long-range or integrated goals are to relate the technical to the aesthetic, and to question existing divisions between art and technology.

The observation post was intended to be exhibited at a military expo, and to function primarily in peacetime military maneuvers. Actual combat specifications were not adopted as they implied substructures more than superstructures.

Three site situations were offered: the post was to (1) span a 25-meter-wide ravine; (2) cantilever from the side of a high cliff; or (3) rise 25 meters high above ground level. These situations implied different structural (and formal) solutions, which were then explored in the design process of the post.

This particular concept combined both a bridge and a tower into a solution that allowed observation from two different positions. It also responded to both ravine and "high-rise" requirements by being a bridge and a tower within one structure.

To this end, a trussed beam with observation decks for three soldiers, confined to the deepest part of the structure, could be swung into a vertical position as a tower given a pin-jointed base stayed with cables to three separate anchors. The observation decks are "foldable" to accommodate both horizontal and vertical positions of occupancy. Access is designed to occur along the compression element in one of two ways: (1) through the spine of the tower, which comprises a bundle of three hollow tubular steel elements spaced only wide enough to allow one man to climb up the tower structure; or (2) along a cantilevered catwalk when the structure is in its bridge mode.

This scheme is an exercise in space, form, and structural idea in response to its use and place in the military context. Its process may be summarized as follows:

use—> structural mechanism—> architectural object

PROJECT 2: A BRIDGE AS DWELLING

The immediate goal of this project is to develop a structure for spaces that questions the conventional notion of a dwelling. The long-range or integrated goal of the project is to illustrate how technical matters may influence and enhance intangible matters. This process allows the student to oscillate between ideas conceived in aspects remote from structure, and ideas in consideration of structure.

The scheme was intended to be a study of a structure spanning over a ravine and its implications on the interior spaces of the dwelling. In this context, the spaces-suspended-in-space provide the opportunity for redefining the enclosures and the structure of the dwelling, which now addresses several points:

1. The structural elements are configured in a way that minimizes physical intrusion into primarily linear organizations of space.
2. The structure can be developed to minimize visual obstruction to the exterior.
3. Floors can now become windows.
4. Balconies can now be suspended in space as in hot-air balloons.

The design was approached from two directions:

1. There was an exploration of the different spaces possible within the geometry of a linear structure.
2. There was the configuration of the elements of the structure itself, in response to the spatial concept.

PROJECT 3: A SPACE FOR ROALD DAHL

The immediate goal of the project is to compose a rational structure as a series of interrelated tectonic elements. The long-range or integrated

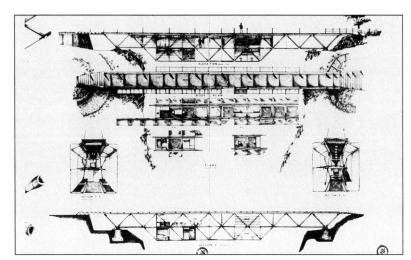

Image 106. Bridge as dwelling.

goal of the project is to merge art with technology in the creation of architectural objects.

This project exemplifies the "pendulum" approach, which swings between the intangible concept and the tangible structure. The spatial concept encapsulates the essence of Dahl's writing, which renders familiar the unfamiliar. Likewise, the spaces typified by the Singapore shophouse* are transformed into unfamiliar ones by *contrast* and by *inversion* .

Contrast

The old structure (masonry party wall) becomes a mere screen with a texture markedly opposite the proposed steel-framed roofs and their supports, which are expressed as separate entities. Although the shophouse outline is retained, the structural frame that forms itself into this familiar outline has no existing precedent. Old forms in new structures here give new spaces that become the unfamiliar.

Inversion

The roof form and entry space in the front half of the shophouse has its relationship inverted in the rear half of the house. The rear spaces and forms become inverted mirror expressions of those in the front. The entire roof structure is linked by a common lower beam,

130

which is the only unifying element between familiarity and unfamiliarity. The process may be summarized as follows:

the intangible idea—> allegorical use of structure—> architectural object

*For those unfamiliar with the cultural phenomenon of a shophouse, please refer to the project of Desmond Hui and Lye Kum Chew entitled "Between Tradition and Modernity."

Serendipity: Accidental Discoveries and Sagacity!

Darla Lindberg-Berreth and Robert D. Hermanson
University of Utah
Salt Lake City, Utah

SUPPLEMENTARY INFORMATION

THE VOICE OF THE PLACE

The philosophical objectives at the University of Utah correspond to the three pedagogical components outlined in this project: (1) that of receiving (seeing): vocabulary, architectonic elements, formal organizational strategies, materials, etc., and their arrangement appropriate to a particular time and place; (2) that of integrating (knowing): relating and reinterpreting an individual awareness and compassion for the experience of form and space; and (3) that of making (doing): communicating an acquired knowledge by sketching, drawing, making models or alternative media.

THE INTENT OF THE PROJECT

For Part 1, the intent is to get them started, getting them, talking, get them thinking. In Part 2, students explore architectural language using a kit of parts. In Part 3, they explore the haptic experiences of

space centering on the body (the dance), and the contemplative inner reflections in contrast to the outer contextual experiences of the mind (The Tabula Rasa).

THE DURATION OF THE PROJECT

Part 1 lasts one week; Part 2, three weeks; Part 3, six weeks.

THE UNIVERSITY OF UTAH CURRICULUM

The program is a three-to four-year first-professional Master of Architecture degree designed for students from diverse backgrounds.

THE PLACE AND LEVEL OF PLATFORM COURSES

Courses are offered in the first year of graduate studies. The students have taken a Design Process course—"legendary in teaching the fundamentals of seeing"—prior to their first studio. The students have had no other architectural history, graphics, or foundation lectures in architecture. Many students come from other career tracks with a completely different approach to problem-solving, and thus are regarded as true beginners.

THE PEDIGREE OF THE PROJECT

While ideas used in formulating this project derive from various sources, including Jonathan Friedman's kit of parts in his *Creation in Space* and Paul Klee's evolution of point, line, plane, and volume, along with other sources noted later, the project itself is original.

THE EVALUATION

(1) What was significant in this particular studio's pedagogy? We believe the pedagogy suggests the notion of moving from the evidence (and authority) of others to the evidence of self—imperative in the development of invention and ingenuity. (2) How was the studio structured to achieve results? We found this through analogy—the "Tale" as a paradigm for the studio process. Implied in this, of course, was the notion of getting prepared for the journey. (3) Finally, how did the projects nurture these results? This occurred in sev-

eral ways: through the celebration of play—"Serendipity" encouraged free thinking; through the exploration of language and meaning in architecture; through alternative, interdisciplinary investigation, i.e., storytelling, writing, and dance; and, perhaps most important, through the act of doing—the making of architecture."

—*Darla Lindberg-Berreth and Robert Hermanson*

THE PROJECT

"King Giaffer of Serendip had three sons. He loved his sons so dearly that he wanted them to have the best possible education, not only in ways of power but in the other virtues which princes in particular are apt to need. And so he employed skilled tutors to train them in each of many special fields" (Austin, p. 195). Thus begins the tale of The Three Princes of Serendip who were ultimately sent out into the world by their father to experience the wonders of foreign lands. In their travels the three sons became known for their wise and insightful observations of the world. The heroes were "always making discoveries, by accidents and sagacity, of things they were not in quest of" (Remer, p. 6) noted Horace Walpole, who, upon reading the story, coined the word *serendipity* to describe the phenomenon. The tale suggests what Pasteur called the "prepared mind." Such a mind is capable of receiving and recognizing fortuitous events through the quality Walpole referred to as sagacity, or "a keen, farsighted penetration and judgment" (Webster, p. 1036). The tale also suggests that sagacity did not happen through the gaining of external knowledge or the knowledge of others alone. The three sons' success and ultimate wisdom and fame came through the implementation of their own internal evidence.

This simple yet elaborate tale suggests a paradigm—a pedagogical journey vis-à-vis the studio experience of the beginning student. The apparent "chance" discovery that serendipity represents is transformed in the design process when students acquire the ability to recognize a newfound "something" as their own creative idea. Distilling this information, they begin to deal with these discoveries as a series of fortuitous opportunities. It is this process of informed discovery that subscribes to the conditions of sagacity.

Image 107. Serendipity: a tale.

The princes' keen observations seemed all the more incredible when the people of the land recognized the obviousness of their clues. This raised several questions for the students: how do I know that I know? (Descartes); what is the source of all knowledge? (Locke); how does information acquired through experience become knowledge? More important, how do I recognize it as an idea? What is the role of culture, philosophy, education, etc., in shaping my ideas in order to communicate? The context of these questions reveals the relationship of the individual to the collective. We may acquire knowledge through others (often an institutionalized "authority"). But there is also the quest for self—those discoveries through innate abilities of the creative self (intuition, ingenuity, etc.) that "let the inside out and the outside in" (Belenky, et al., p. 135). Students learn from others and know through their own evidence.

In the tale, the king deliberately sent his sons on a journey after realizing they "had reached the peak of their book knowledge" (Austin, p. 195). Now the princes had to experientially discover their world and demonstrate their judgmental abilities.

PART 1: SERENDIPITY

Exploring an event or tale (a day's journey, a memory of an experience, etc.) through two- and three-dimensional "found" objects, the students revealed preconceived notions (mental "baggage") about the investigated and transformed the found material into architectonic expressions capable of communicating an individual experience to the collective.

PART 2: VISUAL THINKING AND THE LANGUAGE OF FORM

Continuing with the notion of the design process as a journey, the second project explored the language of architecture by using a kit of parts (architectonic elements as mental and spatial communication systems). Through two interrelated phases, students first explored knowing the elements (words and their meaning), and later transformed these concepts as words via syntactic relationships (analogous to the sentence) to create meaning. The kit of parts allowed students to experiment through principles such as solid/void, figure/ground, displaced space/implied space, etc., within the limits of a specified abstract territory (the universe in an 8" spatial cube). This resulted in a variety of investigations that suggested the role of play in the conceptual process (Image 108).

A modest program and site (a ski pavilion) were introduced in the transformation phase to emphasize spatial relationships and their meanings, in addition to the perfunctory roles of function and context. Consequently, a rather rigorous organization of spatial modules commenting on performance and promotional strategy was juxtaposed with a statement that explored ordered randomness. A change of scale and a shift in emphasis encouraged the students to work directly with each other in orchestrating an overall site strategy as well as developing their own individual designs.

Emphasis was placed on conceptual and intellectual rigor (receiving and integrating) in exploring spatial concepts as well as materials and craft (making).

The serendipity tale in which the king deliberately sent his sons out on their own conveys the notion of self-reliance and judgmental capabilities. The first two problems reflected a received and procedural process of knowing (book knowledge). Emphasizing the acquisition of a language, the problems involved ways of seeing through other authorities' methodologies, ordering systems of form and space, and experimentation with materials to communicate meaning structures through architectonic investigations. The second half of the quarter placed more emphasis on the connected and integrated process of knowing involving the notion of centering through both the mind and the body. Using both mind and body, we bring the outside in when

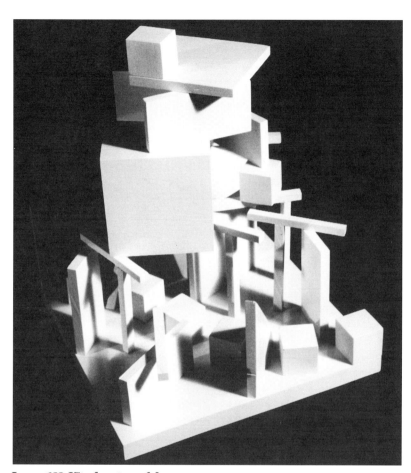

Image 108. Kit-of-parts model.

world observed around them. One student simulated a cultural situation involving home, television, and gender that revealed a concern for authenticity he wasn't originally in quest of (Image 107). Others saw opportunities to "read a story" into elements, or discover underlying ordering systems that could be translated into an architectonic language. Yet another student vividly described the conscious and semiconscious stages experienced in a head injury. Color, repetition, datum, texture, two- and three-dimensional surface, etc., were discovered as architectural language systems used to communicate a personal experience. The first phase involved simply gathering found objects and arranging them intuitively in order to tell the tale. The second phase we interact through our physical sense, as well as our contemplative sense of past and present. Therefore, centering involves the body as a container—the corporeal being (body) moving in another spatial container—the world around us.

PART 3: THE FINAL PROJECT

For the final six weeks, the class was divided into two expedition groups taking simultaneous journeys through two modes of discovery: (1) the haptic experiences of space centering on the body (The Spatiality of Movement), and (2) the contemplative inner reflections in contrast to the outer contextual experiences: inner and outer stories (The Tabula Rasa).

THE SPATIALITY OF MOVEMENT

The first journey, titled "The Spatiality of Movement," was the design of an experimental dance studio and involved members of the Modern Dance Department as visiting critics. Following a series of movement exercises with the dancers, each student developed a study based on Rudolf Arnheim's commentary in differentiating the methodology of constructing a spatial container—namely, the egg versus the burrow. Using the analogy of the burrow, in which the occupant engages in the constructing process (in contrast to the egg—a form independent of its occupant's presence), one student developed a series of radiating planes that conveyed the aspect of "moving out" from a center—in this case the body, into a new spatial territory through movement. Extending the notion of a body center rediscovered through experiential and reflective sequences, the dancers' notion of centering involves a kind of inner spirit moving out through choreographed movement patterns or notations. This suggested for another student the development of his or her own notion system (based, in part, on Laban's original studies) that included a vocabulary consisting of pathways, temporal intervals, directionality, and spatial conditions responding to body movment through the idea of "addressing"—qualities that a dancer explores vis-à-vis gesturing, touching, supporting, surrounding, holding, etc. This vocabulary reinforced the initial premise of this particular studio's journey—namely, the haptic experiences of space centering on the body.

Such a vocabulary was transformed by one of the students into a series of architectonic studies that suggested developing a neutral

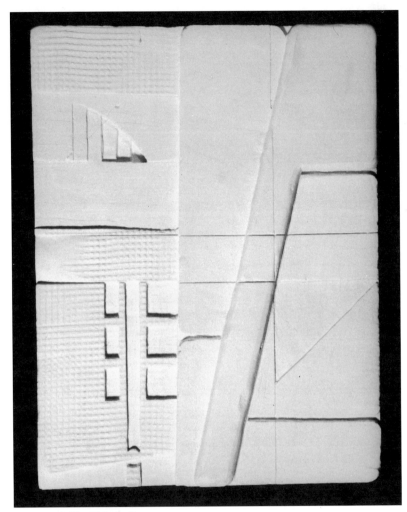

Image 109. The Tabula Rasa.

structural framework within which numerous spatial and movement patterns could be experienced. The framework, like the neutrality of the dancer's stage setting, provided a datum from which the various spatial and movement patterns could be experienced. Within this datum the sequences conveyed a variety of spatial and movement patterns that reinforced many of the notation strategies developed earlier.

The project, like many others within the studio, yielded a paradoxical condition: the duality that exists between man's mobility, a

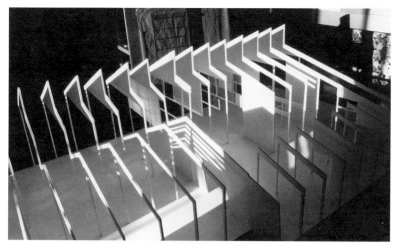

Image 110. The sectional properties of spaces.

and formal ordering strategies (Image 109).

The tablets became texts—written impressions carved into the plaster surface. Students carved into the plaster tablets many layers of information that recorded the site and surroundings as context, as well as notions about the project—the text. Students differentiated margins where "notes" on materials, details, and proportioning systems were carved. The plaster carving became a conceptual sketch that was informed continuously through the act of making (several carvings took eight to ten hours) and revealing new relationships through the materials.

Synthesizing these knowledge processes, the Tabula Rasa studio concluded with an investigation of the sectional properties of the various spaces. The architectural volumes were "read" as a series of incremental "pages" beginning with the cover—the facade (Image 110). Perceiving the wall and plan simultaneously through the sectional readings suggested an integrated process. Students were asked to consider the abstract construct of building in plan and section as a representation of the perceptual and mental processes of experience. The simultaneous journeys involved a learning process that focused on a rediscovered center—an informing of the mind by the body and the body through the mind, as well as interdisciplinary use of the same language (often perceived as foreign).

Upon returning to Serendip, following their adventures, the three princes were ultimately rewarded—they inherited the kingdom. In keeping with Walpole"s comments on their serendipitous nature—the faculty of making discoveries by accident and sagacity—the princes with their "book knowledge" and through their subsequent keen, judgmental actions achieved wisdom and its consequential rewards.

diachronic condition (especially in dance), versus architecture's synchronic constancy in attempting to transcend these changes. The studio, therefore, challenged these perceptions regarding space, time, and movement through a series of photographic journeys imparting the mobile as well as constant aspects of a perceived reality as interpreted by the student.

THE TABULA RASA

The second of the simultaneous journeys was titled "The Tabula Rasa." In conjunction with faculty in the University Writing Program, the project involved John Locke's assertion that all ideas come from experience, both external and internal. The program involved the design of gallery spaces for artistic works that would tell the stories of experiences and then challenge those works through writing. Correspondingly, two processes of knowing were emphasized: sensations imprinted on the mind, the tabula rasa, that provide us with ideas emanating from the world outside of us, and inner reflections that provide ideas as part of our inner world. Following a site investigation, students began an exploration of the facade as a vertical poché, the dialog between inside and outside. Contextual images became part of the generating force informing the facade studies. These studies initiated a series of plaster tablets (8 1/2" x 11" x 1") recording carved images based on conceptual ordering principles derived from site, program,

SOURCES

Arnheim, Rudolf. *The Dynamics of Architectural Form*. Berkeley: University of California, 1977.

Austin, James H. Chase, *Chance and Creativity: The Lucky Art of Novelty*. New York: Columbia University Press, 1977.

Belenky, M.F., et al. *Women's Ways of Knowing*. New York: Basic Books, Inc. 1986.

Remer, Theodore G. *Serendipity and the Three Princes*. Norman: University of Oklahoma Press, 1965.

Webster's Ninth New Collegiate Dictionary. Springfield, Mass.: Merriam-Webster, Inc., 1988.

Avatars of the Tortoise

Bruce Lindsey and Paul Rosenblatt
Carnegie Mellon University
Pittsburgh, Pennsylvania

SUPPLEMENTARY INFORMATION

THE VOICE OF THE PLACE

Picture a department of architecture within a college of fine arts, under the same roof as drama, music, art, and design, and you have one picture of the Carnegie Mellon Department of Architecture. Picture a predominantly research faculty in a major research university that was once, not so long ago, a technical institute, and you have another picture. Picture the forms a belief in fundamental architectural truths—like firmness, commodity, and delight—might take, and you have a third picture. Picture the relationship between form and technology. Picture architectural historians in the department. Picture computers.

Picture all of these pictures superimposed on each other.

That's the spirit of the place.

THE INTENT OF THE PROJECT

The immediate goals of Part 1 are the fostering of an understanding of connection and detail, the concept of hierarchy, and construction as a group activity; for Part 2, resolution of the intersection of two different geometries, and the making and developing of projects using physical and computer models. The integrated or long-range goals of the entire project center on relationships of part to whole, of model to real, of designing to building; on the relationship between form and representation; and on the examination of the frame as spacemaker.

THE DURATION OF THE PROJECT

Part 1 lasted five weeks; Part 2, four weeks.

THE CARNEGIE MELLON CURRICULUM

The curriculum consists of a five-year professional Bachelor of Architecture degree program, and a three-year first professional Master of Architecture degree program.

THE PLACE AND LEVEL OF PLATFORM COURSES

The courses were offered in the first semester of the first year of a five-year Bachelor of Architecture program. The two parts of this project were preceded by a few simple two-dimensional design problems. They were given simultaneously in three studios of approximately thirty students with two faculty members. In addition to studio, the students were studying calculus, introduction to world history, and computer modeling. The computer modeling class was taught by Paul Rosenblatt. The students used public computer clusters for the computer work and the architecture shop, which is located adjacent to the studios, for the construction work.

THE EVALUATION

The project was given twice, in the fall of 1990 and fall of 1991. Part 1 was a "very successful fusion of 'building something big,' design fundamentals, and computer modeling." Part 2 "resulted in effective integration of different physical and computer modeling strategies in the design process."

—*Bruce Lindsey and Paul Rosenblatt*

THE PROJECT

PART 1: 9-SQUARE: CUBE CONSTRUCTED

This project attempts to deal with a few fundamental issues that move between the concrete and the abstract, from the part to the whole, from the small to the big, and from the individual to the group. Past experience provides the place of beginning, quickly moving from the particu-

Image 111. Full-scale models in the great hall of the College of Fine Arts (with other class-level models in the foreground).

lar in the act of making, to abstraction, and back to the particular as stated by the object. Existing experiences are carried forward into new perspectives adding new systems of understanding brought to bear on new experiences.

The student starts with what he or she knows by constructing a 12" nine-square cube in balsa wood of two sizes only. The logic of the connection of the pieces guides the construction and the expression. Gravity is the critic. The literal structure is the conceptual structure. The balsa has materiality, dimension, and proportion. The problem, and therefore the goal, can be seen clearly from the outset.

In the first act of discovery, the cube reveals distinctions that were not anticipated. The center, the corner, and the edge are unique due to the geometry. These distinctions hold possibilities.

Next, an act of brainstorming, a violent mental aberration; the joint is studied at a larger scale in 3/4" balsa wood. A family of situations—3-legs, 5-legs, 6-legs—are explored. Because of the new size, new possibilities for connection are provoked. Connections now deal with distinction as well as construction.

Now comes negotiation, in which groups of five students throw their joint studies on the table and look for collective possibilities. They must construct a 3' cube with "an attitude." They must "create" distinctions, they must say that the cube should be this way as opposed to any other way. They give this action value. The end is not clearly seen.

Anarchy threatens as the group builds a 3' cube. It is both more than they imagined and less than they expected, and it took three times longer to build than anticipated. It is beginning to be more than a model.

Anarchy turns into democracy as the studio of six groups (thirty students) chooses one of the 3' cubes to build 9' to the side. Two other studios do likewise. The cubes must be built on a budget of $20 contribution per student. They must be designed and built within a week's time. They must be extraordinary.

In an act of refinement, the connections are studied full-size. Mysteriously, they look different from their 3/4" predecessors. The cedar does not work like the balsa; the joints are unstable. Necessity provokes invention: John Coltrane, Alexander Calder, and Magic Johnson come to mind.

The construction process becomes one of group therapy, as "architecture remembers the childish dreams of building great towers and climbing high mountains."

The three structures sit in the great hall of the College of Fine Arts. They can be physically occupied. They are extremely large.

Image 112. 9-square : Grid: Intersected; two-dimensional graphic.

PART 2: 9-SQUARE : GRID : INTERSECTED

Space is the medium of architecture, geometry is the order of space, and composition is the arrangement of geometry. Geometry is distilled from nature in an attempt to understand the underlying structure of things, and then reapplied to create new things with underlying structure. Geometry holds wonders that make magicians envious.

This project explores paired constructs in a way that reveals the implications, possibilities, and limitations of each. In this way a "bridge" is built, one that is based on complementarity as opposed to duality. The first stage uses two grids to explore the possibilities of ordered structures to produce beautiful relationships. Beauty lies somewhere between boredom and chaos, the intentional and the fortuitous, the simple and the complex.

The second stage takes a two-dimensional representation and provokes three-dimensional implications using visual transparency,

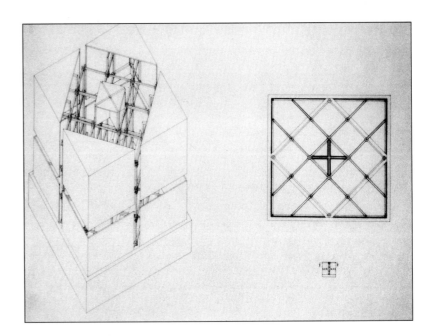

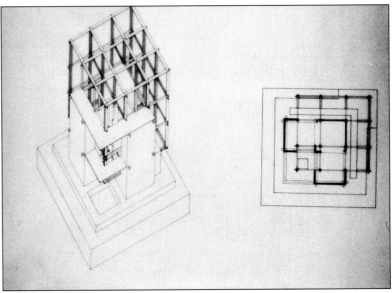

Images 113 and 114. 9-square : Grid : Intersected; plans and axonometric drawings (hand-drawn).

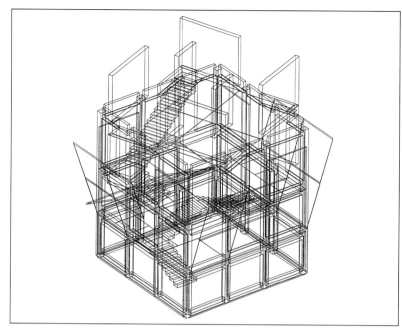

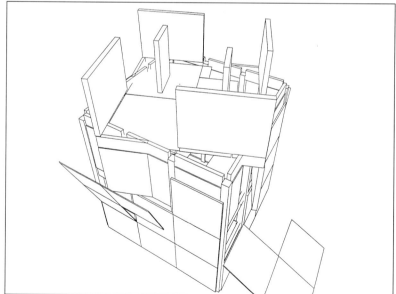

Images 115 and 116. 9-square : Grid : Intersected; computer-generated axonometric drawings.

overlap, and occlusion. These drawings are taken into three dimensions and the implications become literal: order/disorder, two-dimensional/three-dimensional, literal structure/conceptual structure.

The third stage gives the abstract three-dimensional grids a program: to define a dominant interior space and a secondary exterior space. The grids become loaded with architectural possibilities. They are constructed and drawn in axonometric view. Again the object is looked at, this time in three mutually limiting ways—in the model, in the hand drawing, and in a computer drawing. Each mode of representation is examined for the particular insight of its view but also for the possibilities it may suggest. Possibilities are both concealed and revealed by any particular point of view. To approach the potential richness of any idea, a number of points of view are required. The computer drawings were done as part of the computer modeling course taught by Paul Rosenblatt. In this modest organizational connection complementarity is shown to exist between courses.

The fourth stage requires the students to extend the object into a site. The site is meant to exhibit a reciprocal relationship with the spaces and the structure. It is also considered in a subtractive way, providing a contrast to the linear elements of the cube structure. Each student presents his or her project verbally and visually. The critique of the final project is done in architectural terms: abstract/concrete, drawing (computer and hand-drawn)/model, object/site, intention/representation, verbal/visual.

Joining the authors of this project in its realization in the studio, other faculty include: Douglas Stoker, Mark English, Ken Doyno, Jill Watson, Dina Bonefacic, Laura Lee, Rob Woodbury, Gary Carlough, Claire Gallagher, and Sherri McKibben.

The Promenade

Nicholas Charles Markovich
Louisiana State University
Baton Rouge, Louisiana

SUPPLEMENTARY INFORMATION

THE VOICE OF THE PLACE

Marked by a pragmatic emphasis in curriculum development during its early years, Louisiana State University is now developing its theoretical base. LSU is noted for a strong five-year undergraduate program in which students have been asked to carry a heavy technical course load. New directions and philosophies of the School of Architecture have set forth an agenda for the future that shows respect for creative and interpretive theory in design, and strengthened design methodology. Combined excellence in technology and aesthetic theory stands to make LSU a premier architectural experience for the student. The recent addition of the Master of Science in Architecture program is considered a welcome addition in the quest for achieving ongoing goals.

THE INTENT OF THE PROJECT

Immediate goals include the integration of the functional aspects of design into the design process, while providing the student with an initial understanding of site/design relationships with an emphasis on the manipulation of form and path within a given context. Longer-range or more integrated goals focus on a broader understanding of site/design relationships, attainment of visual, spatial, and connected behavioral understanding; and the realization of the link between aesthetic and visual vocabulary and the functional aspects of design.

THE DURATION OF THE PROJECT

The project lasts for two and a half weeks (eight class sessions).

THE LOUISIANA STATE UNIVERSITY CURRICULUM

The curriculum is a five-year Bachelor of Architecture degree program.

THE PLACE AND LEVEL OF PLATFORM COURSES

Students begin the design sequence in their first year of college. "The Promenade" is given in the middle of the first semester of the first year. Thus it is preceded by about a half-semester of freehand drawing and the study of basic design issues.

THE PEDIGREE OF THE PROJECT

The project was created by Professor Markovich in 1985.

THE EVALUATION

This project has been offered to over twenty basic design classes in the first year, from 1989 to 1992. [It] has exhibited a high degree of success in synthesizing "abstract" notions of visual literacy and architectural form with the very "real" concepts of site and behavior.

—*Nicholas Markovich*

THE PROJECT

As in earlier projects, as well as all subsequent projects in the first and second years at LSU, the student is not given a written handout. The project is discussed verbally and the students are required to disseminate information on their own, with appropriate understandings. In the experience of the LSU faculty, this helps to ensure verbal/visual comprehension.

The basic elements of design and their properties in two- and three-dimensional composition have been explored earlier; "The Promenade" is the first project in which human and behavioral references,

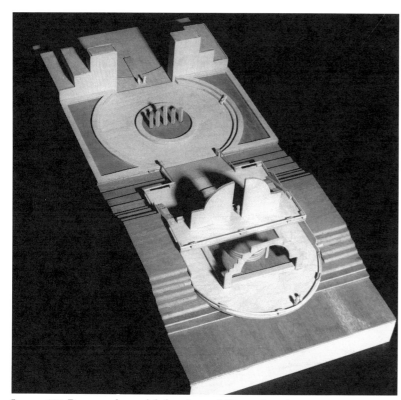

Image 117. Promenade model showing axiality and stasis.

and the issue of site, are introduced. The behavioral factors of walking, stopping, pausing, and resting are offered as definers of spatial sequencing and design decision making. The student is encouraged to take principles of design that they have explored in "abstract," or non-functional terms, and apply an anthropometric dimension to them.

In this problem students are offered a park-like setting as a site. In this setting they are to create a promenade; that is, a place to walk, rest, view, meet, and engage in general social activities.

The students are provided with a set of definers regarding human behavior that must be represented in an architectural construct on the site. They are asked to work within parameters of design knowledge explored in previous two- and three-dimensional shape and form studies.

This is the first time students have had the opportunity to move beyond visual linguistics to the application of primary behavioral criteria, and to respond to a specific site.

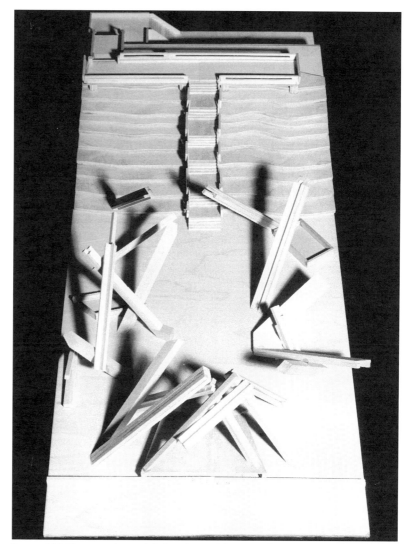

Image 118. Promenade model showing axiality into dynamism.

The students are required to work with foam-core board and museum or Strathmore board, in white only. Removing the elements of materiality, tone, and color accentuates the play of light and shadow, thus allowing the finished construct to read more clearly and generally giving the student a greater degree of accomplishment as well as clarity in visual interpretation.

Thinking Hands

Lorna Anne McNeur
Cambridge University
Cambridge, England

SUPPLEMENTARY INFORMATION

THE VOICE OF THE PLACE

Cambridge strives to instill in the student the importance of creating architecture that contributes to the dignity of people's lives, acknowledging the inherent intimate relationships between the inhabitant and the space inhabited, thus leading to an understanding of architecture as the physical embodiment of a culture. Cambridge has a history-, theory-, and philosophy-based program that is integral with design studio.

THE INTENT OF THE PROJECT

The project is meant to introduce the student to the numerous layers that contribute to the quality of inhabitation of place and space through design and the study of the history, theory, philosophy, construction, structure, and meaning in architecture.

The architect must be prepared to use a great deal of imagination, not only regarding design solutions but also in the approach to problems. The unconventional forms of the first six projects stretch the imaginative capabilities of the students and encourage them to discard some of their preconceptions about buildings which can sometimes be a hindrance to them in discovering more innovative solutions to previously unresolved problems in architecture.

"Throughout the year the underlying assumption is that one thinks with one's hands, rather than predetermining a design in one's head. While the hands build, the eyes perceive and the mind learns, constructing more ideas for the hands to think about, while building. Thinking, making, perceiving, and learning occur simultaneously in the thinking hands, the precious gift of the architect."

THE DURATION OF THE PROJECT

The project lasts for one full academic year (three terms, 8 weeks + 8 weeks + 6 weeks). Projects 1 through 3 are given in the first term; Projects 4 through 6 in the second term. Project 7 occupies the entire third term, with five weeks for development and one week for presentations.

THE CAMBRIDGE CURRICULUM

The curriculum is a five-year program in which students earn a Cambridge degree after three years of design studio and support courses. Third-year students must submit a 7,000- to 10,000-word dissertation prior to completion of the course. After one "year out" working in an office, there is a two-year Diploma degree that gives the student the RIBA qualifications to work for one more year and take the equivalent of American licensing exams.

THE PLACE AND LEVEL OF PLATFORM COURSES

Beginning design studios occur in the first year of college study. There is no art foundation course or any other course to prepare students for work in the first year. Since about half of the students come from science or math backgrounds with no art, while others have had limited art training in the British equivalent of high school, they are all essentially true beginners.

THE PEDIGREE OF THE PROJECT

"Thinking Hands" harks back to the classic nine-square project, although in a reactive rather than a derivative manner. Professor McNeur, having studied this project under John Hejduk at Cooper Union, went on herself to teach it for four years at Carleton University in Canada. When she returned to Cooper Union, now as a teacher, Hejduk asked that she *not* teach that project. Thus her first-year program was completely redesigned into the present project, although the core issues established early on remain constant here: analysis, place, path, monument, section, facade, and home.

THE EVALUATION

The first version of this project was taught for three years at Cooper Union. It further evolved during the author's one-year return to Carleton, and its development continued at Cambridge from1989 to 1992. The evaluative criteria applied to the project are: (1) demonstrated ability to interpret the project conceptually in a significant manner; (2) evidence of comprehensiveness, cohesiveness, clarity, and a high degree of resolution in the project solution; (3) the ability to embody meaning in form; (4) attention to detail, form and materiality, which serve to reinforce the ideas; (5) high quality of craft in construction; and (6) demonstrated ability to plan a work schedule that allows for a completed project by the due date.

> *My subjective evaluation of the success of the project is that its inherent principles seem to be deeply needed and therefore warmly received by both students and professors alike. Cultural differences between North America and England are such that the former seems more enthusiastic about the imaginative challenge of the structure while the latter has a stronger interest in building-oriented projects. However, transforming the project to suit cultural differences adds an intriguing complexity to the story while it is still possible to retain its underlying intentions.*

> —*Lorna McNeur*

THE PROJECT

"Thinking Hands" is not a single project, but a series of accretive projects embracing the entire first year. This first-year program is designed to introduce the student to a number of architectural issues and methods of working in preparation for subsequent years in architecture. Out of seven projects assigned during the year, the first six are cumulative and sequential, introducing the fundamental issues of analysis, place, path, monument, section, and facade. The projects encourage the student to focus on individual places or spaces in each design to ensure that he or she has a thorough understanding of these issues prior to working simultaneously with the numerous complexities of architec-

Image 119. Home for Albrecht Dúrer by Jose Esteves de Matos.

143

ture. Throughout the course of the year, the student becomes familiar with these issues through designing, constructing, and researching.

The culmination of these first six projects is an architectonic building that contains two rooms, vertical circulation, and a facade, as well as drawings that document it in plan, section, and elevation. Each project is a culmination of everything learned in the previous project, as well as those new issues introduced in the present project. The last project, which lasts for the entire third term, is considered a synthesis of the year and includes the design of a building with a site and a program.

One primary intention of this sequence is to encourage the student of architecture to consider seriously the implicit relationships between culture, architecture, history and human inhabitation as integral to the process of designing a building. Despite the intentions of some of the original thinkers of the modernist movement, its popularization has resulted in a preoccupation with systems, technology, efficiency, finance, function, and formal design. The issue of human beings living their lives in the buildings that we make has been subordinated to the point of deprivation. Too many cities and landscapes have been built up with clever products of efficient systems, ignoring the necessity to respectfully cohabit with the environment in which they have been built. If we are to return to a civilized understanding of the role of architecture, one essential consideration would be its contribution to the quality and dignity of people's lives. Acknowledging the necessity for efficient systems in the twentieth century, this program aims to establish a healthy balance of considerations, to reinstate inhabitation as one of those primary factors in the making of architecture.

Although these projects require a great deal of building with carpentry tools and materials such as wood, metals, concrete, plaster, etc., the students do not need a knowledge of construction or architectural drawing prior to beginning this design course. Regardless of previous experience, each student is taught all that is necessary to complete the requirements of the projects.

PROJECT 1: ANALYSIS

The first project includes the analysis of a painting or print from the Late Medieval to early Renaissance period. Owing to this period's particular location in history, the student becomes familiar with some of the issues of symbolism and perspective, and their historical and theoretical relevance to the twentieth century. This project is designed to integrate history and theory into the process of design and to introduce the student to some of the relationships between architecture and art. Through researching and then constructing a space that has been created by one of the masters, the student will soon become familiar with such phenomena as qualities and sources of light, perceptual and symbolic weight of objects and space, materiality, and meaning of place. Through dwelling in a period of time substantially different from our own, the student begins to gain some insight into the state of contemporary architecture.

Image 120. Home for Albrecht Dúrer, lower room, by Jose Esteves de Matos.

PROJECT 2: PLACE

While the first project includes the intellectual and perceptual analysis and construction of an "existing" space, the second project, "Place," introduces the students to the process of design. After researching and discussing some of the twentieth-century art and architecture movements having to do with perspective and Cubism, they then proceed to design a significant space called "A Room of One's Own" (inspired by Virginia Woolf's work of that name).

Although it might initially seem to be a rather large leap from the late medieval–early Renaissance period to Cubism, it is easily understood when one remembers that the shift of perceptions between the Middle Ages and the Renaissance was marked in the art world by the shift of two-dimensional symbolic space to three-dimensional perspectival space, and that Cubism marked the shift in perceptions from three-dimensional perspectival space into four-dimensional simultaneous space (see John Berger's "The Moment of Cubism," from The Sense of Light).

PROJECT 3: MONUMENT

Having now created two rooms, the student is required to design and construct a structure to house them. Whereas the two previous projects involved the use of materials to create a small scale place that

Image 121. Home for the Master of Flemalle by Jane Thomson.

implied that it could actually be a full-scale room, the third project introduces the student to the use of materials on a scale closer to "one-to-one." The focus of his or her attention is primarily on the design of details, as well as the gesture and form of the structure. In that the two previous spaces were inspired from markedly different points in history, there remains the possibility of this structure metaphorically representing the bridging of the centuries that lie between.

PROJECT 4: PATH

Once the two rooms of Projects 1 and 2 are positioned within the structure constructed in Project 3, the issues of movement in architecture are now introduced. This is a study of the space of movement as a significant experiential condition. This project is intended to counteract the unconscious assumption that the space between rooms is less important than the rooms themselves, which results in non-spaces called corridors. This particular project focuses on vertical circulation, employing the use of elements of intrigue and surprise. Students design an experiential path as the inhabitable space of transition between the realities of the "Medieval" and "Cubist" spaces that have been created thus far (see J. E. Cirlot for an interesting definition of "path").

PROJECT 5: SECTION

After completion of this architectonic building of two rooms, a path, and the structure, it is now appropriate to construct measured drawings of the building in plan and section. This project exclusively discusswa and studies various kinds of drawings such as measured drawings, historical sections, and perceptual drawings involving qualities of light, shadow, and texture. The section is discussed relative to the structure of the human body and architecture, along with interiority and the inhabitation of space.

The body can be seen as the house for the mind and the soul. The building can be seen as the house for the body, the mind, and the soul. Providing the house for one's entire being, architecture can embody both our physical needs for shelter and our intellectual and emotional dreams and desires. A self-portrait can reveal the nature of one's physical state as well as the spirit of one's existence. The section of a building can reveal both the structural composition and the quality of the spaces, which contain the intimate stories present in the journey through the structure. Architecture can be seen as the physical manifestation of human space.

PROJECT 6: FACADE

Returning to the structure, the design of facade is discussed relative to its ability to reveal and conceal the structure, the spaces, and the qualities of the interior. Upon completing the design of facade, the student then constructs drawings of it. Having studied section as a way of revealing the structure and perceptual qualities of the spaces within bodies and buildings, facade is now studied, first through the making of a self-portrait, and then through the constructing of a facade.

In a self-portrait, the face, the hands, and the gestures of the body can reveal or conceal the feelings, the thoughts, and the perceptions of the being within. The facade of a building can reveal or conceal the qualities of the spaces within. The face of the building is the mask that reveals or conceals. A sixteenth-century author of emblems discusses this phenomenon in another way, perhaps implying that it is possible "to conceal in order to reveal" (Giles Corrozet, *Hecatomgrahie*).

PROJECT 7: A HOUSE FOR AN ARTIST

This project is designed as a transition between architectonics and architecture, as well as a "bridge" between the first and second years, particularly focusing on physically manifesting conceptual issues into inhabitable form and space. After dwelling upon the phenomena of analysis, place, path, monument, section, and facade, and the numerous issues associated with them, the student is now prepared to design a building dealing with all of these issues simultaneously—as is the case in the design of architecture.

The student is asked to choose an artist and design a house and studio for him or her. This house is to be a retreat from the complications of city life, a place where the artist will be able to concentrate on his or her work in the quietude of a peaceful setting (see David Coffin, *The Villa in the Life of Renaissance Rome*). The house should reflect the sensibilities of the artist chosen as well as be respectful of the context in which it is created. The considerations of the context include such things as history and character of the "place" and the dialog between the new building and the existing environs, such as building materials, qualities and heights, pastoral views, "city" frontage, etc. Since this project is situated between the "city" and a pastoral view, it affords the

opportunity to develop the design according to the theme inherent in the site—the transition from culture to nature. Therefore, the design can acknowledge this theme in some way appropriate to the artist chosen.

SUMMARY

In the development of this program over the last eight years, experience has shown that the transition from the architectonic structure to the design of a building is very smooth. In approaching the seventh project, the students have developed their confidence in thinking and working creatively, are unintimidated about working with almost any material, understand many aspects of the building through having studied them so carefully during the year, and are very enthusiastic about the prospect of designing a building. They have also practiced their ability to articulate their thoughts through participating in weekly design theory seminars and having been critics during design presentations. They have gained a tangible understanding of the relationships between history, theory, and design through having simultaneously designed, discussed, and written essays during the year. The students proceed into the second year with confidence and enthusiasm.

SOURCES

Berger, John. *The Sense of Light*. New York: Pantheon Books, 1985, p. 171.

Cirlot, J. E. *A Dictionary of Symbols*, 2nd edition, New York: Philosophical Library, 1983, pp. 164–65.

Coffin, David. *The Villa in the Life of Renaissance Rome*, Princeton, N.J.: Princeton University Press, 1979.

Corrozet, Giles. *Hecatomgrahie*. Eited by C. Oulmont. Paris: Champion, 1905. Translation given by Dr. Irene Bergal, as well as the interpretation "to conceal in order to reveal."

Perez-Gomez, Alberto. *Architecture and the Crisis of Modern Science*. Cambridge, Mass.: MIT Press, 1983. Dr. Perez-Gomez introduced the author to the concept of "thinking hands."

Woolf, Virginia. *A Room of One's Own*. New York: Harcourt Brace Jovanovich, 1929, 1957, 1981.

A Pool

Leonard Newcomb
Rhode Island School of Design
Providence, Rhode Island

SUPPLEMENTARY INFORMATION

THE VOICE OF THE PLACE

An Architectural Studies program situated within a school of art and design enjoys certain advantages: Paths of creative inquiry are opened in conjunction with a range of different artistic modes and production techniques. From the outset the student is encouraged to explore and develop visual language and technical means for the expression of ideas prior to beginning focused study in the fine arts or in a design major. The core studio is predicated on the belief that insight and conceptual skills are obtained through development of an articulate architectural language and formal expression. The foundation philosophy assumes that perception can be learned as one can learn any language, that creative intuition can be developed, and that a common visual and formal vocabulary can be built through the handling of diverse materials and techniques.

THE INTENT OF THE PROJECT

The project is meant to establish and represent natural and man-made aspects of "site" as an objective fact; to explore the relation between social order, natural order, and built order, and built order versus social order; and to establish clear definitions of context and the public realm. Through a sequence of exercises in which basic modeling materials are employed in a kind of constructive play, choices are made among material and spatial connections in order to define the internally driven and spontaneous motives of form-making and their coherence with social meanings and cultural production observed in the real world. Through ideas about movement, space, connection, and scale (such as approach, entry, and horizon) —ideas that integrate sensuous and intellectual perceptions—virtual occupation and human presence are re-presented by the designer-as-observer.

THE DURATION OF THE PROJECT

The project lasts four weeks.

THE RHODE ISLAND SCHOOL OF DESIGN CURRICULUM

The curriculum is a five year program consisting of the one-year foundation course; three more years to receive a Bachelor of Fine Arts degree; and the fifth year, upon completion of which a professional Bachelor of Architecture degree is conferred. This model applies to all three programs at RISD: architecture, interior architecture, and landscape architecture.

THE PLACE AND LEVEL OF PLATFORM COURSES

The freshman foundation year, which precedes the first year of architectural design (the core studio), concentrates on a range of artistic disciplines: two-dimensional design, three-dimensional design, and especially drawing as the language of visual thinking, fundamental to all the disciplines in the school. The core studio explores design principles common to architecture, interior architecture, and landscape architecture. Projects are developed to provide a basis for discerning and investigating both the differences of focus suggested by the three disciplines and their common concerns. Design principles from this first semester are reexamined in the second semester, during which a basic understanding of physical and cultural context is developed, and specificities of site, program, construction, and precedent are successively introduced. A third semester was begun in the fall of 1992 for architecture students only. The projects illustrated are chosen from the student work in the final problem of the first semester.

THE PEDIGREE OF THE PROJECT

The pool project assignment was written by Silvia Acosta with Professor Newcomb, who is the first-semester core design studio coordinator, in conjunction with the teaching faculty. The objectives and syllabus are reviewed each year and problems rewritten jointly by the faculty members and the coordinator.

THE EVALUATION

The pool project has been given four times, from 1988 to 1991, as the last of six projects in the first semester. At first the pool was used as the central element in a community center, but by the second year the uses unrelated to the pool itself were discarded in favor of investigating more fully the potential for enlarged drawings and models, which then became the basis for research in problems of construction, material connections, and surface quality. Through the emphasis on a range of scales and development of drawing and modeling techniques, the language of architecture becomes more fully enriched through its precise two- and three-dimensional representations.

Leonard Newcomb

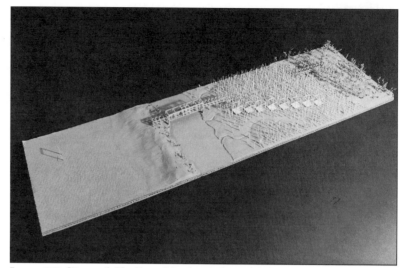

Image 122. Site model by Peter Norris, student of Colgate Searle, fall 1990.

THE PROJECT

A dialog within the studio begins to shape the interaction between formal vocabulary, language, and critical discussion. At mid-semester an analysis problem is introduced in order to examine and clarify these critical relationships through study of and visits to buildings and their sites including, in recent years, those of Aalto, Gropius, Kahn and Le Corbusier. Focusing on techniques and processes for abstracting formal themes, spatial and material components, and structure and construction, the analysis provides an effective framework for investigating and re-presenting complex works at different scales and levels of abstraction. Its position in the sequence serves to ground emerging themes and ideas in a broader cultural and historical context, and to initiate personal research.

THE POOL PROJECT: APPROACHES AND PATHS TAKEN

"The pool" is defined by human occupation; the project thus opens opportunities for insights into social attitudes. The pool is a membrane that separates, excludes, or permits events to enter. Presuppositions about public space and public nature are reexamined in a way consistent with the intuitive and rational development of the foregoing projects in the semester. In an attempt to move beyond the architectural project as an object—something the designer looks down upon on the desktop—the investigation of conditions and the means of representation reveal that the author was there, that she or he saw, touched, and recorded with the same degree of sureness with which the study buildings were observed. The notion of public, then, is rooted in individual perceptions and self-awareness. That the idea of public—including the communal as a special configuration of public—is a projection, an expression of our sense of belonging to and being part of society, is what interests us as architects: how it manifests itself in our speech, writing, actions, artifacts, claims to space, and uses of landscape.

The first week of the project is spent in constructing individual site models. No history is given of the settlement from which the users will come, nor of the site. The (hi)story is derived from the student's own sensibility and process. Constructing a landscape at the edge of the sea elicits laws of nature and her features and initiates tectonic speculations, or propositions, as if the underpinnings of gravitational force would illuminate the necessities of our own physical supports. The site model, then, is more than surface; it articulates both apparent and actual structure.

Students show early preferences en route to the reconciliation of the built work and the landscape: Some choose local sites so that ideas

Image 123. Charcoal drawing by Jonathan Rosenbloom.

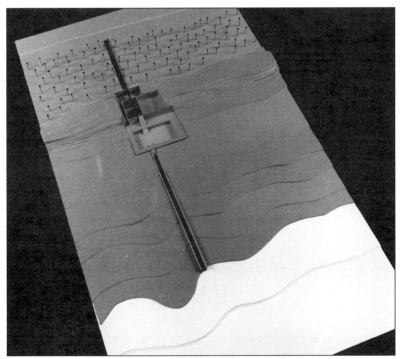

Image 124. Site model by Philip Photiadis, student of Silvia Acosta.

can be tested in the actual places; others "remember" sites and explore places of particular meaning in the past. An occasional urban site implies a preference for a landscape culturally transformed: The dynamics of natural elements are already interpreted in terms of buildings, parks, and infrastructure; geologic interpretations often rely on marking ancient boundaries between sea and land.

SPECULATIONS

At the risk of oversimplifying the broad range of problems and creative thought brought out in the various approaches to site and program, some reflections are offered on the narrative themes that emerge, and certain limitations and opportunities suggested by these are observed. First, the approaches to establishing the human presence in the landscape take different and revealing turns. A recurring tendency is to "find" that the pool already exists, perhaps by combination of given features—topographic, climatic, hydraulic. But where the accommodating conditions for occupation (involving, for instance, scale, exposure, and shelter) have been "foreseen" and provided by nature herself, the designer then is presented with the difficulty of being in a kind of paradise with little need for architectural, engineering, or landscape intervention. This seeming impasse can be successfully negotiated only upon the realization that landscape is a human conception, and that the challenge inherent to architectural design is to constructively mediate differences between social needs and existing conditions of the landscape.

For others, the project begins with exploring ideas of natural process through graphic and three-dimensional means prior to specific concern for occupation. This tendency may not view the pool site as a singular, ideal event, but may invite instead research and speculation on typical geologic formations (faults, erosion, uplift, tidal action, deposition) as primary forces and phenomena within which the site is to be determined. These strategies often lead to interesting speculations on the relation between scientific thinking (geology, archeology) and creative design processes. Having to construct a model of landscape provides the basis for a reflexive or dialectical view of built and natural environments, and results generally in a more articulate, comprehensive production.

One can imagine a site, for instance, that does not at the outset offer amenities for occupation and in fact may be preferred exactly for its "difficulty" of material, scale, or remoteness. This approach often suggests experiments with structures (footings, grounding, framing,

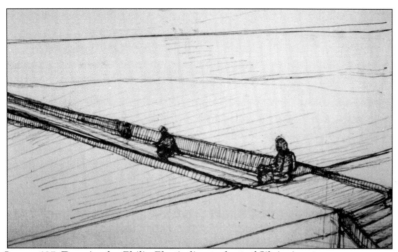

Image 125. Drawing by Philip Photiadis, student of Silvia Acosta.

containing, excavating, lifting) that would maintain the integrity of both new and existing forms with the freedom to substitute materials not actually found in nature. The latter approach usually allows greater breadth of investigation, not only in terms of structural and material possibilities but in the conception of a public use and public domain. On the question of approach to site, then, one concludes that being able to articulate a distinction between what is given and what must be created is fundamental to working definitions not only of site but also of public and communal zones.

Although the problem requires a minimum functional program, conception of the program that is there plays out in divergent and revealing ways. Following the designation of site, some begin with proposals for the functional elements by exploring constructional techniques in relation to, say, observed materials and methods peculiar to the chosen locale; or perhaps through ideas of construction one gains a sense of place defined in part by climatic concerns and issues of permanence and temporality.

For still others, the program is driven by social concerns. The project can be seen as a system of codes in which the transition from the settlement to the landscape, from landscape to pool, from public to private, is seen as a framework for the investigating and structuring of social combinations, encounters, and observation. All deal with defining critical thresholds or transitions. Perceptions about social formations with landscape are revealed as the supporting medium and

measure, and the pool as the perceiving subject's connection to the natural world, with the social or public as its mediation.

Precedents and other historical references are cited in antiquity, mythology, literature, in our contemporary media, and, of course, in our immediate buildings and landscapes. These are encouraged for consideration, inclusion, and transformation in the individual's substantive grounding of the project. This is considered to be the beginning of a personal research that may become more defined in the pursuit of the student's own field of interest or chosen discipline.

Derived from this "personal research," a statement of belief is driven by internal forces—spontaneous, accurate, powerful. Clear, incisive images are the medium of the artistic sensibility; to the extent that they endure, they are the key to architecture's vitality. To embody these images in the architectural work, we need a precise and articulate language. Precision in "seeing thought" is then possible only with testing the work on all levels, the passion to reexamine, to use one's particular discipline to strip down again to simple, inevitable truths.

The Otherside of Seaside

Judith Reno
Savannah College of Art & Design
Savannah, Georgia

Michael Kaplan
University of Tennessee
Knoxville, Tennessee

SUPPLEMENTARY INFORMATION

THE VOICE OF THE PLACE

The mission of the five-year undergraduate architecture program at the University of Tennessee is to provide rigorous professional training, with an emphasis on the acquisition of technical skills.

THE INTENT OF THE PROJECT

This project is concerned with the development of (1) the imagination, based on a belief in the possibility of teaching artistry by applying the principle of "reflection in action"; and (2) a sense of community, both within and between individuals, that supports intrinsic motivation. Other goals include the creation of artifacts representing the expression of self within the context of a community; examination of the issues of structure, space, and enclosure; and an exploration of the interplay between (1) two and three dimensions, (2) the compositional (abstract) and the utilitarian (physical), and (3) convention and invention.

THE DURATION OF THE PROJECT

The project lasted for a total of nine weeks: Part 1, three weeks; Part 2, two weeks; Part 3, four weeks.
The University of Tennessee curriculum
The University has a five-year undergraduate curriculum, leading to a Bachelor of Architecture degree.

THE PLACE AND LEVEL OF PLATFORM COURSES

The University of Tennessee is on a quarter system. The first design studio is given in the third quarter of the first year. "The Otherside of Seaside" was preceded by two quarters of freehand and constructed drawing study, but there is no previous basic design study. The student is introduced to architectural design itself as a problem-solving procedure.

THE PEDIGREE OF THE PROJECT

"The Otherside of Seaside" is an original hybrid of compositional, theoretical, and problem-solving pedagogy. It is the invention of Professors Reno and Kaplan, who developed and team-taught the project at the University of Tennessee-Knoxville.

THE EVALUATION

The course, as described and illustrated, was taught at The University of Tennessee during spring quarter, 1986. A second iteration was taught during spring quarter, 1987. "The Otherside of Seaside" was presented at the plenary session of the 1986 Southeast Regional ACSA Meeting, and the fifth National Beginning Student Conference. It was published in the third edition of Best Beginning Design Projects.

The projects and constituent exercises described [below] may seem, on the surface, to reduce the teaching of artistry to a "set of procedures," yet their formulation was subject to the same reflection in action demanded of our students. While our vision of an expressive, detailed architecture remained constant, the content and format of the exercises was continually and interactively examined and revised. During the second (1987) iteration of the course, we formulated a correction to enable the students to better understand and explain their solutions. An analysis was made to identify consistent formal, spatial, structural, or metaphorical themes in the earlier exercises; this knowledge, once tacit but now conscious, was then applied to the design of the house. Donald Schön describes this process as reflection in action, marking both the distinction and the analogy between learning and teaching. As reflective instructors, we became students. And our students, rationally understanding what they had done intuitively, developed skills in self-criticism and correction that, in effect, enabled them to become their own teachers.

—*Judith Reno and Michael Kaplan*

THE PROJECT

"The Otherside of Seaside" was a program consisting of three interrelated and interconnected projects, formulated jointly by the two instructors and shared by students in both labs.
The immediate goal of the program was to fulfill the requirements of the course description: "Development of imagination in designing simple objects and buildings. Studies of simple structures. Presentations requiring concept diagrams, sketch and refined models, and constructed drawings." With its emphasis on the acquisition of technical skills, this statement reflected the mission of the architecture program at the University of Tennessee to provide rigorous professional training, yet the inclusion of the term "development of imagination" suggested an

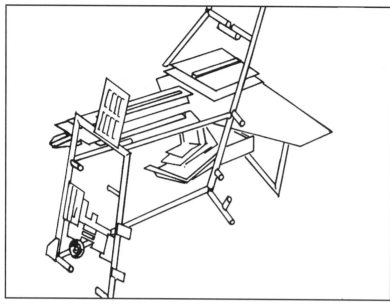

Image 126. Step 3, perspective drawing.

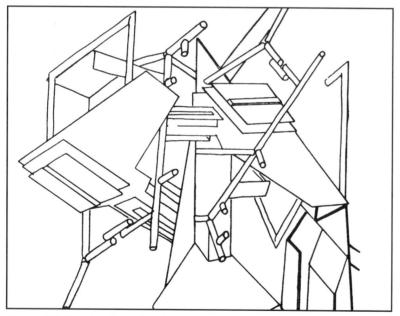

Image 127. Step 4, collage drawing.

Image 128. left to right: model constructed of model kit parts; balsa model; house model.

opportunity to explore alternatives to traditional design pedagogy. Three goals were defined for such an alternative: (1) to validate the instructors' belief in the possibility of teaching artistry; (2) to develop a community — both within and between individuals — that supports intrinsic motivation; and (3) to create artifacts representing the expression of self within the context of that community.

STRATEGY: REFLECTION IN ACTION

In *Educating the Reflective Practitioner*, Professor Donald Schön suggests that *artistry* is necessary for the solution of problems in professional practice that occupy the indeterminate zones of uncertainty, uniqueness, and conflict. The two traditional approaches to the teaching of artistry, however, are problematic. The first, its elimination from a curriculum based on technical rationality, is predicated on the belief that artistry is mystical and essentially unteachable. The second, its reduction to a set of procedures, has proven not to work with indeterminate phenomena that are inherently unmanageable. Schön proposes a third strategy: *reflection in action,* based on his observations that considerable tacit knowledge is already built into practice. By entering the condition of action and reflecting on what has been done, one can resolve "indeterminate" problems in situ by doing.

PROJECT 1: MODELING THE SALVAGE OF CONVENTIONS

As an introduction to the design process, a series of abstract, non-programmatic transformation exercises propelled the students into the action of designing, enabling them to immediately develop confidence in their intuitive and creative abilities. Charged by the supplementary course description to address structure, space, and enclosure, we defined *structure* initially in a general sense, related to composition: the arrangements of parts in a defined pattern of construction capsulizing thought unique to the individual.

Step 1:

The first exercise was a three-dimensional manipulation of conventional, familiar elements: plastic scale-model kits of autos, airplanes, boats, and rocket ships. The two kits selected by each student were to be of different color and scale in order to establish hierarchical relationships when combined.

Step 2:

A selected piece of the collage model was enlarged using planar and linear materials, continuing the exploration of composition and hierarchy.

Step 3:

Perspective drawings were constructed of this third model, depicting movement around it to represent its volumetric form.

Step 4:

These drawings were overlayed and combined into a single collage drawing.

Step 5:

As a final transformation, a carefully crafted balsa wood model was "extracted" from the last collage.

Each transformative step — involving startling moves between two and three dimensions, and through diverse media — represented an evolution of the student's visual and spatial consciousness, recording the interplay between convention and innovation. Each became, too, a realization of *reflection in action* wherein each step permitted the student to test his or her design premises and effect correction if desired. *Modeling the Salvage of Conventions* created a model of the design process to which the students would be required to refer in subsequent assignments.

PROJECT 2: TRANSITIONS

As a matrix for the continuation of the process and a device for social critique, we created a hypothetical community located adjacent to Seaside, Florida. Like Seaside, it occupied 80 acres and would be developed at the same density as its neighbor. The community's major built elements included a gridded central business district, commercial strip, boardwalk, and housing. The Seaside building code imposes a rigorous and unusual set of constraints on the designer, which include deep front yard setbacks, a specified percentage of front facade given over to porch, and mandated picket fences. Coded convention bounded by picket fence isolates our ability to be and express ourselves; rather than provide privacy, the picket fence *invades* our privacy. In contrast to Seaside, our community established codes to support a balance between individual expression and communal interaction. We called our community "Otherside."

The boardwalk was the transitional element in the design of the community. It provided a link between the lake and the sea, a bridge over the highway, and passage between the private domain of the house and the public domain of the beach.

Teams of three students were asked to design a length of the boardwalk that would derive its formal and structural language from the final collage models of Project 1 and appropriately connect to its neighbors at each end. Functional requirements for access, seating, viewing, and shading were to be satisfied. Each team developed a tower node that contained access from ground level (by stair and ramp) and a viewing platform; vertical structure and circulation were to be resolved.

Transition may be defined as passage from one state, place, or subject to another. The boardwalk was thought of as an element of passage in every sense. It marked the move from basic to architectural design in its addition of utilitarian and programmatic requirements; it began the consideration of structure and span in physical, rather than purely compositional, terms; it permitted the student to work, for the first time in his or her academic career, as a member of an interpersonal community.

PROJECT 3: HOUSE

The final project represented the conclusion of the design process: the ordering of an expression of self into house. Each student was asked to design a beach house for himself or herself using a rule sys-

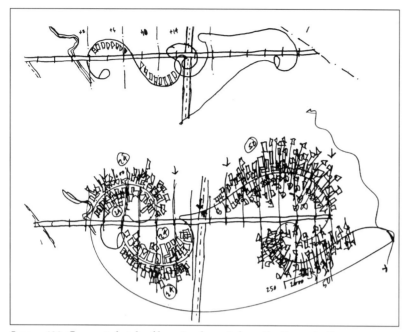

Image 129. Concept sketch of housing layout, from the Reno studio.

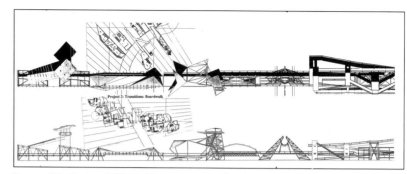

Image 130. Project 2: Transitions: Boardwalk. Plan and elevation.

tem (project statements provided by the professors) to guide the location and organization of the design, but not its formal outcome. The student was again required to summon prior knowledge: the visual vocabulary developed in earlier exercises. There was an intent to support the ideas of community and minimal impact on the natural landscape: the clusters of houses were compactly sited and lifted off the ground on poles.

The physical program was defined not by specific square-footage areas but by activities: eating, sleeping, living, working, and bathing. Its enclosure would provide natural light, ventilation, and view to the boardwalk, lake, and ocean. One-third of the house was required to include a cabaña or a screened porch, and a carport was provided. Lot size and shape were determined geometrically; Professor Reno established guidelines for frontage and the development of physical connections between lots, while Professor Kaplan began with the inscription of the letters otherside on the site as an arbitrary footprint.

Space and *enclosure* were considered pragmatically for the first time, as responses to functional requirements. The detailed formulation of the program, the rule system for the development of the house,

and, ultimately, the design outcome in each lab reflected the different backgrounds and interests of the two instructors. Reno, in Southern California tradition, emphasized post-and-beam/infill construction, while Kaplan translated Middle East bearing-wall into vernacular balloon-frame construction. Final presentation artifacts included complete schematic drawings, framing diagrams, and a highly detailed model. Work from both labs was exhibited together on a large base model that included the boardwalk, a demonstration of our belief that individual expression could both add to, and defer to, the collective.

Architecture, as art and construction, permits the synthesis of thought unique to the individual and objects of conventional usage. Invention in modern architectural language implies the exploration of three-dimensional space in all its volumetric and sectional complexity and energy. *House* was the culmination of a process enabling the beginning student to invent forms that would translate into detailed architecture through the initially intuitive, but ultimately conscious, development and application of a personal vocabulary.

SOURCE
Schön, Donald A. *Educating the Reflective Practitioner.* San Francisco: Jossey-Bass, 1987.

Design and Build a Sky: A Tensegrity Project

Alan Stacell
Texas A&M University
College Station, Texas

SUPPLEMENTARY INFORMATION

THE VOICE OF THE PLACE

Texas A & M stresses learning by doing, and doing it from a knowledge-based design paradigm.

THE INTENT OF THE PROJECT

The tensegrity project is called "build a sky," or "design a sky," because the metaphor links architecture to structure. Tensegrity—"tensional integrity"—is a place to begin exploring what structure is all about, and the idea of a sky, or a shelter, is a place to begin pondering what architecture is all about.

THE DURATION OF THE PROJECT

The project lasts for five weeks.

THE TEXAS A&M CURRICULUM

The curriculum is a 4 + 2 model: a professional Master of Architecture degree, following a nonprofessional Bachelor of Environmental Design degree.

THE PLACE AND LEVEL OF PLATFORM COURSES

The courses are given in the first year of the Environmental Design degree program. The "Tensegrity" project is given in beginning design, and also in an elective second-year conceptual structures course, which contains a mix of students from second to fourth year.

THE PEDIGREE OF THE PROJECT

While tensegrity principles have been used in the study of structure at many schools for a number of years, they are normally addressed in a straightforward, pragmatic manner. It is the poetic and metaphoric approach of this author that sets him apart, and that makes his project a true original.

THE EVALUATION

This project is always popular among students, and enjoys an unusually high success rate.

THE PROJECT

The problem statement handouts for this project state, in part:

Your next assignment is to design and build a sky.

Sky-building began some several days past among gaseb needs, waddling ducks, and the settlers of the Tigris-Euphrates delta. It began because people began building communities that remained in a single location; it began in a marshland settlement later to become a city with a name; it was called Ur. For the past four millennia, give or take a couple of centuries, there have been people who nurtured the idea of a roof, a shelter, canopy, lid, or sky erected to provide a large gathering place. Each generation of dreamer imagined a lodge, a hall, an arena, a coliseum bigger than the last one, or bigger than the one in another city. The dream is still alive, even though technology will now allow us to erect an auditorium large enough so that people on one side cannot see across to people on the other side.

You must decide how much sky to design and build. Your assignment is to model a prototypical example, not necessarily a whole system. So we are into a scale situation where if an inch equals eight feet we can build a working model that presents a reasonable description of the structure. Some ideas could work at a smaller scale—it is negotiable.

The structure twins, Concept and Image, are children of our perception. Elephants, bluejays, apples, and beans; arches, domes, vaults, and beams are their progeny. The diatom and the woodpecker share between them a thousand shadows. The dog's ear and the cistern gather rain. How many closets can a push broom have?

When students of architectural design begin thinking of their structures as force diagrams, they are beginning to think structurally, which adds physical credibility and visual authority to their products. In his classic book *On Growth and Form,* published in 1942, D'Arcy W. Thompson gave the injunction "to think of physical form as the consequence of forces, or force diagrams." Three hundred years earlier, in 1632, Galileo started down the same path in his book *Two New Sciences.* The beginning design student can enter the vast territory of structural thinking by building force diagrams, setting aside for a time continuous compression systems in favor of continuous tension systems.

Tensegrity is a physical and visual force diagram. Tensional integrity, from which the author of *Synergetics,* R. Buckminster Fuller, coined the term *tensegrity,* reveals force pathways and their dual action/reaction nature: tension and compression.

Tensegrity is somewhat like executing graphic statics in three dimensions. The force polygons, funicular polygons, and other familiar features of elementary vector mechanics are present and accounted for.

There is no equivalent substitute for the formal study of statics, strength of materials, and structural theory with the precision of math, but what tensegrity models and other kindred tensile figures do for the design student is to demonstrate the principles behind equilibrium and stability. Tensegrity opens doors by closing the gap between what architectural school curricula deem separate—namely, statics and aesthetics.

When the beginning design student grasps that abstract concept and sensory experience have common ground in design of structures, it enables the integration of structural thinking and design thinking in the tutorial studio, even when the courses are separate.

The energy transfer process endemic to all physical structures begins in a tensegrity figure with the system being prestressed—the stored energy distribution. The diagram of forces is right there to look at and reflect upon. This kind of energy reservoir is a graphic descrip-

tion of force pathways, and at once a felt image for the student. We mortals haul ourselves into upright postures by pulling in order to push. Tensegrity literally reaches us where we live, and it is only a short trip from bone and tendon and muscle to brain, where structural theory lives in the four fundamental ways to handle loads—arch action, truss action, beam action, and suspension.

The arch may owe its origin to the discovery that a horizontal piece of material that is curved upward against the normal deflection of gravity will span a greater distance than a flat member without camber, or arch. Such a load-carrying device also develops thrust at each end. This thrust can be countered with a mass equal to or greater than that required to resist it. The historical arch was mass against mass. The arch was essentially a masonry structure, whether the stone was natural or man-made, and it transferred its load to the ground through a pressure line down the middle third of its mass. Thus, it maintained its shape as a stable structure, rather than a mechanism. Corbelling, or stair stepping the stones, may also account for the origin of the arch.

By shape and general configuration a dome is 360 arches arranged to transfer loads down arch meridians accumulating mass, which will be prevented from bursting out of the pressure line by hoops or belts that cross the meridians at right angles. Massive arches, domes, and vaults of circular shape were often used because that shape controls thrusts or reduces them to a negligible amount, and the circular shape presented a standard method of centering or constructing the scaffolds. The Romans used the half circle most of the time. The pointed Gothic arch is two circular arcs or segments of equal arc resting on each other. Probably the Romans and other early builders had some reference to elliptical and parabolic shapes and the catenary curve, but they did not build them.

The dome remains an effective and efficient way to leap across space. It has evolved into a variety of sophisticated forms in steel, concrete, and aluminum— no longer the mass of material shaped to best take advantage of all that bulk, but still arching. A dome wraps a volume of space with a rather ideal ratio of material to volume. It is really that fact added to its ability to transfer loads by arch action over long spans, that keeps the dome a credible way to build, as long as there is reason to enclose large spaces. The desire to do so has not yet diminished.

The dome-shaped device that I want to describe and show for examination has many of the features outlined above, but it is basically doing its load-carrying backwards. Instead of pushing itself up into a volume of arches by sustaining pressure lines of compression, it is pulling itself up into continuous lines of tension and discontinuous islands of compres-

Image 131. Tensegrity model.

sion. Only the island struts and the base are in compression.

It may have been only an accident of history to put massive materials to use prior to lighter ones. Nevertheless, we humans have acquired a mind-set about domes being arches in compression and not bubbles or balloons. The structure described and shown here is behaving like a balloon. It would be a more ideal balloon if it were a *geodesic;* i.e., if instead of meridians and hoops of differing diameter, it were made from circles of the same diameter. Meridians and hoops are not confined to circles or segments of circles, but are free to assume most of the great family of funicular shapes that cables naturally take under various distributed loads. The model examined here has a shape somewhere between a parabola and a catenary.

One way to make an arch is to use a cable to create a parabola or a catenary curve, then turn it upside down, reversing it from a funicular curve in tension to an identical one in compression. The value of creating funicular shapes with cables actually loaded or by a graphic force polygon is that they will yield an arch pressure line. Sustaining that pressure line may make it necessary to shape an arch of several funicular curves, if the loading is not going to be uniform or evenly distributed at all times.

What our model really does well is to employ cables and struts to their greatest structural advantage in enclosing a volume. The stress pathways created to transfer loads are all either axial tension or axial compression, and this remains the case if the loading shifts and redistributes stress. This system has a great capacity to deform without loss of efficiency. It can flex or not flex, because all joints in the superstructure will translate and rotate without developing secondary stresses.

The prestressing tensile and compressive forces are equal to or greater than the combined dead and live loads, using a higher percentage of material to greater advantage.

That we are able to measure forces and describe, as well as predict and control, their behavior with a great deal of accuracy does not separate them from being largely experiential. The most abstract and sophisticated studies require a visceral, empathic response to be appreciated.

Model-making is an act of informing; it precedes form; it is perception in duration. What appears are the tracks left by the acting out. The seeing was accomplished during the act of modeling. To see a model or a structure is to act it out, to reenter the informing.

Show what it is that vaults; show what it is that spans. Show that leg, wing, thigh, and sole of dragonfly cannot be counted on to preempt the grubworm's style. Structure, as imaged, is not to be disenfranchised any more than the prayers of children. It is simply the pathway of forces, full-formed in the shape of God's eyebrow.

Structure is from seed to blossom; structure is young to aged. Structure is built by unfolding centuries of April. A triangle is maintained by counting to three and a sphere is determined by turning around.

—*Alan Stacell*

The Generic Possibilities of Artistic Pattern

Janez Suhadolc
University of Ljubljana
Ljubljana, Slovenia

SUPPLEMENTARY INFORMATION

THE VOICE OF THE PLACE

The School of Architecture was established after World War I in 1921 by architect Joze Plecnik (1872–1957), a leading personality in Slovenian architecture. Plecnik, a student of Otto Wagner's, was completely devoted to aesthetic problems in architecture. He rejected the so-called "functional style," instead developing a very personal and expressive style based on Art Nouveau, and the Renaissance and Baroque periods. After Plecnik's death, his work was often the brunt of mockery and scoffing, and the "functionalists" seized power in the school. Reverence for the old master's architecture was pushed into oblivion under the school's leading personality of this period, Edvard Ravnikar (born 1907). More recently, the postmodern movement vindicated and rehabilitated the old master Plecnik, now widely recognized in Slovenia and abroad. The mainstream of the school is now, slowly but surely, shifting back to the principles of the old master, all the while remaining vigilant and conscious of architectural movements worldwide.

THE INTENT OF THE PROJECT

The immediate intention of the exercise is to encourage students to develop a pattern of their own choice, and to document the stages of its transformation. The goal of this particular method of teaching is to have the student creatively convert a generic pattern into a meaningful architecture or design. The objective is to confront the students with a method of architecture/design development radically different from the functional-analytic method previously prevailing at the school. This exercise, presented in seminar, is based on deductive rather than inductive methods of teaching, and stresses architecture as an eminently artistic, intuitive, creative act wherein aesthetic aspects dominate the secondary, utilitarian ones. Basically, this method was developed in opposition to the predominantly functionalist "modern" architecture of past decades.

THE DURATION OF THE PROJECT

This exercise is represented by three different but closely related projects of one semester's total duration.

THE UNIVERSITY OF LJUBLJANA CURRICULUM

A Bachelor of Architecture degree takes nine semesters. After four semesters, the student selects one of three specializations: General Architecture, Architecture of the Interior, or City Planning. The ninth semester is dedicated to the preparation of B.A. work. M.A. and Ph.D. degree programs are also available.

THE PLACE AND LEVEL OF PLATFORM COURSES

The courses are given in the first four semesters, in which a common foundation is offered for all three specializations. In the first year the students study drawing for two semesters, four hours weekly, and take a one-semester design seminar that meets five hours per week. If there is any preceding or concurrent influence on this exercise, it is the drawing studio, which is also taught by Professor Suhadolc.

THE PEDIGREE OF THE PROJECT

To quote Professor Suhadolc: "I hope that the method 'Generic Possibilities of Artistic Pattern' is an original one, [or] is almost original. [It] is supposed to be original."

THE EVALUATION

While the specific methodology described above and illustrated in the following projects has evolved in the first-year design seminar since the late 1970s, Project 1 was assigned to twelve students in the 1990 summer semester. Of twelve submitted projects, the one illustrated in this book was evaluated as outstanding among the three best. Project 2 was given in the 1989 summer semester; the one illustrated was awarded a maximum grade (on a scale of 1 to 10). Project 3 was assigned to the class in the 1985 summer semester. The project illustrated was evaluated as the best of the entire academic year from the design seminars and was awarded the highest grade.

THE PROJECT

The pedagogical methodology of these projects encourages the students to consider architecture as an eminently artistic creation. The making of architecture is conceived as an intuitive, creative process guided primarily by its inherent aesthetic code, and only secondarily subject to utilitarian, functional, technical, and scientific standardization. In short, it seeks an architecture of socially relevant dimensions, with a goal of rescuing architecture from the world of *techne* and moving it to that of *poesis.*

In the design seminar classes, work begins with an arbitrarily chosen pattern, of either the instructor's choice or the student's. The task of the student is to develop compositions, flat or spatial, whose inherent characteristics invariably lead back to the basic design. Put differently, the student is asked to explore the "hidden" possibilities in an element or pattern, and thus to establish what the generic qualities of an artistic pattern are.

The results of such work are diverse, and may include children's toys, objects of everyday use, furniture, residential houses, hotels, or model towns. The finalized works are generally represented in drawn form, but prototypes, models, and maquettes are equally common and welcome—one solution was even knitted.

The results are always compared with previous student works, and with achievements in local and international architectural and design production. At times, students are given exercises that expressly demand the inclusion, either direct or paraphrased, of local cultural tradition.

The students involved in the work of the design seminar generally profess to be unfamiliar with the work of, say, John Nash, the postmodernists, or Sullivan and Mendelssohn, or even with some renowned architectural works in Slovenia. But it would be naive to think that their works spring entirely from their own imagination. A certain amount of information may, consciously or not, affect their creative potentials. However, the dilemma of the role of formal education

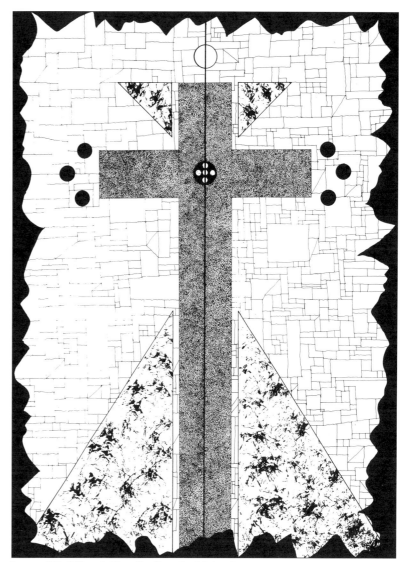

Image 132. "Church Door" collage by Mahovic.

and the forms of positive knowledge transmission remains open as to the essence of creative mechanisms. In any case, the works of the students are all made with great enthusiasm and often in quantity and quality that surpass all expectations.

PROJECT 1: UPWARD, DOWNWARD, AND AWAY

This project (Image 13) consists of eight phases and discusses the beginning and transitory nature of the world—and the architecture within it. Its language is as clear, transparent, and even moving as it can be in a student who still believes in revelations.

The starting point is a quadrant divided into two parts along a slanted line. Next, the two fields, black and white, begin to change—to merge into one another with lines, hatchings, and slabs, which eventually crystallize into architectural elements and shapes. Stage 5 is the culmination of positive development. Thereafter, the architectural creation is gradually dissolved with the intrusion of foggy dots that finally pervade: away, and into the mist.

PROJECT 2: FROM A CHURCH DOOR TO AN ON-WATER SETTLEMENT

The exercise (Images 132 and 133) began with a collage whose central figure was a symmetrically placed cross. It was stated that the collage would be a quite suitable starting point in designing a metal church door. A wooden base covered with bits of various metals, processed and structured in different ways, was provided.

In Phase 2, the collage underwent a transformation that allowed it to serve as a sketch for a theatrical scene. In the maquette, the cross evolved into stairs, and dots transformed into pillars that retained on their surface the elements of the original church door. The rhapsodic contents of this theatrical scene and its vague reminiscence of antique remnants seemed an appropriate setting for ancient tragedies. In the third, conclusive stage of the project, a part of the theater scene floor was transformed into water surface, while one of the original platforms increased substantially in size and was elevated on the pillars to produce an illusion of a mansion built above the water surface and accessible by means of a monumental staircase. Some of the remaining pillars were left to be used for various possible additional dwelling places. The latter was named "The Pillar Water House."

In the course of work, a precedent emerged of a fascinating Slovenian architectural heritage. South from the center of Ljubljana there was, in prehistoric times, a lake. According to archaeological findings, around 800 bc the lake was inhabited by a people who lived in complex above-surface dwellings on pillars, an architectural solution

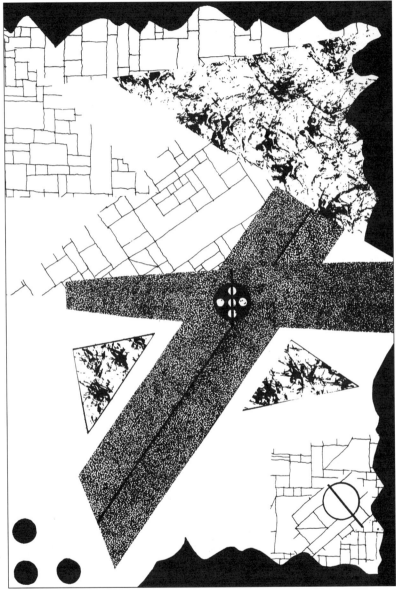

Image 133. Collage transformation of church door by Mahovic.

Image 134. Top: theatrical scene maquette; below: "Pillar Water House" maquette by Mahovic.

Image 135. Top: illustration of a village of ancient Slovenian water dwellings; below: photomontage simulation of Mahovic's "Pillar Water House" village.

still functional in certain more exotic places. A possible reconstruction of these water-settlements is illustrated.

Finally, a photomontage was made, depicting a group of above-water dwellings raised on pillars. Thus, the project began with a collage representing a church door, and ended in above-water-surface dwellings: a panoply of meanings and functional relations.

Image 136. "Ime Roze," original pattern by Irena Vesel.

PROJECT 3: THE NAME OF THE ROSE

The student began her exercise (Images 136 through 140) with an embroidered floral design. Stage by stage, the pattern was transformed into an array of architectural creations. While the general process itself

Images 137 through 140. Irena Vesel's "Ime Roze" transformations (other transformations can be seen in Images 42 and 43).

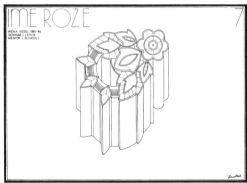

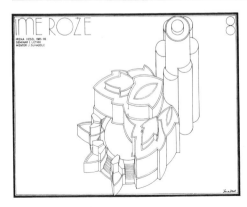

is standard in the design seminar, unusual originality and inspiration guided the transformation from two-dimensional pattern into three-dimensional solids. The student was advised to draw a Renaissance, Gothic, and columnar variation of her spatially developed study. An additional variation was made based upon the Futura typeface.

The exercise concluded with a developed botanical variation of the original pattern. Thus the whole thing began, and ended, with flowers, a paraphrase of the biblical "ashes to ashes" cyclical thinking.

Basic Design
Munehiko Taniguchi
Kogakuin University
Tokyo, Japan

SUPPLEMENTARY INFORMATION

THE VOICE OF THE PLACE

The School of Architecture's objective can be characterized as "the practical approach to an architectural design philosophy." The entry-level course is dedicated to helping students develop their own creativity by following a very logical and practical approach to education.

THE INTENT OF THE PROJECT

The various components of this course of study have different, yet interrelated intentions. The opening exercise causes the students to realize the adequacy or inadequacy of their memory, and to recognize their strong and weak points, causing them to be more serious toward the exercises that follow. They proceed to an understanding of the principles of rational architectural beauty and to the building of a design vocabulary (proportion, symmetry and asymmetry, contrast, etc.), and are encouraged to unleash their imaginations and to have fun in the act of creating. Practicality is stressed instead of theory in

the generation and free expression of idea after idea. In the last project, architectural structural principles are introduced.

THE DURATION OF THE PROJECT

The project lasts for one semester (twelve weeks).

THE KOGAKUIN UNIVERSITY CURRICULUM

The curriculum is a four-year program that, upon completion, confers a professional Bachelor of Architecture degree.

THE PLACE AND LEVEL OF PLATFORM COURSES

Basic Design is taken in the first semester of the first year. In addition to developing creativity and imagination, another goal of this course is to address, and ultimately turn around, a rather pervasive psychological problem. Because it has only one college, unlike other multicollege universities in Japan, Kogakuin is sometimes viewed from the outside as lacking in prestige and thus is frequently the beginning student's second or third choice for university studies. By quickly building the student's sense of confidence and self-esteem through studio projects, and by identifying the achievements of distinguished architects and engineers who are alumni of this university, Kogakuin soon replaces such negative attitudes with a healthy sense of pride.

THE PEDIGREE OF THE PROJECT

"Some ingredients of my Basic Design course are attributable to design education given in some Japanese art universities. Based upon those methods, I have modified the course, especially from the viewpoint of how students can express their solutions efficiently and beautifully."

THE EVALUATION

Basic Design has been given seven times, from 1985 through 1991. This course enhances the students' familiarity with fundamental design and architectural terminology, as well as their interest in and understanding of color—particularly the effects of color on design. The project also increases their interest in architectural design and structures.

I will of course further modify the class, because in my view much energy must be applied to imagination rather than production.

—*Munehiko Taniguchi*

THE PROJECT

This semester-long course consists of twelve lectures, which are divided into three major stages. The following describes the course in general terms.

Stage 1 is composed of the first three lectures, which introduce the course and the teacher, general orientation, and explanations of principles of design structures and methods. In this stage, students also study color and color schemes. The students' understanding is gauged by mini-tests administered during the lectures.

Stage 2 includes the fourth through seventh lectures. Here the relationship between environment and color is explained in slides shown during the first thirty to forty minutes of each lecture. In the latter half of these lectures the teacher gives an explanation of exercises that are assigned and due by the next lecture the following week. In this stage all design exercises are strictly two-dimensional. During this process, a number of other resource slides are shown to help students generate their own solutions, while the teacher provides a detailed explanation of the slides being viewed by the students.

In Stage 3 the lectures focus on a method for generating ideas. The process of the lectures is identical to those in Stage 2, except that here students work with volumetric designs.

The students are required to turn in their solutions to the following exercises at the beginning of each lecture. These exercises are done under very strict rules and guidelines. Although unique ideas are welcome, the students may copy — but not completely — the compositions and the color patterns shown in the lectures.

Image 141. Student sketches for Exercise 5.

EXERCISE 1: REPRODUCTION OF A SLIDE

A slide of a composition by a famous twentieth-century artist (such as Mondrian or Vasarely) is shown to the students, who are given about ten minutes to sketch the image and to take notes on the colors used by the artist. Using their sketches as a basis, the students

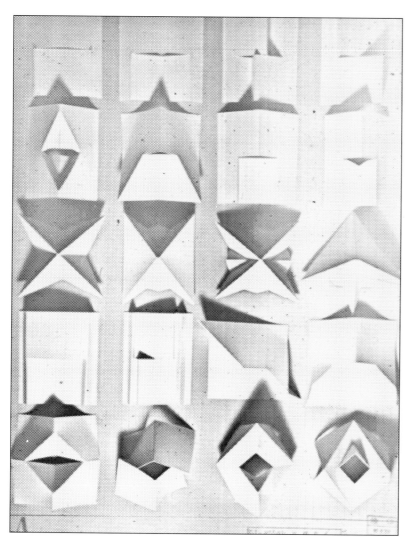

Image 142. Student reliefs, explorations done in Exercise 6.

must reproduce the composition on a sheet of paper 120mm by 120mm. The compositions chosen as models have been carefully selected by the teacher. The main criterion for selection is that they must be based on a simple ratio (e.g., 1:2:3), and the colors used must be readily understandable. If the student observes the system, the module, and the colors carefully, he or she will be successful in reproducing the

composition. This exercise is designed to enhance students' concentration, all the while discovering the system, proportion, and module used, and to develop an accurate and clear understanding of a specific coloristic environment.

EXERCISE 2: PROGRESSIVE AND RHYTHMICAL COMPOSITION USING LINES

The most important requirement of this exercise is the creation of a beautiful composition consisting of horizontal and vertical straight lines, while thoughtfully engaging the planes defined by these lines. As in Exercise 1, the picture area or field is 120mm by 120mm, and work is done in colored paper collage.

To begin, a typical set of progressions, such as harmonic progression, geometric progression, Fibonacci series, and logarithmic progression, are shown as examples using a video/slide projector system. These progressions serve as an underpinning, or guide, for this set of exercises. In some solutions the distance between adjacent lines varies sharply according to the given progression, while the widths of the lines themselves are also progressively changed, resulting in the expression of dynamic movement. In other successful projects a gradated color pattern is detectable in the ground, or those areas surrounded by lines. Some solutions failed to express parallel lines clearly and accurately owing to poor craft in paper cutting, while others were unsuccessful because of their failure to express dynamic movement, attributable to the fact that arithmetical progression (n+1, n+2, n+3 . . .) was used.

EXERCISE 3: TWO-DIMENSIONAL PATTERN USING SQUARES

The students must come up with two beautiful yet systematic patterns using at least five squares as a design motif. Each must illustrate different design principles and color pattern. Again, these studies are done on a 120mm by 120mm field. The solutions that provoke rhythm and movement created by the employment of an appropriate system receive the highest evaluation.

EXERCISE 4: CUBIC EXPRESSION

In this study, designed to investigate cubic effects, the students must freely express their own ideas. To provide inspiration, several

Image 143. Student "Cubic Imagination" model (another model can be seen in Image 44).

possible in this process to create a number of complex forms, the more complex they become the more they begin to resemble each other. Therefore, the students are encouraged to strive to make simple forms in which the differentiating characteristics may be clearly observed.

In the initial stage of this project, the students may make as many shapes as they can imagine. Their forms are then scrutinized, edited, and classified into a hierarchy. In this process the students can find a key to new ideas. In the final stage, twenty reliefs are selected, classified, and mounted onto a rigid board 364mm by 257mm.

EXERCISE 7: CUBIC IMAGINATION

This project is realized fully in three dimensions. Students are required to make two different undeformable three-dimensional forms using a square of paper 150mm by 150mm. They are allowed to cut and fold the paper, but no part of the original square may be removed. Pieces of colored paper may be attached to some parts of the forms in order to emphasize the configurations.

Applications of architectural construction techniques— pin joint and truss-like structures— are introduced to prevent these three-dimensional constructs from deforming. Explanations of these techniques are provided by the teacher. Here, as in Exercise 6, it is recommended to the students that they begin with simple cuts and structures, which may become appropriate guidelines for more complicated and beautiful configurations later on.

examples of cubic effects are shown. The most successful solutions include multiple cubic images that emphasize harmonious colors.

EXERCISE 5: HOW TO COME UP WITH IDEAS, PART 1.

The students are asked to imagine what form an isometric solid with proportions of 1:2:3 would take if it is made of paper, metal, string, clay, wood, etc. They are then asked to draw as many images as possible in their sketchbook. One image is selected for further development and modification.

EXERCISE 6: HOW TO COME UP WITH IDEAS, PART 2.

The students now work for the first time in three dimensions: in low relief using pieces of slit and folded paper, 60mm by 60mm . The goal is to create a range of relief forms of high visual interest by making the most imaginative use of the placements of the slits, which can be made anywhere on the sheet so long as they do not affect the sides, and of the cubic effect achieved by folding the paper. Although it is

Vocabulary of Space

Kurula Varkey

Centre for Environmental Planning and Technology
Ahmedabad, India

SUPPLEMENTARY INFORMATION

THE VOICE OF THE PLACE

The school seeks the rediscovery in the past of the essence of India's ethos, and then its redefinition and reinterpretation in a new light. What is sought is a creative renewal, for each period must reinvent its own language.

THE INTENT OF THE PROJECT

This project is aimed at understanding the basic principles of establishing spatial order and its correlation to the order of form.

THE DURATION OF THE PROJECT

The project is of four weeks' duration, nine contact hours per week.

THE CENTRE FOR ENVIRONMENTAL PLANNING AND TECHNOLOGY CURRICULUM

The five-year (ten-semester) program awards the Diploma in Architecture, the equivalent of the Bachelor of Architecture degree.

THE PLACE AND LEVEL OF PLATFORM COURSES

First year is considered the "Foundation Year," with two semesters of six credit hours each devoted to the development of design skills and design vocabulary. The "Vocabulary of Space" project is the first problem given in the first semester.

THE PEDIGREE OF THE PROJECT

The project was first developed by Professor Varkey in 1976–77 at Ahmedabad. He made variations and modifications on it at the University of Nairobi from 1977 to 1987. It was further redeveloped into its present form at Ahmedabad from 1987 to 1990, in association with Professors M.C. Desai and Sharad Sheth.

THE EVALUATION

The average student joining the architecture program in India comes from twelve years of science-based high school education, with the rational logical faculties developed and the intuitive and sensory faculties given very little opportunity for development. Thus it becomes necessary to introduce architecture and its disciplines from a seemingly rational and logical base, gradually opening up sensory acuity and intuitive judgment. This time-tested project has proven very successful in beginning to bridge this gap.

THE PROJECT

INTRODUCTION

Architecture can be talked about as order—spatial order, dimensional order, geometric order, material and structural order, proportional order, and the order of symbols and meaning systems. Such orders establish the appropriate relationships that unite parts into a totality and establish appropriate character.

Architecture is a three-dimensional response to forces of social organization, technology, and the nature of the environment, and as these forces differ from place to place, and culture to culture, architectural expressions differ. Yet the need to order parts into a meaningful total is basic to all architectural design.

In this project the students are introduced to a basic alphabet of space making elements—the wall and the column—and the possibilities through combinations of these elements for the evolution of different spatial types exhibiting varying degrees of enclosure and openness.

Students begin Stage 1 by choosing one basic spatial type (cubic, cylindrical, etc.) from a given list that includes basic dimensions. There

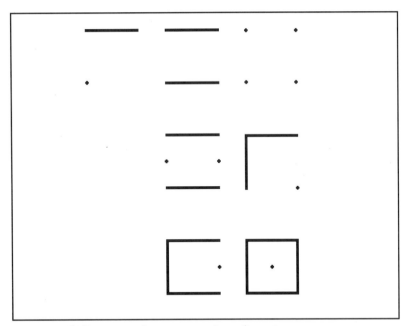

Image 144. Differences owing to geometric configuration.

Image 145. Permutations and combinations of elements.

is a limit on the number of elements of a given type that may be chosen—from nine to twelve. Students then explore the inherent character
of these elements and the principles that govern their interrelationships.

In Stage 2, students choose two geometric types, again with related dimensions, along with linear and curvilinear elements. The goals
are to develop forms as a result of the types chosen, and to study their
character and the principles of interrelationships between them.

The concepts of design as "Theme," "Organizational Order," and
"Sensorial Variation" are explored through these excercises.

PROJECT AIM

This project is aimed at understanding the basic principles of
establishing *spatial order*, and its correlation to the *order of form. Space,*
as distinct from *form*, can be seen to be made by the plane or wall that
directs space, and the point or column that defines *position*.

These two elements in combination define space of different
kinds, each exhibiting differing degrees of *enclosure* and *openness*.

The permutations and combinations of the basic space-making
elements—the wall and column, as seen above—yield what may be
termed basic *"spatial words."* These "words" can be put together to create different organizations—"sentences"—each with distinct meanings. The law or principle by which the words combine can be related
to "grammar," which in Architecture approximates to order.

In this project students will examine the individual spatial elements or words, their character, the manner of their combination relative to position, the terms of position, connections, and
interrelationships—dimensional relationships, geometrical relationships, movement as connector, etc. They will also examine principles
that are used to establish unity, variation, and sensorial stimuli.

All examination will be in reference to three basic principles of
design:
1. *theme/idea* that unifies parts into a totality.
2. *order/discipline* by which they are related to each other, and
3. *variation* and *sensorial stimulus*.

PROGRAM 2

Part 1

Students are to choose as basic elements one of the following
groups:
1. cubes of 2.5 M and 5.0 M sides,
2. cylinders of 2.5 M and 5.0 M diameter,
3. hexagonal or octagonal prisms of 2.5 M and 5.0 M sides.

No more than nine elements are to be used from the chosen
group. However, in each case a maximum of three elements from
another group can be included, resulting in a total of twelve elements.

Partial units that imply a whole may be used. The employment of
level changes, and freestanding walls or columns to signify entrance,

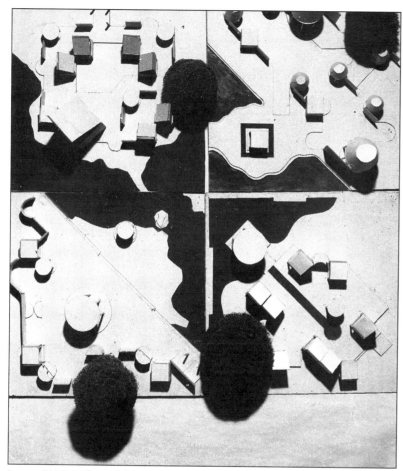

Image 146. Part 2, model.

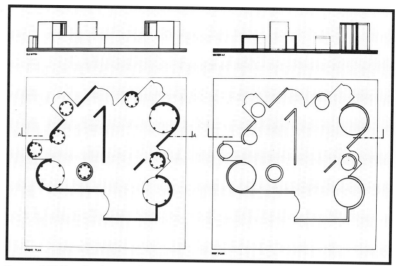

Image 147. Part 2, plans and elevations.

movement, direction, transition, foci, interval, termination, etc., are encouraged.

With these elements the student is to explore issues of space and spatial order.

Part 2

In the second part of the exercise, the design is to be modified to include roof forms that relate to the basic geometries chosen in the first part of the exercise. It will be observed that the relationships of mass

and space alter substantially because of the introduction of these roof forms, which have their own values of position and direction.

For this part of the exercise the student is to introduce both a water body of desired shape and a tree in a suitable position. The exercise explores the relationships between space and form and the distinctions of spatial order and order of form.

SCHEDULE

The project is of four weeks' duration, nine contact hours per week. All work consists of three-dimensional models, which are later translated into drawings. Design issues introduced are illustrated through both analysis of historical buildings and slide presentations.

Studio and Dwelling for a Bookbinder

Betsy Williams
University of Michigan
Ann Arbor, Michigan

SUPPLEMENTARY INFORMATION

THE VOICE OF THE PLACE

One unique aspect of the undergraduate program at the University of Michigan lies in the nature of the studio sequence. Undergraduate studios are taught by a diverse group of young faculty members, several of whom are on invited fellowships. Although the group meets to discuss the common studio issues to be addressed, each studio instructor determines precisely how these issues will be covered by writing independent studio problems. This atmosphere leads to healthy experimentation and dialog among and between faculty and students.

THE INTENT OF THE PROJECT

In the creation of this studio problem, an attempt was made to address the common student question of *how to begin* the design process. The ideal was a project type that asked students to draw relationships between architecture and other, different creative pursuits, and that was conducive to individual interpretation and the search for meaning. By starting with an abstract yet related project of *making*, the students would be encouraged to think about conceptual issues that could inform their architecture. In a way, they were "tricked" into thinking about architecture before they knew that they were.

THE DURATION OF THE PROJECT

The project lasts for four weeks.

THE UNIVERSITY OF MICHIGAN CURRICULUM

The curriculum is a 2/4 (or 2/2/2) program, in which undergraduates enter the Department of Architecture in their junior year, following two years of liberal arts course work. After two years of architectural studies, students receive a nonprofessional Bachelor of Science degree. They may then continue for two more years as graduate students to receive a professional Master of Architecture degree, or they may pursue their graduate work at another institution.

THE PLACE AND LEVEL OF PLATFORM COURSES

The first two years of architectural studies consist of four semesters of studio course work combined with an intensive array of support courses including structures, construction, environmental controls, and history/theory. Thus, the beginning design studios occur in the student's junior year. "Studio and Dwelling for a Bookbinder" is given in the first semester of the second year of undergraduate architectural studies. Prior course work includes one term each of construction, environmental technology, history, and design fundamentals, and two drawing courses and two design studios.

THE PEDIGREE OF THE PROJECT

The binding project was an experiment of the author's invention, inspired by her personal interest in paper constructions. As mentioned earlier, the nature of the program at the University of Michigan allows for this kind of exploration.

THE EVALUATION

The project has been given twice, in 1990 and 1991. My sense was that at this point [the students'] general and technical knowledge exceeded their design abilities (and experience) and the binding project was a response to this apparent imbalance. It was an attempt to assign a simple yet sophisticated project that could capitalize on both their knowledge and their naiveté. For an experimental first-run project, I was pleasantly surprised by the outcome. I found that the introductory project of "binding" had an enormous impact on the success of the students' projects. Tricked into thinking about architecture before they knew that they were, their initial ideas were more in keeping with their intellectual abilities. Students were also introduced to the relationship of craft and idea, while developing an understanding of and respect for the work of their proposed client. One of the inherent difficulties of a project of this type is the tendency for students to draw very literal analogies that result in diagrammatic or clichéd projects. I fought this tendency with several students, and found that this presented a convenient forum to discuss the potential dangers of this kind of design strategy.

—Betsy Williams

THE PROJECT

In this second of three four-week projects, students were asked to design the studio and dwelling spaces for a hand bookbinder on an urban site in Ann Arbor, Michigan.

After touring a local bindery, the students were given the program statement in the form of small (4.25" by 5.5") unbound sheets of paper, carefully wrapped in brown paper and sealed with a postage-stamp-sized set of initial instructions: "Read the following pages. Begin to consider the problem and the way you are going to go about solving it. . . . You are to assemble or bind these pages in a way that explores or challenges the concept of binding. Take great care and effort in this first assignment."

The contents of the handout package included a miniaturized reproduction of "The Art of Bookbinding," from *Bibliopecia* by John Hannet; the assignment, in narrative form; site information; the project objectives and requirements; project schedule; an outline of information on bookbinding process and required equipment; a bibliography; illustrations of bookbinding apparatus and examples of modern bookbinding; and "Roger Payne" from *Bibliopecia*.

The assignment narrative reads as follows:

A local bookbinder has purchased 101 West Liberty Street (assume that this is a vacant lot.) She would like to set up her shop and studio there, as well as make this her home. The owner is a hand binder who does book conservation and various other projects on commission. She is especially well known for her beautifully constructed sketchbooks, folders, boxes, and portfolios, which she sells commercially. Her programmatic needs fall into three general categories, although they need not be seen as distinct and necessarily separate.

The bookshop will require display space for books and other items that are available for purchase. There will be a need for both linear shelving and case work, as well as an area for the display of the owner's noted collection of bookbinding tools. There should be an area where customers purchase items and bring in books for repair. Both a small business office and a conference/waiting room are also necessary.

The owner's bookbinding studio is currently located in a three-car garage. She looks forward to the additional space her new location will afford. This space should accommodate the equipment and process outlined under "Requirements," as well as a storage room.

The owner's domestic needs are conventional: eating, sleeping, bathing, and entertaining. She is an avid gardener and hopes there will be an opportunity to continue the hobby in this urban location.

The project objectives are stated as follows:

As in the preceding studio assignment, both craft and idea will be stressed. However, unlike that assignment, the heart of this project lies in the exploration of spaces within given urban constraints. The building is "bound" by three sides, and can go no higher than its neighbor on the left. Designing the remaining edge, or facade, will provide an opportunity to explore the interaction of spatial organization and exterior expression. The section, the drawing type that best describes this interaction, will be the primary design tool.

Things to consider: the investigation of, and more important the establishment of the power of vertical circulation; extracting and abstracting relationships between bookbinding and architecture; and the mixed-use nature of the program.

After presenting the bound books, which make up the first stage of this project, students engaged in a discussion about the relative design issues of binding and architecture. They then proceeded with the design of the building. For some, the ideas explored on this introductory project became the generator for their building development.

Image 148. Book designed by Laura Giezentaner, and her model of the studio/dwelling for a bookbinder.

For others, the binding project served as a point of departure for the architectural project. In either case, the process of using a handcrafted object at artifact scale as a metaphor for a building was an effective tool in breaking down stereotypes, which should be clearly seen in the illustrations.

DESCRIPTIONS OF STUDENT SOLUTIONS

Image 147: Ken Nye

Ken appreciated the distinct relationship between the pages and cover of a book, and drew an analogy to the interior and skin of a building. Both the binding and the architectural model articulate the relationship between a fragile interior protected or bound by a solid enclosure.

Image 148: Laura Giezentaner

Laura was inspired by the potential rituals of books and architectural space, and began by celebrating this notion in her binding. This then led to an investigation of the rituals and related sequence of spaces associated with the life of the inhabitant.

Understanding Structures Through Models

David T. Yeomans
University of Manchester
Manchester, England

SUPPLEMENTARY INFORMATION

THE VOICE OF THE PLACE

This project was given at the University of Liverpool, where "the approach of the first year is to introduce the students to building design as soon as possible on the principle that it is buildings that attracted them to architecture, and to spend the first year designing cardboard chairs or whatever would be frustrating."

THE INTENT OF THE PROJECT

The immediate goal is to make students aware of the role of structure in architecture. The long-term goal is to provide a foundation for later structural design teaching. This project involves modeling the structure of existing buildings in order to explain, and thus understand, the structural actions involved.

THE DURATION OF THE PROJECT

The project lasts for two weeks.

THE UNIVERSITY OF MANCHESTER CURRICULUM

As British schools have not yet gone over to a modular structure for their courses, there are no course numbers or official titles for most projects. The overall architectural program is a three-year Bachelor of Arts degree, followed by a two-year Bachelor of Architecture degree.

THE PLACE AND LEVEL OF PLATFORM COURSES

There are no "platform courses" or general courses for most English university architecture programs at the present time. The project described is set in the second term (quarter) of the first year.

THE PEDIGREE OF THE PROJECT

Professor Yeomans created this project at the University of Liverpool, and it has evolved over more than two decades (see below, under "Evaluation").

THE EVALUATION

This project has been given over a period of about twenty years, with only occasional breaks. The principal development during that time has been the comparative element, as described in the project, which although not completely successful in its primary aim, has had some beneficial side effects.

THE PROJECT

Instead of beginning with a lengthy preamble, the basic aim and description of the exercise that students were given will be stated at the outset. The intention is to introduce architectural students to the role of structures in buildings, and to give them an idea of the influence that the choice of structure might have on the resultant architectural form. The essence of the exercise is that students select a building from a list provided, make a model illustrating its structure, and use that model to explain this in a class seminar.

The rationale behind the exercise is founded on the belief that it is important to introduce structural design to architecture students by (1) giving them some idea of the physical realities described by abstract structural mechanics, (2) showing them the scope of the structural problems that buildings pose, and (3) making them aware that there is always—or nearly always—more than one way of solving any structural problem. This means, simply, beginning to explore the relationship between structure and architecture.

It is arguable that this approach may be equally valuable for other technological aspects of architecture as well. It is common to begin teaching engineers with the basic physics of their subjects—structural mechanics or thermodynamics—presumably on the assumption that they are able to cope with such abstract ideas. However, if we are teaching designers it seems a good idea to demonstrate the nature of the problem on the grounds that they come into design because of an interest in those problems. An extension of the argument is that the subjects might profitably be introduced to engineering students in similar ways.

The premise is that integration of technology and architecture should not be left for the students to work out for themselves, but should be more actively and directly engaged in teaching. Others may take the opposite view, and clearly this kind of exercise would not be for them. If we are to attempt such an integration, then what are the immediate issues (i.e., the issues to be addressed at the beginning of the course)? What aspects of structural design may be drawn to the students' attention? At this stage of their development, one is not attempting to teach some body of theory. The intention is simply to open up a field of inquiry and suggest simple techniques that the students may be able to apply for themselves. The purpose is to give them a way of looking at buildings and learning for themselves. Perhaps it could be said that this attitude is based upon the philosophy that design is largely a craft activity—that is, an activity in which we learn by seeing how it has been done by others.

These concepts provide the starting point: (1) Students need to be introduced to some simple ideas about structures (i.e., the division between beams and columns)—the idea of arches; the idea that while structures are three-dimensional, they may be composed of three-dimensional as well as two-dimensional elements; and the idea that the shaping of the materials may be as important as the amounts used; (2) students need to be encouraged to look at actual buildings to see how their designers have tackled structural issues, or indeed any other technological issue; (3) they need to be able to see the structure, services, or whatever, as an integral part of any building and not simply view buildings as a series of spaces or planes into which someone else must insert the bits that make it work; and (4) in seeing that similar problems may have been solved in different ways, they will appreciate the fact that the designer has some choice in the matter, and that the choice needs to be related to his or her architectural intentions.

The first of these aims is often tackled by the kind of exercise that asks students to design and make a structure of paper, balsa wood, or some other simple material, to support a given load over a given span. Such exercises may be given a competitive element by awarding a prize to the structure with the greatest strength-to-weight ratio. But while this sort of problem certainly gives students some feeling for structure per se, the students do not relate this to architectural form. The same can be said of the exercises that were developed by Barry Hilson, although these did have the merit of showing simple quantitative relationships between structural form and load-carrying capacity that less structured exercises do not—fun though they may be.

Only with actual buildings can we explore the relationship between architecture and structural form, and this can be developed further by looking at more than one structure of a similar type. Thus the list from which the students select has groups of similar structures, usually three, and while they create a model of just one of them, they are asked to compare its structure with the others in the same group. The study of real buildings still has an element of fun because students select buildings that interest them. Admittedly, this is a limited range of choices, but such limitations allow the instructor to be confident that certain lessons can be learned, so specific structures need to be carefully selected to facilitate this. There will also be an element of fun because students are being encouraged to think for themselves instead of simply following a set experimental route. Indeed, thinking for oneself is an important part of the exercise: Students will not be able to find the answers in a textbook.

How, then, are the buildings selected? What is needed are groups of buildings with some similarity in their structures so that students can see the differences that are possible within the same basic theme (which introduces students to Yeomans's design motto No. 3: "There's always more than one way to skin a cat"). It is important that the students be able to find sufficient information about the buildings, normally from journals or books, but also from examples near at hand. Students can visit and examine these buildings for themselves, and they provide good lessons in observation as well as in structural interpretation. However, sometimes the information may be incomplete, resulting in some uncertainty about the actual structure. This may not matter because it is then possible to suggest alternative arrangements, and also alternative ways in which the same form may be handled structurally.

The subjects on the list given to the students date from Roman times to the present day. If there is any weakness in it, it is the relative

174

Image 149. Structural analysis model.

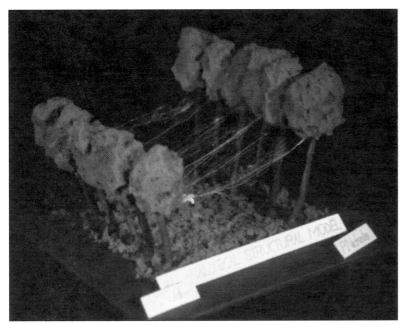

Image 150. Dulles Airport conceptual model.

paucity of more recent buildings. This is not because they are not interesting, but rather because of the occasional difficulty of finding good structural information. Students are given a list of sources that have proved useful—books for the earlier buildings, and journals for the more recent ones. One useful source has been Howard's excellent book on structures for architects, which unfortunately is no longer in print. Orton's The Way We Build Now is similarly useful, but rather more complex in its presentation.

It is also worth noting that the exercise does not stand alone; it is associated with a series of lectures on historical structures. This is presented as a brief history of structures, but the intention is as much structural as historic, demonstrating that it is possible to make approximate assessments of the forces and stresses in quite complex structures using very simple means. For example, a simple analysis of a dome or a vault is possible just by using the triangle of forces (which introduces Yeomans's design motto No. 2: "A job worth doing is worth doing badly," an exhortation to early back-of-envelope calculations). This lecture course ran in parallel with the course on structural analysis given by another faculty member, which it was designed to complement.

Not all the structures chosen will have simple explanations, and it is useful to include some examples of these to provoke discussion. It is also interesting to include structures that are not as they appear to be. The Sainsbury building at the University of East Anglia, for example, appears to be a portal frame but is in fact just trusses resting on large "columns."

It is necessary to stress that it is not the quality of the model itself that is important; it is the quality of the visual explanation (Yeomans's design motto No. 1 is, "Work is no substitute for thought"). Thus it is critical to emphasize that this is not an exercise in fine model-making. A frequently used example is that of the men demonstrating the structure of the Forth Bridge as a possible way of illustrating a structure. It is not a permanent model. Many may also know of that wonderful demonstration given by a tour guide who explains the structure of a French Gothic cathedral by using the very bodies of the tourists to represent vaults and buttresses. Fortunately, this has been filmed, and is available as a classroom aid. Regrettably, no students have ever shown such imagination; perhaps there is a limit to the number of structures that can be demonstrated in this way. However, some of the more interesting models have been designed to self-destruct in order to demonstrate the structural actions.

The importance of the final seminar, when students explain their structures, cannot be over emphasized. While it does involve an element of assessment, that is of minor importance at this stage of the course. First, the seminar enables all students to see a range of structural types. Second, it is important to uncover any misconceptions that they may have about the behavior of structures. These can be identified so much more easily by getting students to talk about the structures and then asking pointed questions. Sometimes curious imagery is used by those trying to get a grasp on something they don't understand. Of course, it is not always clear how some historic structures actually behave (Jacques Heyman has even argued that asking how an existing structure actually behaves is a meaningless question), and more than one interpretation may be possible. There are also some structures that were not fully understood even by their designers, resulting in details that may suggest structural actions that are not correct. Using such examples naturally presents a more difficult challenge to those students who select them, but it produces interesting lessons in the seminar. For this reason it is useful to have an engineering colleague present who may take a different view of the behavior of some structures based upon different initial assumptions.

It must be confessed that the instruction required to compare the structure modeled with the others in the group is not often done well. This is partly because students become too absorbed in the particular structure that they are modeling and partly because in the seminar pressure of time tends to prevent more than a discussion of the model itself. It is possible to ask for simple calculations, but the difficulty here is that the instructions would have to be tailored to suit each structure. In a timber barn, for example, one might ask the ratio of the wind load to self-weight to emphasize the significance of the bracing. Such a calculation would not be appropriate for a structure like Dulles Airport, where the horizontal forces on the columns are a direct result of the shape of the structure.

Then there are the questions that may be asked. It is important to have architectural colleagues in the seminar, because they often ask questions that had not occurred to instructor, questions sometimes directed to the students but sometimes asked about the comments of the instructor or the explanations that he has provided. It is also interesting to see how other people "see" things, and although this exercise has been done over a number of years and with the same group of buildings, there is always something new to be learned at the seminar.

SOURCES

Hilson, Barry. *Basic Structural Behaviour Via Models*. London: Crosby Lockwood, 1972.
Howard, H. Seymore, Jr. *Structure: An Architect's Approach*. New York: McGraw-Hill, 1966.
Orton, Andrew. *The Way We Build Now: Form, Scale and Technique*. Wokingham: Van Nostrand Reinhold, 1988.

ANNEX 2
Biographies

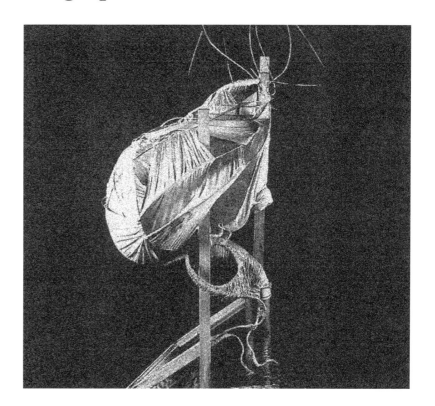

This section is dedicated to brief biographical notes on the professional and personal lives of the thirty-four contributors to this book. In keeping with the format used in the preceding two sections, *"An Annotated Anthology of Beginning Design Projects"* and Annex 1, the biographies that follow are organized alphabetically by the individual contributors' last names.

JOHN ANDREWS
Professor and Head of Interior Design
Royal Melbourne Institute of Technology
Melbourne, Australia

JOHN ANDREWS was born in Central London in 1950. He studied at the Chelsea Art School and also at the Architectural Association (AA), where he graduated with honors and the year prize in 1977 (shared with Zaha Hadid).

Following a period of residence in Mexico City, and several subsequent exhibitions in New York, Andrews returned to London to establish a practice and to head an instructional unit at the AA. Over the next decade he designed and built a significant number of key commissions in tandem with a continuing academic involvement with institutions such as Cambridge University, the Royal College of Art (London), Cornell University, Bennington College, Curtin University (Australia), Pratt Institute, and the AA.

From 1988 to the present, Andrews has been focusing on a personal research program embracing world design, looking at both indigenous and hybrid forms in relation to contemporary culture. This has taken him to India, Thailand, Mexico, Spain, North Africa, Russia, and Australia, where he is now living.

Andrews is currently Head of the Department of Interior Design in the Faculty of Environmental Design and Construction at RMIT, where the wealth of his educational and traveling experience, combined with his passion and enthusiasm for students and design, generate an extremely vital, intense, and creative environment.

JAMES R. BAGNALL
Professor of Architecture and Head
Department of Architecture
School of Architecture and Environmental Design
California Polytechnic State University, San Luis Obispo
San Luis Obispo, California

JIM BAGNALL is currently Head of the Architecture Department at Cal Poly in San Luis Obispo. He received a Bachelor of Arts degree in psychology from Occidental College, and a Master of Architecture degree from the University of California, Berkeley.

Bagnall worked in architecture, design for print, exhibition design, and architectural graphics until he joined the Cal Poly faculty in 1969. He has focused on foundation courses in design since that time.

Coauthor (with Don Koberg) of the entry-level design process books *The Universal Traveler* and *Values Tech.*, Bagnall's interests remain with the beginning design student.

PETER BEARD
Unit Master, First Year
Architectural Association
London, England

PETER BEARD was born in Oxford, England, in 1960. He received his Bachelor of Arts degree from Cambridge University with First Class Honours in June 1982. He continued his studies at Cambridge and the Harvard Graduate School of Design, receiving his Architecture Diploma, Awarded with Distinction, from Cambridge University in June 1985. Beard successfully completed his Royal Institute of British Architects final professional exams in October 1987.

Beard has been a first year tutor at the Architectural Association in London since 1987, and is currently Unit Master at that level. His previous teaching involvements include Cambridge University and the Rhode Island School of Design. His work has been published and exhibited widely, most recently at the Royal Academy and the Architecture Foundation in London. As of January 1992, his most recent theoretical work was included in the latest edition of *AAFiles*.

WILLIAM R. BENEDICT
Assistant Professor of Architecture
Department of Architecture
School of Architecture and Environmental Design
California Polytechnic State University, San Luis Obispo
San Luis Obispo, California

WILL BENEDICT received a Bachelor of Architecture degree from Kansas State University in 1967, and a Master of Architecture degree from The University of Texas at Austin in 1989. He is currently an assistant professor in the School of Architecture and Environmental Design at Cal Poly in San Luis Obispo, having previously taught in the Department of Architecture at Texas A&M University, and the Department of Art and the School of Architecture at the University of Tennessee.

Benedict's teaching experience has been focused in foundation design and communication. His interests are dominated by a search for conceptual schema of fundamental design principles and a pedagogy that would facilitate their communication to and/or discovery by others. In these areas he has presented papers and given lectures on the principles of design and the development of corporate identity programs.

Benedict has worked as a designer in government, as an architect for the Tennessee Valley Authority, Knoxville, Tennessee; in private industry, as the corporate designer for Special Instruments Laboratory, Knoxville, Tennessee; and in private practice, as a senior designer for Ross/Fowler, Knoxville, Tennessee. His work has included architectural, interior, graphic, and product design, and he has received awards in the areas of graphic and product design.

OWEN CAPPLEMAN
Associate Professor of Architecture
Interim Assistant Dean, 1992–93
School of Architecture
University of Texas at Austin
Austin, Texas

OWEN CAPPLEMAN (B.A., Florida State University; M.F.A., University of Texas) is a painter and craftsman, a graphic designer, and a cultural historian in art and architecture. Throughout his thirty-three-year career as an educator, he has worked with all age groups, from preschool children to retirees in settings that have ranged from museums to public school classrooms, from university studios to the tropical rain forests of north Borneo. While maintaining an active exhibition schedule, Cappleman's teaching energies since 1964 have been primarily devoted to the study of architecture. For the past ten years his ongoing interest in the platform-level education of the beginning design student has placed him in the forefront of this rapidly developing specialization. In the mid-1980s he cofounded the School of Architecture First-Year Computer Imaging Lab, a unique facility at the time, and was coeditor of Volume 3 of *Best Beginning Design Projects.*

In Cappleman's own artistic endeavors, his work has been as eclectic and diverse as his teaching experiences and lifestyle. He has worked in a variety of techniques and materials, including painting and drawing, various mixed media, batik and other dyecraft, leaded and resin-encased stained glass, and, most recently, computer graphics. In addition to twenty solo, two-, and three-person shows and twenty group exhibitions, his work has been included in numerous invitational and competitive exhibitions in all parts of the United States, Canada, and Mexico, has garnered fifteen awards, and appears in private and public collections worldwide.

Beyond teaching and creating, Cappleman's greatest passion is travel. Over the years he has roamed by plane, train, boat, car, donkey, and elephant on four and a half continents in thirty countries with visits to and stays in hundreds of cities. The climax of his travels (thus far) was a two-year teaching assignment in Southeast Asia in 1987 and 1988.

ELIZABETH PATTERSON CHURCH
Assistant Professor of Architecture
Department of Architecture
Vermont College at Norwich University
Montpelier, Vermont

ELIZABETH CHURCH received her Master of Architecture degree from Columbia University in May 1986 and her Bachelor of Arts degree from Duke University in May 1978. She has been assistant professor of architecture at Vermont College at Norwich University from the fall of 1991 to the present. Prior to coming to Vermont, she was a visiting assistant professor of architecture at Mississippi State University from the fall of 1990 through the spring of 1991.

Church's teaching is involved with a wide array of course work, including not only the first-year design studio but first-year Introduction to Architecture and a first-year lecture course, Passive Building Systems. Other courses include first- and second-year honors seminars, second-year design studio (of which she is coordinator), a second-year lecture course on Human Issues in Design, and a second-year lab course entitled Computers in Architecture.

Church maintained a private practice in New Hampshire and Vermont from the Spring of 1986 through the fall of 1990.

ALAN R. COOK
Associate Professor of Architecture
Department of Architecture
Auburn University
Auburn, Alabama

ALAN COOK, a native Nebraskan, was born in 1948 virtually in the shadow of Bertram Goodhue's magnum opus, the Nebraska State Capitol building. He grew up experiencing the values of his region as well as those of France, owing to his mother's European roots.

After graduating with a Bachelor of Environmental Design from the University of Nebraska in 1971, Cook apprenticed in Phoenix, Arizona, and then in Lincoln, Nebraska. He eventually returned to Lincoln to complete graduate studies in architecture, where he was involved in the Nebraska Capitol and Environs Plan. That project was accorded a First Design Award for Planning by *Progressive Architecture* in January 1978. Cook completed his Master of Architecture in 1976, including a written thesis entitled *The Roots of Design*, which was an investigation into the nature of psychology and the design process.

After teaching for three years at North Dakota State University, Cook moved to Auburn University, soon assuming the role of directing the freshman architectural design sequence. In 1983 he presented a paper at the ACSA National Meeting entitled "Mastermime: the Paradigm of Personification in Design," which explicates the dominant role that the development of human psychoanatomy plays in the appreciation of architecture.

Cook currently teaches elective seminars entitled "Imagery, Aesthetics and Expression in Architecture" and "Geometry and Architecture," and coordinates the junior level of architectural design at Auburn.

DAVID COVO
Associate Professor of Architecture
School of Architecture
McGill University
Montreal, Quebec, Canada

DAVID COVO is a native of Montreal and a graduate of McGill's School of Architecture. He has worked across Canada and abroad as a teacher and an architect. Since joining McGill's faculty in 1977 he has taught a wide range of courses, including sketching, computer-aided design, and the first-year design studio, which he coordinates. He has at the same time maintained a private consulting practice, working both alone and in partnership with other architects, and has built a number of residential and institutional projects in Quebec and Ontario.

Covo's research activities are related to his teaching and architectural practice. They address drawing and the design process, the role of computers in design, and the special architectural requirements of the disabled, and they have contributed to the development of several new courses in these areas. His particular interest in drawing also finds him sketching in pencil and watercolors at every opportunity.

Covo is extremely active in university and community affairs. He is especially committed to the sport of sailing, as both competitor and volunteer, currently serving on the executive board of the national governing body of the sport.

DEREK DRUMMOND
Professor and Director
School of Architecture
McGill University
Montreal, Quebec, Canada

DEREK DRUMMOND, a Fellow of the Royal Architectural Institute of Canada, is the Macdonald Professor of Architecture at McGill University. He was Director of the School from 1976 to 1985, and was reappointed to this position in 1990 for a third term of five years. He teaches two elective courses, Civic Design and Site Usage, as well as design studios in the first and final years.

Drummond's principal research is concerned with the impact on our urban environments of entrepreneurial initiatives and corporate incentives. He is a regular contributor to scholarly publications, and writes architectural criticism for the Montreal *Gazette*.

Drummond also holds several administrative posts at McGill, and serves on the boards of directors of a number of businesses, schools, institutions, and nature organizations.

ZAFER ERTÜRK, Ph.D.
Professor of Architecture and Head,
Department of Architecture
Faculty of Engineering and Architecture
Karadeniz Technical University
Trabzon, Turkey

ZAFER ERTÜRK, Ph.D., M.Sc., M.Arch., graduated in architecture and received a Master's degree in Human Sciences from LUT in England, and a Ph.D. in Building Science from Istanbul Technical University. He is currently the Dean of the Faculty of Social Sciences at the Karadeniz Technical University in Trabzon, Turkey. He is also Head of the Department of Architecture, and serves as full professor in architectural design in that department.

Ertürk is also the designer of many kinds of buildings in Turkey, particularly a number of university buildings. The scope of his numerous publications includes environmental problems, ergonomics, Anatolian architecture, and the theory of design activity and design techniques.

Ertürk has taught in the College of Architecture of Texas Tech University as a visiting professor, where he lectured on the ancient civilizations and architectural heritage of Anatolia, and also took part in architectural studio teaching. He is a founding member of the International University for Bio-Environment at Athens, and also is a member of the Bio-Politics International Organization.

JONATHAN BLOCK FRIEDMAN
Professor of Architecture and Dean
Center for Architecture
New York Institute of Technology
Old Westbury, New York

JONATHAN FRIEDMAN graduated cum laude with a Bachelor of Arts degree from Princeton University, where he was a National Merit Scholar, in 1967. In 1968 he received his Diploma in Architecture from Cambridge University, and in 1980 he completed his Master of Architecture at Princeton. He is a registered architect with memberships in the American Institute of Aeronautics and Astronautics, SIGGRAPH (a graphics organization), and ACM, the Association for Computing Machinery. In addition to his role as an educator, Friedman has maintained an active professional career over the past twenty years.

Friedman has taught at NYIT since the early 1980s. Before that, he held teaching posts at the New Jersey Institute for Technology and the University of Kentucky. He has been a guest critic at Cooper Union, Ball State University, Columbia, and Harvard.

The bibliography of Friedman's writings fills two pages. Perhaps his crowning achievement in this area is his two-volume set on first-year architectural pedagogy—*Creation in Space, Volume 1: Architectonics,* and *Volume 2: Dynamics.*

Friedman has a long history of public service, and is the recipient of numerous honors and awards.

CHARLES P. GRAVES, JR.
Assistant Professor of Architecture
School of Architecture and Environmental Design
Kent State University
Kent, Ohio

CHUCK GRAVES was born in 1952 in Atlanta, Georgia. He received his Bachelor of Architecture degree from the University of Kentucky, and his Master of Architecture from Cornell University.

Prior to joining the faculty at Kent State in 1987, Graves taught for two years at the Eidgenoessische Technische Hochschule (ETH) in Zurich, Switzerland.

Graves's professional experience includes work with Stephen Potters, Architects, New York, New York, from 1979 to 1983, and with Welton Becket Architects, New York, New York, from 1983 to 1985. Since 1987 he has been a principal at Zix/Graves Architects in Kent, Ohio.

MARY HARDIN
Assistant Professor of Architecture
School of Architecture
College of Architecture and Environmental Design
Arizona State University

MARY HARDIN is coordinator of the design fundamentals program at Arizona State. She teaches beginning design studios as well as upper-division studios. Her research interests include beginning design pedagogy and affordable housing design.

Hardin maintains a small professional practice in the Phoenix metropolitan area, specializing in affordable housing projects that range in scale from single-family units to institutional facilities. She obtained her Master of Architecture degree at the University of Texas at Austin in 1983.

ROBERT D. HERMANSON, AIA
Professor of Architecture
Graduate School of Architecture
University of Utah
Salt Lake City, Utah

ROBERT HERMANSON received his Master of Architecture degree from the University of Pennsylvania following undergraduate studies at the University of Minnesota. Subsequent to a position as associate and director of design in the firm of Thorsen and Thorshov, Minneapolis, he presently teaches in the Graduate School of Architecture at the University of Utah in addition to conducting a private practice. He is the recipient of several AIA design awards.

Hermanson has directed his attention within academia to interdisciplinary studies incorporated within the design studio as extensions of a pedagogical interest in the design process. These have included narrative literature, music, dance, film, and video in collaboration with architecture as part of an integrated studio experience.

Hermanson also conducts lecture classes in Scandinavian architecture and related design disciplines and participates as a visiting professor at the Catholic University of America in Washington, D.C., each summer as director of the American Studies program. He is a member of the American Institute of Architects and a registered architect in the state of Utah.

DESMOND HUI, Ph.D.
Assistant Professor of Architecture
Department of Architecture
University of Hong Kong
Hong Kong

DESMOND HUI was born in Hong Kong in 1958 and emigrated with his parents to Canada in 1980. Educated at Wah Yan College, Kowloon, in Hong Kong, he began his studies in architecture at Cornell University in 1977 under an international student scholarship, receiving his Bachelor of Architecture degree in 1982. At Cornell he was a Dean's List student, holder of the Edward Palmer York Memorial Prize, and winner of the AIA award for outstanding academic performance.

After graduation, Hui worked briefly for Raymond Moriyama in Toronto on the winning design of the North York Civic Centre competition before joining Barton Myers Associates, where he worked on several large-scale urban development projects. He won the Robert James Eidlitz Fellowship from Cornell in 1985 and went to England to study with Joseph Rykwert at Cambridge University. He obtained his Master of Philosophy degree in 1986, and continued for a Ph.D. degree under the Commonwealth Scholarship. In 1989, he was elected Research Fellow at St. Edmund's College, Cambridge.

Hui took up his present teaching appointment in the Department of Architecture at the University of Hong Kong in 1990. He has been invited to speak at several academic conferences in China on traditional dwellings, and at an international conference on theory of architecture in Australia. He has also lectured and published widely in Hong Kong. He became a registered architect of the Ontario Association of Architects in 1985 and is a member of the Royal Architectural Institute of Canada.

LAURA E. JOINES
Assistant Professor of Architecture
Department of Architecture
School of Architecture and Environmental Design
California Polytechnic State University, San Luis Obispo
San Luis Obispo, California

LAURA JOINES received her Master of Architecture degree from North Carolina State University in 1987. She also pursued her education at the Architectural Association, London; in the Master of Science in Historic Preservation program at Columbia University; and in the anthropology department of the London School of Economics. In 1981 she graduated from Vassar College with an A.B. degree in geography/anthropology.

Joines's teaching interests are in the fundamentals of design and in processes of making intentional relationships between things. She has written on the subject of design methods, most recently on the "Disaggregate Method of Design." She believes that the fundamentals of design are not concepts that remain at the beginning of one's career, but constantly inform it. She has successfully used these concepts in other architectural and urban design applications, such as the Prague Urban Design and Housing Seminar, which she instituted in 1990. The seminar continues as a summer study studio in Prague, Czechoslovakia. This program adopts a "vernacular" approach to urban design by focusing on the relationships between the buildings of medieval Prague in order to integrate new architectural development into a spatially and culturally distinct city.

Currently Joines teaches design studios and communication graphics in the fundamentals of design program at Cal Poly in San Luis Obispo.

MICHAEL JACK JORDAN
Professor of Architecture
College of Architecture
University of Oklahoma
Norman, Oklahoma

MICHAEL JORDAN received his Bachelor of Architecture degree from the University of Texas at Austin in 1970, and his Master of Architecture degree from Yale University in 1974. Jordan is a veteran of nearly twenty years of teaching beginning design, having taught in this area at Auburn University, the University of Texas at Austin, and, most recently, the University of Oklahoma, where he is full professor. At each of these institutions he has served as coordinator of foundation studies.

From 1986 through 1989, Jordan was the stateside architecture coordinator for a cooperative program in Malaysia under the auspices of the Texas International Education Consortium and the Institut Teknologi MARA. In this role he functioned as liaison between five Texas schools of architecture and the government of the Federation of Malaysia. He has visited parts of Asia—most notably in three trips to Japan to conduct research in an area of ongoing fascination for him, Japanese gardens.

In addition to being an architect, Jordan has written numerous articles on beginning design education, and has been editor or coeditor of two editions of *Best Beginning Design Projects*. In 1986–87 he combined his continuing involvement in first-year studies with a then-new interest in computers to co-found the University of Texas First-Year Architecture Imaging Lab, a facility that was unique at that time. His current research extends this interest to include computer visualization and animation of energy usage on the campus of the University of Oklahoma, a project undertaken in collaboration with CRSS Architects in Houston.

Michael Jordan is also a frustrated—and sometimes frustrating—painter, and has heard every basketball joke known to the human race, generally delivered by telephone at 3:00 AM.

MICHAEL KAPLAN
Associate Professor of Architecture
College of Architecture and Planning
University of Tennessee at Knoxville
Knoxville, Tennessee

MICHAEL KAPLAN is associate professor of architecture at the University of Tennessee at Knoxville, where he teaches architectural design and theory. He received a Bachelor of Arts degree in Fine Arts from Brandeis University and a Master of Architecture degree from Harvard University. Following service as a Peace Corps volunteer architect in Tunisia from 1967 to 1969, he worked with Hardy Holzman Pfeiffer Associates as project architect of the Mt. Healthy School in Columbus, Indiana. While establishing a practice of his own in Israel, he taught at the Beersheva Technical College and conducted research in earth construction at the Ben-Gurion University of the Negev. He has been a regular participant at multidisciplinary conferences, addressing issues of architecture and power in the Middle East.

JOSEPH LIM, Ph.D
Associate Professor of Architecture
School of Architecture
Faculty of Architecture and Building
National University of Singapore
Singapore

JOSEPH LIM received an Honours degree in architecture from the National University of Singapore in 1982. He was an assistant architect in a Singapore practice until 1985, when he was offered a teaching scholarship by the same university. He currently holds a doctorate degree in architecture from Heriot-Watt University in Edinburgh, and is an architect registered with the Singapore Board of Architects.

Lim's interest lies in the relationship between art and technology, with particular emphasis in architectural structures. The samples of his studio work are an indication of his ongoing experimentation with second-year beginning architecture students, in which highly theoretical concepts are balanced with the teaching of basic pragmatics.

DARLA LINDBERG-BERRETH
Assistant Professor of Architecture
Graduate School of Architecture
University of Utah
Salt Lake City, Utah

DARLA LINDBERG-BERRETH received her Bachelor of Science in Architectural Studies and Bachelor of Architecture degrees from North Dakota State University, and her Master of Architecture degree from Iowa State University.

Prior to Lindberg-Berreth's appointment at the Graduate School of Architecture, University of Utah, she was involved with practice and teaching at NDSU and Iowa State. She has held several state and national AIA appointments, and has maintained active association with local organizations committed to excellence in art and architectural design. She is also a registered architect. Involved with both practice

and academia, she is dedicated to teaching both instrumental knowledge necessary to uphold professional standards and visual thinking skills critical to advancing knowledge in the field. Lindberg-Berreth's research interests in architectural education and writing have centered around an exploration of the processes of creative problem solving and resource building through three-dimensional and interdisciplinary models. In addition, her recent efforts have involved *Architecture and Children*, a curriculum-building activity in grade schools focusing on architecture as a paradigm for resource building, visual thinking, and learning as a process-versus-product orientation. Actively involved with students, she was selected as the 1987 Mortar Board Honor Society Outstanding Academic Advisor from the College of Engineering and Architecture at NDSU and has been an AIAS advisor for the past six years.

BRUCE LINDSEY
Assistant Professor of Architecture
Department of Architecture
Carnegie-Mellon University
Pittsburgh, Pennsylvania

BRUCE LINDSEY is an assistant professor of architecture at Carnegie-Mellon University and a principal in the architectural firm of Bruce Lindsey Paul Rosenblatt Associates, Pittsburgh. Born in Geneva, New York, and raised in Nampa, Idaho, he attended Boise State University for two years, before going on to receive his Bachelor and Master of Fine Arts degrees from the University of Utah, and his Master of Architecture from Yale University. In 1987, he began teaching architecture at Carnegie-Mellon University, where he became head of the first-year program, and Bruce Lindsey Paul Rosenblatt Associates was formed.

Lindsey and Rosenblatt's major projects have included the "College of Fine Arts Niches Project," a CAD-CAM stonecarving project cited in *Architectural Record* and *Engineering-News Record*, and the "Piers" project, a series of proposals for the Pittsburgh riverfronts that received a 1991 AIA Honor Award.

In addition to his collaborative work, Lindsey's metalsmithing has been exhibited throughout the United States, and he has received a national teaching prize from the ACSA, in addition to the Henry Hornbostel Teaching Prize from Carnegie-Mellon University.

LYE KUM CHEW
Professor of Architecture and Head
Department of Architecture
University of Hong Kong
Hong Kong

LYE KUM CHEW was born in Malaysia in 1934. Educated at the Raffles Institution of Singapore, he pursued his undergraduate and postgraduate studies in the United States under Victor Olgyay, Jean LaBatut, and Louis Kahn. At Princeton he was awarded the AIA medal and the Henry Adams Prize for general excellence in architecture.

Lye's work has taken him to the United States, Britain, the Netherlands, Canada, and Singapore. He has taught at the Architectural Association (AA) in London and at the Leverhulme Department of Urban Design. From 1968 to 1976, he was Head of the Department of Architecture at the University of Manitoba. In 1972 he was awarded a research fellowship to SAR at the University of Eindhoven in the Netherlands and also lectured at Delft at the invitation of Professor Jos Weber. Appointed Chair of Architecture at the University of Hong Kong in 1976 and Dean of the School of Architecture from 1978 to 1989, he is at present Head of the Department of Architecture.

Lye was engaged in design consultancy to several practices and is now in private practice. He was a member of the winning team for the design of the Hong Kong University of Science and Technology in 1987. He has served as a member of the government Town Planning Board and the Building Committee of the Hong Kong Housing Authority as well as External Examiner and a member of visitation boards to various universities around the world, including those in Singapore, Malaysia, India, Sri Lanka, and China. He was also invited to several international conferences in architecture and served as judge for an international design competition.

Lye is Fellow of the Royal Architectural Institute of Canada and Fellow of the Hong Kong Institute of Architects, as well as a member of the RIBA. and various professional bodies around the world. Recently he was appointed as a member of the Accreditation Board by the Chinese Ministry of Construction.

NICHOLAS CHARLES MARKOVICH, Ph.D.
Associate Professor of Architecture
School of Architecture
Louisiana State University
Baton Rouge, Louisiana

NICK MARKOVICH was born in Syracuse, New York. He attended undergraduate school at Syracuse University, where he studied industrial design. He then transferred to the State University of New York at Buffalo to finish his Bachelor of Fine Arts. He later pursued his Master of Architecture and Ph.D. at the University of New Mexico.

Markovich has taught at several universities, including the University of Texas at Arlington, Cornell, the University of New Mexico, the University of Colorado, and now Louisiana State University. His most extensive academic activity has been the development of programs in beginning design education. He has hosted several conferences on beginning design, and has published extensively in that area.

Markovich's other research interests are in the field of American regionalism and architecture. He was chief editor for the publication *Pueblo Style and Regional Architecture,* published by Van Nostrand Reinhold in1991.

TIM McGINTY
Professor of Architecture
School of Architecture
College of Architecture and Environmental Design
Arizona State University

TIM McGINTY was one of the founding fathers of both the annual Beginning Design Student Conference (celebrating its tenth convention in New Orleans in 1993), and the School of Architecture and Urban Planning at the University of Wisconsin-Milwaukee, where he taught for over a decade. He currently teaches at Arizona State University, and has been a visitor or young teacher at the University of California at Berkeley, Temple University, and the University of Nebraska.

While he also teaches architectural design, urban design, and architectural programming, McGinty has enthusiastically taught beginning students survey courses about architecture, perspective, design drawing, and design fundamentals. As a career "beginner," he has

185

championed using the "laws" of visual perception as the point of departure for teaching both drawing and design as well as using architectural themes as the subject of "Basic design" exercises. His book *Drawing Skills in Architecture* —unfortunately now out of print — illustrated these views.

As an architect, McGinty worked on the 1980 and 1981 *Progressive Architecture* award-winning research project on design guidelines for Child Play Centers. He currently consults on the areas of concept design and environmental graphics for Kiku Obata and Company in St. Louis. Recent projects include the award-winning design of the children's bookstore, P. B. Pages, for Barnes and Noble.

Educated at the University of Kansas, where he received the Thayer Medal in 1966, and at the Louis Kahn studio at the University of Pennsylvania in 1967, McGinty recently received, along with colleague Mary Hardin, an AIA Honors in Education Award for the Design Fundamentals Sequence at Arizona State University.

LORNA ANNE McNEUR
First-Year Studio Master
Third-Year Lecturer
Department of Architecture
Cambridge University
Cambridge, England

LORNA McNEUR (Bachelor of Architecture, Cooper Union; Master of Philosophy and M.A., Cambridge University) currently teaches the History of the Inhabitation of Public Space to the third year in addition to her duties as First-Year Master. Since graduation from Cooper Union in 1980, she has taught at all levels of design and practiced architecture: at Carleton University in Ottowa, Canada; the Cooper Union in New York; and Skidmore, Owings and Merrill in New York. Her primary profession is now teaching and research, although she maintains her interest in building with a few choice projects. She is currently involved as architectural advisor to Lucy Cavendish College at Cambridge for a new residence and dining hall.

McNeur has published and exhibited her work in the United States, Canada, and Europe. Her publications include "Central Park City," *AA Files* No. 23; "The Cambridge First-Year Design Programme," *The Architects Journal*, March 1991; "Women and Men in Architectural Education in the Late Twentieth Century," *Scroope, The Cambridge Architectural Journal* 1990; "Student Projects: The Nine-Square Grid and Central Park City," *Education of an Architect: The Irwin S. Chanin School of Architecture*, Rizzoli 1988; a presentation of student and faculty work, *Carleton Folio* 1985; a review of the Whitney Museum exhibit "MetaManhattan," *Art Forum*, New York 1984; "New York Project," *Section A*, Montreal, 1984; "The Nine-Square Grid and a Teaching Methodology," *Section A*, 1983; a review of Artist's Space Exhibit "Sequences," *Art Forum*, New York 1981; and "Nine-Square Grid," student issue of *Lotus International*, Italy 1981. Her exhibitions include Public Image Gallery, New York; SOHO 20 Gallery, New York; Whitney Museum of American Art, New York; Ohio Foundation on the Arts, a one-year traveling exhibition of five architects shown throughout the United States; Artist's Space, New York; the Houghton Gallery of the Cooper Union, New York; International Design Center, Berlin; and the Architecture League, New York.

McNeur has given lectures, seminars, critiques and/or workshops at the following institutions: the Central European University Foundation in Prague; Birmingham Polytechnic, England; Carleton University, Ottawa; Carleton University Rome Programme, Italy; the Architectural Association, London; the Martin Centre Research Society, Cambridge, England; North London Polytechnic; Sheffield University, England; University of Toronto; Waterloo University, Canada; Waterloo University Rome Programme, Italy; University of Ottawa School of Art; Calgary Architecture and Urban Studies and the University of Calgary, Canada; the Cooper Union for the Advancement of Science and Art, New York; Institute for Architecture and Urban Studies, New York; and Columbia University, New York. She has traveled to Australia, Canada, Czechoslovakia, Egypt, England, Fiji, France, Germany, Greece, Holland, India, Italy, New Zealand, Scotland, Spain, and the United States (including Hawaii).

LEONARD S. NEWCOMB
Associate Professor of Architecture
Division of Architectural Studies
Rhode Island School of Design
Providence, Rhode Island

LEONARD NEWCOMB is a landscape architect in Boston, Massachusetts. He is associate professor at Rhode Island School of Design, where he teaches design studios and seminars focusing on contemporary issues in landscape and architecture. He has been coordinator of the first-semester core design studio for four years.

Professor Newcomb's research and design work focuses on urban and environmental issues and public landscapes through design studios and seminars, design competitions, and private commissions.

Newcomb received his Bachelor of Arts degree from Ahmerst College and is currently pursuing his interests in history and theory in the Master in Design Studies program at the Harvard Graduate School of Design.

JUDITH E. RENO
Professor of Architecture
School of Architecture
Savannah College of Art and Design
Savannah, Georgia

JUDITH RENO is professor of architecture at Savannah College of Art and Design where she teaches architectural design and theory. She received a Bachelor of Arts degree in Psychology from Boston University and a Master of Architecture degree from the University of California, Los Angeles. Her stay in Los Angeles included study at the Southern California Institute of Architecture and professional practice in the office of Daniel Dworsky Associates, where she worked as designer on the Tom Bradley International Air Terminal. Her teaching career has included posts at California Polytechnic State University at San Luis Obispo, Auburn University and the University of Tennessee at Knoxville. Her numerous papers and publications address interconnections of design, culture and construction in architecture.

PAUL ROSENBLATT
Assistant Professor of Architecture
Department of Architecture
Carnegie Mellon University
Pittsburgh, Pennsylvania

PAUL ROSENBLATT is an assistant professor of architecture at Carnegie Mellon University and a principal in the architectural firm of Bruce Lindsey Paul Rosenblatt Associates, Pittsburgh. Born and raised in New York City, he received both his bachelor's and master's degrees in art and architecture from Yale University. In 1987, he began teaching architecture at Carnegie Mellon University, where he became head of introductory computer modeling and the second-year program, and Bruce Lindsey Paul Rosenblatt Associates was formed.

Rosenblatt and Lindsey's major projects have included the "College of Fine Arts Niches Project," a CAD-CAM stonecarving project cited in *Architectural Record* and *Engineering-News Record*, and the "Piers" project, a series of proposals for the Pittsburgh riverfronts that received a 1991 AIA Honor Award.

In addition to his collaborative work, Rosenblatt is a former editor of *Perspecta*, the Journal of the Yale School of Architecture, and advisor to the new Carnegie Mellon Journal of architecture, *Aris*.

ALAN L. STACELL
Professor of Architectural Design
Department of Architecture
College of Architecture
Texas A&M University
College Station, Texas

ALAN STACELL received his Master of Fine Arts degree from the University of Illinois in 1960. Painting, the history of art and architecture, and the philosophy of art were the subject areas of his formal education. The history of strength of materials, statics, and structural theory have been Stacell's informal interests over his three decades of teaching studio courses to introductory level architectural design students.

Stacell states his personal philosophy as follows: "I thought that schematic visual design theories without connections in the empirical world of physical science lacked credibility and vice versa, but I have not found that equivalencies exist."

Stacell has been Department Head of Environmental Design and is currently Interim Head of Landscape Architecture and Urban Planning. He makes paintings, drawings, and writings, and is one of four people working on an electronic computer book about an imaginary city.

JANEZ SUHADOLC
Professor of Architecture
Faculty of Architecture
University of Ljubljana
Ljubljana, Slovenia

JANEZ SUHADOLC was born in Ljubljana in 1942. He graduated from the University of Ljubljana, Faculty of Architecture, in 1968, in the class of Professor E. Ravnikar, and was employed at the same school in 1970 as assistant professor. He was promoted to the rank of professor in 1989.

As Suhadolc so compellingly puts it: "I was born in Ljubljana, the capital of the recently established Republic of Slovenia, on July 3, 1942. In this town I went to schools, here I am employed, married, and as it looks, I will also die here.

"My architectural education was so perfected and thorough that I spent several years after the diploma getting rid of the carefully nourished rationalism and functionalism, and managed to begin more interesting work. The latter I attempt to do still as I teach younger generations at our School of Architecture in Ljubljana, where I was taught architecture and am in turn teaching it now. I would not go into details of my work since I have not as yet quite decided what to do with my life; aside from my pedagogical career, my fellow countrymen know me as a graphic designer. At times, I also draw or paint, make scenery, exhibitions, interiors, museums, etc. [Sometimes] I indulge in writing, especially when the issue [is on the] "urbanist structure" of my town.

"In the cellar of my house I keep a woodworker's workshop. There I make wooden furniture, mainly chairs, after my own plans. This activity of mine is pretty renowned at home, and also in some other parts of the world. I was recently invited to appear with these pieces on the American market...

"My mother, age 89, often says to me, 'You shall yet see what life is all about once you are older' And I think to myself, I might then find a serious job to do—and perhaps become a real pro in it.

"That is the time I still wait for, for the ultimate revelation and final station, the asylum... of my being."

MUNEHIKO TANIGUCHI
Assistant Professor of Architecture
Department of Architecture
Kogakuin University
Tokyo, Japan

MUNEHIKO TANIGUCHI has a deep involvement in architectural design education, while at the same time working as an architect. It is his belief that design can be taught most effectively when the teacher contributes to society as an architect. The scale of his architectural projects is quite wide, ranging from large-scale public architecture to interior design and furniture for a small house.

Taniguchi is particularly interested in the design of the urban house in an overpopulated area. When designing a house under such unfavorable conditions, he employs his own simple — but deliberate — solutions to transform a bad situation into one that is more than acceptable. His gauge of success is "if the owner can be proud of the house designed."

Taniguchi goes on to state: "When I feel tired from an urban life [on] the twenty sixth floor of the university building, I go climbing. Mother Nature always makes me refreshed and remotivated, giving me momentum for another design [project]."

KURULA VARKEY
Professor of Architecture and Hon. Director
School of Architecture
Centre for Environmental Planning and Technology
Ahmedabad, India

KURULA VARKEY received his Bachelor of Architecture degree with honors from I.I.T. Kharagpur in India, and his Master of Architecture degree in architecture and urban design from the Helsinki University of Technology in Finland.

Varkey has worked as senior designer with Balkrishna Doshi from 1968 to 1977; as visiting faculty in the School of Architecture and School of Planning, Ahmedabad, from 1974 to 1977; as senior lecturer in the Department of Architecture at the University of Nairobi from 1977 to 1984; and as professor and honorary director of the School of Architecture at the Centre for Environmental Planning and Technology in Ahmedabad from 1987 to the present.

In addition to serving as department head and supervising the first-year foundation program, Varkey teaches architectural design, urban design, the history and theory of architecture, settlement history, and urban design theory.

BETSY WILLIAMS
Adjunct Assistant Professor of Architecture
College of Architecture and Urban Planning
University of Michigan
Ann Arbor, Michigan

BETSY WILLIAMS received a Bachelor of Environmental Design at Miami University in 1983, and a Master of Architecture at the Harvard University Graduate School of Design in 1986. She began teaching at the

University of Michigan in 1990, after working for five years as an architect in Boston. The making of books and other paper constructions has been an interest of hers for a number of years.

DAVID T. YEOMANS, Ph.D.
Senior Lecturer in Technology
School of Architecture
University of Manchester
Manchester, England

DAVID YEOMANS graduated in civil engineering and worked for Ove Arup and Partners in London, at the same time engaging in part-time teaching. His first full-time teaching post was at the Oxford University School of Architecture, lecturing on structural design, and then at the University of Liverpool School of Architecture. He used the project featured in this book at both schools.

An interest in the history of structures led Yeomans to write a Ph.D. thesis on the development of structural carpentry in England. In 1980 he was seconded to the Timber Research and Development Association as Chief Education Officer, and on returning to Liverpool established a graduate course in building conservation (historic preservation).

Yeomans is now at the University of Manchester in charge of the technology faculty. He also teaches classes in both history and construction technology. His current research includes work on the relationship between standards of workmanship and building performance.

ANNEX 3
Systematics: A Taxonomy of Educational Design Objectives

Systematics: A Taxomony of Educational Design Objectives

"Systematics," a typology of design intentions, scales, and methods of representation, has been developed to serve a variety of purposes. The two most important of these are (1) as an organizational tool for examining the projects featured in this book and (2) as a rational aid for instructors in the first year, or at any other year level, in the development of meaningful design problems.

Organizationally, the Systematics approach is used in this book in two ways. First, in Section 2—"An Annotated Anthology of Beginning Design Projects"—the taxonomy is presented as a band of text along the bottom of each double-page project synopsis. Here the specific Systematics descriptions of the project under all five Taxon categories are highlighted in italics as a typological summary of the project. Systematics is seen again in the final section of this book, the matrix, which is organized in the same order as the Taxonomy described here. The matrix can be used to locate specific projects in particular areas of concern. For example, if one were seeking only architectural project types dealing with human concerns at a social scale, or perhaps any actualized projects represented at full scale, the matrix would provide ready access to such information.

"Systematics" consists of five Taxons: the nature of the problem; subject matter; scale, both in terms of the problem itself and in its representation; and the mode, or method, of documentation of design solutions. Within each Taxon is an array of specific project types. These typologies are ordered from the most vague to the concrete, or from imprecise to precise, from the smallest to the largest, or from qualitative to quantitative, in an effort to maintain a tenuous measure of consistency among five related, yet disparate, realms.

TAXON ONE: NATURE OF THE PROBLEM

The "nature of the problem" is an early—possibly the first—choice made in problem-seeking, and is related to the problem's intentions and educational goals. It is also arguably the most difficult decision for the project creator, who must have these goals and intentions clearly defined. Once the problem's nature has been determined, the task of

decision making in regard to the other characteristics of the problem (subject matter, scale of the problem, and scale and methods of documentation) becomes much easier. Five fundamentally different problem natures have been identified.

Conceptual

The idea *itself* is the issue. The problem may exist at the earliest ideational stages, and may not have clearly realized visual form. Analogous to conceptual art, it is extremely intellectual, possibly even obtuse.

Analytic

The problem dissects one or more larger issues, examines the parts from an objective point of view, and increases the student's powers of abstraction and discrimination. Examples could be diagrammatic models, studies of underlying geometries and partí, or of relationships between mass and void, or of color harmonies.

Nonobjective/Compositional

Traditionally referred to as "abstract" problems. Generally (but not necessarily) two-dimensional or low relief in format, nonobjective/compositional projects explore relationships of parts, and foster the development of the student's eye/mind/hand acuity. They facilitate the building of a visual vocabulary to support informed discussion of visual interactions and relationships. Examples include Bauhaus-based positive and negative shape explorations, studies in pictorial space or pictorial composition, or exercises in page layout.

Compositional/Architectonic

Problems that explore compositional issues abstractly, but within an architectonic framework. Generally in three-dimensional format (either drawn in axon or perspective, or realized in model form), compositional/architectonic problems have a "building–*like*" character with few or no programmatic elements. Examples might include non-site specific massing studies, explorations of form/space relationships, path and movement studies, or more purely abstract manipulations of three-dimensional forms. Scale may be relative, or vague, and may range from artifact to full-scale.

Architectural

Problems with clearly defined programs (whether simple or complex) that result in a useful object realized at a specific numeric scale (see Taxon Four: Scale of Documentation). Architectural projects may range from artifact scale to edifice scale to the scale of the city (urban scale), as noted in Taxon Three: Scale of the Problem. Examples include design of a toy (simple program, artifact scale), design of a restaurant interior (somewhat complex program, social scale), design of a block of row houses (complex program, neighborhood scale), or tower/bridge type structural explorations that exist at hermetic scale.

TAXON TWO: SUBJECT MATTER

The particular type of subject matter in a project depends on a number of variables, the most important being the nature of the problem (Taxon One). In most projects, irrespective of their nature, there is wide latitude in choosing a subject type to fit a given studio environment or a particular group of students. It may be drawn from an intuitive sense of appropriateness, or by simply following one's own biases. The typologies listed below are organized from the possibly vague, or at least "soft-edged," at one end of the spectrum, to the more specific and technical at the other.

Poetic

This subject term embraces problems that are characterized by either an unrestrained search for beauty, with no felt need for justification, or an expedition toward an unknown goal. Often there is the element of serendipity, or of whimsy.

Metaphoric

Problems that are loaded with layers of meaning beyond the obvious. Sometimes this subject type is seen hand in hand with the poetic (above), and frequently is linked with referential subjects (below).

Referential

Problems with sources other than architecture as their prime (or ancillary) subject matter, or as a point of departure. These can include literary sources, paintings, music, forms found in nature, or any of an infinitude of sources limited only by the imagination.

Human Concerns

This problem type embraces all aspects of human-based design: measurable physical attributes of the design (anthropometrics or ergonomics); psychological concerns relative to human interaction within the built environment (proxemics); the sociological implications of architecture (territoriality); human use of the built environment (circulation, activity accommodation); and, finally, purely humanitarian issues such as low-cost housing or shelter for the homeless.

Environment

The category of environment ranges from pragmatic issues (site analysis, site design, site development) to issues of conscience and social consciousness (environmentalism).

Visual Vocabulary

Investigations and studies in the elements of form (point, line, plane, volume, texture, color, etc.), the language of form (focalization, symmetry/asymmetry, dominance, hierarchy, etc.), the expression of form (line, tone, texture, color, etc.), and formal and spatial organization (ordering systems).

Procedural

This category refers to multistage processes, usually accompanied by planned steps of accretive knowledge that builds in "layers" as the project progresses. It is generally combined with one or more other substantive subject-matter types.

Programmatic

A typical architectural problem with a carefully developed program at a level of complexity commensurate with the scope and intentions of the project.

Tectonic

Either studies of particular structural systems and materials in isolation, or an architectural project that emphasizes construction and materials.

TAXON THREE: SCALE OF THE PROBLEM

The first issue of scale addresses the scope or size of what is being designed. This is a separate issue from the scale used in the representation of final design solutions, which is discussed in Taxon Four: Scale of Documentation.

Hermetic

Projects in which scale is not an issue. They are self-contained and self-referential. Nonobjective/architectonic projects frequently can be classified under this taxon.

Artifact

An object; usually something that can be held in one or both hands, but generally a thing that is, at its largest, not much larger than a human being.

Individual

"Tight fit." An intrapersonal space, one that accommodates a single person, from a telephone booth to a diving bell.

Personal

"Loose fit." An interpersonal space for an individual, with or without a small group of people, from a bedroom to a dining room to a small living room.

Social

"Public fit." A space for interpersonal interaction on a larger scale, from a small restaurant to a large theater lobby to a park, garden, or playground.

Edifice

Full building scale, from a house to a skyscraper.

Monumental

Usually (but not always) a large building or space with certain characteristics. To be monumental, instead of simply big, an element of symbolism or the sense of awe, wonderment, or of being overpowered must be present.

Neighborhood

Urban scale at a micro-level.

City

Urban scale at a macro-level.

TAXON FOUR: SCALE OF DOCUMENTATION

The scale of representation of a design project.

No Scale

Certain kinds of projects—those that address issues of visual vocabulary, for example, or that test structural capacities (towers, bridges, egg-drop containers), or that exist at a certain degree of abstraction or conceptualization—generally contain no particular scalar reference. In this type of representation, size in relation to other sizes is not an issue.

Ambiguous

A problem in which the scale is unclear, or in which scalar clues offer mixed messages.

Relative

A problem whose scale is indicated by scalar clues (usually a scale human figure), but is not drawn or modeled at any referential numerical scale.

Referential

The most common form of architectural representation. Scale may be indicated in a drawing or model in the language of either the architect (e.g., 1/4″ = 1′-0″) or the engineer (1″ = 40′), or with a graphic bar-scale, or both.

Full

A project realized at its actual size, be it an artifact, an installation, or a monumental sculptural event.

TAXON FIVE: MODE OF DOCUMENTATION

The method of representation used to communicate design decisions.

Nonvisual

Written or oral presentations, or more unorthodox forms of communication such as music, dance, poetry, chants, etc.

Electronic

Computer-generated images. These frequently use or incorporate other methods of representation, but are created within the electronic environment. Certain forms, however, such as animated walkthroughs and fly-bys, virtual reality, and some kinds of solid modeling, are unique to the computer.

Actualized

The actual built thing is the representation (e.g., an artifact), or the scale is otherwise self-referential (e.g., color studies mounted on a 30″ by 40″ board).

Expressive

Images or models intended to communicate the mood, the impression, or the experience of a design. Useful both during the design process as design development tools and later as a means of enriching an architectural presentation, expressive representations are usually character-ized by use of materials and techniques less precise and more informal than those employed in descriptive drawings and models. Examples include sketchy sequential "walkthrough" vignettes in perspective, vigorous charcoal or mixed-media images, "sketch" study models, montaged pastiches of images, etc.

Descriptive

Precise informational drawings or models. Drawing types include working drawings, design orthographic views (plan, elevation, section), clear diagrammatic drawings, paraline projections (isometric, axonometric, etc.), and certain perspective drawings. Descriptive models could be detailed scaled presentation models or very clear analytic models.

ANNEX 4
"Fencing or Soccer?"

Fencing or Soccer?

David Yeomans

During the Foundations in Architecture Conference I posed this question to the conferees: "What kind of skill do you think design to be?" No clear answer was forthcoming. Yet this seems to me to be an important question, because the answer would be indicative of our attitude toward different kinds of student projects and their likely efficacy. So I will try again, this time by way of analogy.

I will draw parallels between soccer and fencing as skills. Teaching the former requires very little up-front instruction. The student can begin playing fairly quickly, because kicking a ball is a relatively simple skill. People may be shown the tactics, and how to refine their ability to control the ball, when they have actually begun to play. This is helpful because they can see, directly and immediately, how development of these skills relates to their play. Some drill exercises may be useful, but their purpose will be so readily apparent that they cannot help but stimulate the motivation of the learners.

In contrast, learning to fence can be rather frustrating because a number of skills must be developed to a reasonable standard before students can begin to engage in contests with others. They have to learn how to stand, how to move forward and back, how to lunge; all possibly without even holding a foil. They then need to learn how to hold the weapon, how to straighten their arm to make an attack, how to parry to defend themselves; all these before doing the thing itself—fighting one's opponent. It's like learning to play the piano: Playing scales hardly resembles playing music.

The question, then, is whether design is a skill like soccer, or like fencing. To judge by the different approaches to beginning the teaching of design, people clearly differ in their views. This is not just a comment on the particular exercises presented at the Foundations conference, but also on the way in which I have seen beginning design approached at different schools in Britain. At the University of Liverpool, where I taught for many years, a program for first-year design was introduced which was based on the belief that since students had come to school to learn to design buildings, we should introduce them to that activity as soon as possible. This approach was not introduced without opposition, but it seemed to work in spite of the arguments put forward by the more conservative staff brought up under a different system. However, elsewhere I have seen students spending much of their first year with exercises that bore little or no resemblance to actual building design, and whose purpose may not have been at all clear to them.

Of course it is possible that design may be treated in either of these ways, because there are skills that are amenable to both approaches. The obvious example is drawing. I cannot remember exactly how I learned to draw, but I had some facility in my teens, when I was already drawing for pleasure. I can remember a friend of my father's teaching me the mechanics of perspective when he saw I needed this. Certainly, for me, drawing was a skill like soccer. I produced drawings and was then shown how to do better. My present drawing skills and technique reflect this learning method.

In contrast, Phillip Thiel of the University of Washington developed a method of teaching drawing that relies on the student first carrying out a series of drill exercises: making dots on paper and joining them up with straight lines, drawing spirals, and so forth. Such exercises, at the beginning, produce nothing resembling representational drawings. Yet this method works well, and for a wide range of age groups; I know an elementary school teacher who has used it with success. Thus, drawing by this method is learned as a skill like fencing rather than soccer.

These two learning methods lead to different techniques in practice, and perhaps to different styles of drawing. For me, producing a drawing has always been a process of first constructing a framework, abstracted from the object or the scene in front of me, which is then progressively "filled in." For those who have learned by Thiel's method, drawing is a process of producing, from the outset, finished lines between points whose relative positions are first carefully observed. If drawing can be defined as seeing and then making marks on paper, the method of observing—of looking—appears to be different, as well as the method of making the marks. This method appears to generate a manner of drawing similar to that used by artist David Hockney. In a program on drawing aired by BBC-TV some years ago—and before I became aware of Thiel's book—Hockney was shown drawing a portrait. He started with the nose and eyes, and worked outward; it was some time before it was clear just what he was drawing. If I were to do a portrait, I would have to start with the shape of the head, and work *inward*.

What is attractive about Thiel's method is that it seems better suited to a medium like pen and and ink than my way of drawing. Thus I would like to learn this technique, but so far have lacked the patience to go back to the beginning and do the drills, even though I can see the purpose behind them. It's like trying to learn to touch-type when one is already fast at hunt-and-peck.

This brings us back to my initial question. I know design can be taught like soccer. That's how it was done in the first-year course at Liverpool in which I participated. Thus I am curious about the effect of starting with compositional exercises that are not linked to clear building design problems. It is not that I doubt their value, just that I'm not sure exactly what is happening. There seem to be a number of possibilities for the exercises:

1. They have no direct relationship to building design activities, but simply prepare the students in a way of thinking. If we can return to the analogy of physical activities, these are like exercises that fencers (and perhaps soccer players as well) go through just to develop muscle strength and joint flexibility.
2. They prepare students so that they come to building design processes with some usefully developed skills, much like a trainee surgeon might usefully learn some elementary needlework before sewing up after an operation. If this is what's happening, then should we assume from the example given by drawing that these skills may affect the subsequent nature of the design process—perhaps even the nature of the designs produced? Alternatively, do they simply make it easier for the student/designer to tread much the same path?
3. They are techniques that students may apply in building design. This is not quite the same as above, as it is not that a skill is being developed (although it may be) but rather that a technique is being demonstrated.

This may not be an exclusive list, and it is certainly a quite different taxonomy from the "Systematics" approach used in organizing this book, because it concerns simply the development of skills and not of knowledge or understanding. Thus it seems useful to define our aims in this way:

1. Do we wish to measure the efficacy of these exercises? How?
2. How are we to define at what future stage they will bear fruit? It is possible that some exercises may not bear fruit during the students' time in school. We may simply be sowing a seed that will develop later.

Some measure of the efficacy of different exercises used in each category seems essential, because it is possible that some exercises may have a negative effect. It has been suggested to me that some abstract exercises are counterproductive because students have difficulty in transferring skills from the abstract to the concrete.

An explanation of my curiosity about this might be helpful here. Perhaps unique among those faculty present at the Foundations conference, I have received no formal design training. I am an engineer, not an architect, and my knowledge of design has been built up by observation and discussion. My own design skills, such as they are, have certainly been learned like soccer. For a long period in history, design was a craft skill; that is, learned from someone already skilled in the art. It is arguable that it remains little developed beyond this even today; while teaching design seems still to be largely the same kind of craft skill, some of those teaching it use techniques remembered from their own early learning experience. This surely suggests a need to look more closely at the methods we are employing, and to consider their effectiveness more than we may have in the past.

It can hardly be disputed that those who are skilled in an activity do not always make the best teachers of that activity. There is a story told by a colleague who attended a training program to teach skilled tradesmen how to teach their apprentices. This fellow was selected from among the noncarpenters present to be instructed on how to remove the iron from a wood plane. To do this, the plane has to be struck on the end with a mallet. A carpenter demonstrated this, after which my colleague tried in vain to release the iron by mimicking the action. After two or three equally unsuccessful repetitions of this performance, the carpenter declared in exasperation, "You're as bad as my f—ing apprentices!" Of course, those responsible for the training program knew this would happen. The trick is to rest the plane on one's knee when you hit it, but this step—unknown to the novice— was taken for granted by the journeyman carpenter, who only demonstrated *where* it has to be hit. Likewise, might not skilled designers be equally unaware of the difficulties involved in learning their skill?

We know that Thiel's method of teaching drawing produces results. We all know that touch typists can produce far faster than hunt and peck, and that it might be to our advantage to *slow down* our typing speed in order to learn, ultimately, to type faster using all fingers. I did that, and now reap some of the benefits (except I never could learn not to look at the keyboard—imperfect training using a teach-myself method). But what are we to say to the forty-year-old students, who just want to be shown how to do design, about the value of design exercises? Can we say that there are well-documented cases of designers using methods relying upon the development of certain skills? We know that in the past, designers learned their trade like craft apprentices, doing a great deal of copying of drawings. There's not much of that done today. We are told that Frank Lloyd Wright played with Froebel's blocks as a child, but can that be a good reason for assigning abstract exercises? Do we really know that these blocks were a significant factor in his development? I am quite willing to assume that they were, but we have eighteen-year-olds to train; it is not at all obvious that similar methods would have the same effect. By that age, I would assume that they need things that are being developed at a much more conscious level. We should recognize that we may be on our own here. I have been told, by a source I assume to be reliable, that cognitive development beyond the age of sixteen is not well understood by psychologists.

We may be able to identify the *objectives* of exercises that would be useful by looking at the deficiencies in students' design tactics or strategies. For example, students frequently are reluctant to explore alternative compositions; sometimes it seems to them that the first idea they produce is the one that they are stuck with. This suggests a need for compositional exercises, perhaps not so much to develop useful skills as simply to demonstrate working methods that they should use in the future. We often find a reluctance on the part of students to let go of ideas that are not working out, and that we have the experience to know cannot be made to work. It has been suggested to me that this is because having got one idea, students are unsure that they will be able to produce another. If so, this indicates a need to develop an ability to generate ideas, and the confidence that they can do this; a need for more sketch design problems, perhaps.

I'm certain that there are numerous such skills of different kinds that can be identified as lacking in students, and that suggest exercises that may be introduced to develop these skills. But this still leaves unanswered the question about how and when these should be introduced—at the moment they clearly need them, or arbitrarily at the beginning—and how might the answer be different for different skills?

So, fencing? . . . or soccer?

Matrices

Systematics Matrix by Author

Author(s)	Project Title	Conceptual	Analytic	Nonobjective/ Compositional	Compositional/ Architectonic	Architectural	Poetic	Metaphoric	Literary	Human Concerns	Environment	Visual Vocabulary
John Andrews	The Journey	■	■			■	■	■		■	■	
James Bagnall, William Benedict and Laura Joines	Nine Square Matrix		■		■							■
Peter Beard	Mapping Tools	■				■	■				■	
Owen Cappleman	A Commemorative Pavilion for Joseph Cornell		■	■	■	■		■	■	■	■	■
Elizabeth Church	The Novel and Architecture		■		■				■			■
Alan R. Cook	Spatial Apotheosis for Apollo and Dionysus				■			■				
David Covo and Derek Drummond	Working with Piranesi		■			■						
Zafer Erturk	Exhibition Area at Cappodocia					■				■	■	
Jonathan Block Friedman	Harmony				■							■
Charles P. Graves, Jr.	House to Street					■						
Mary Hardin	A Nomadic Shelter					■				■		
Desmond Hui and Lye Kum Chew	Between Tradition and Modernity		■			■				■	■	
Michael Jordan	The Metaphysical City		■		■			■				■
Joseph Lim	Teaching Structures for Architectural Application					■	■	■	■			
Darla Lindberg-Berreth and Robert D. Hermanson	Serendipity: Accidental Discoveries and Sagacity					■		■	■			
Bruce Lindsey and Paul Rosenblatt	Avatars of the Tortoise				■							■
Nicholas Markovich	The Promenade				■					■	■	
Lorna Anne McNeur	Thinking Hands		■			■	■			■		
Leonard Newcomb	A Pool					■				■	■	
Judith Reno and Michael Kaplan	The Otherside of Seaside				■					■	■	■
Alan Stacell	Design and Build a Sky: A Tensegrity Project					■	■	■				
Janez Suhadolc	The Gneric Possibilities of Artistic Pattern		■		■	■				■		■
Munehiko Taniguchi	Basic Design			■								■
Kurula Varkey	Vocabulary of Space				■							■
Betsy Williams	Studio and Dwelling for a Bookbinder	■				■		■				
David T. Yoemans	Understanding Structures Through Models		■			■						

Taxon One: NATURE of the PROBLEM

Taxon Two: SUBJECT MATTER

202

				■		■		■					■						■			■		■	■	Procedural
	■					■		■		■		■	■	■	■	■	■	■			■	■				Programmatic
■			■		■	■				■		■			■	■							■			Tectonic
Taxon Three: SCALE of the PROBLEM																										
		■	■	■	■	■																				Hermetic
	■									■	■												■		■	Artifact
																									■	Individual
	■											■			■											Personal
							■						■	■				■				■		■		Social
■	■			■		■	■	■	■		■	■	■	■		■	■	■	■	■	■	■			■	Edifice
																										Monumental
																■										Neighborhood
						■							■												■	City
Taxon Four: SCALE of DOCUMENTATION																										
		■	■																			■				No Scale
								■												■						Ambiguous
	■				■					■						■			■					■	■	Relative
■	■			■		■	■	■	■		■	■	■	■			■	■			■	■			■	Referential
					■					■	■				■								■		■	Full
Taxon Five: MODE of DOCUMENTATION																										
																										Nonvisual
										■						■										Electronic
	■				■					■	■				■								■		■	Actualized
■	■		■			■											■		■	■		■			■	Expressive
■	■	■		■		■	■	■	■		■	■	■	■		■	■	■			■	■	■	■	■	Descriptive

Systematics Matrix by Geographic Region

Region		Author(s)	Conceptual	Analytic	Nonobjective/ Compositional	Compositional/ Architectonic	Architectural	Poetic	Metaphoric	Literary	Human Concerns	Environment	Visual Vocabulary
North America	West	James Bagnall, William Benedict and Laura Joines		■		■							■
		Darla Lindberg-Berreth and Robert D. Hermanson					■		■	■			
		Mary Hardin					■				■		
	West Central	Michael Jordan		■		■			■				■
	Southwest	Owen Cappleman		■	■	■			■	■	■	■	■
		Alan Stacell					■	■	■				
		Nicholas Markovich				■					■	■	
	East Central	Charles P. Graves, Jr.					■						
		Betsy Williams	■				■		■				
	Southeast	Alan R. Cook				■			■				
		Judith Reno and Michael Kaplan				■	■				■	■	■
	Northeast	Bruce Lindsey and Paul Rosenblatt				■							■
		Jonathan Block Friedman				■							■
		Leonard Newcomb					■				■	■	
		Elizabeth Church		■		■					■		■
		David Covo and Derek Drummond		■			■						
United Kingdom		Peter Beard	■				■	■				■	
		Lorna Anne McNeur		■			■	■			■		
		David T. Yoemans		■			■						
Eastern Europe		Janez Suhadolc		■		■	■		■		■		■
		Zafer Erturk					■				■	■	
Asia	West	Kurula Varkey				■							■
	Southeast	Joseph Lim					■	■	■	■			
		Desmond Hui and Lye Kum Chew		■			■				■	■	
	East	Munehiko Taniguchi			■								■
Australia		John Andrews	■	■			■	■	■		■	■	

Taxon One: NATURE of the PROBLEM

Taxon Two: SUBJECT MATTER

204

Procedural	Programmatic	Tectonic	Taxon Three: SCALE of the PROBLEM	Hermetic	Artifact	Individual	Personal	Social	Edifice	Monumental	Neighborhood	City	Taxon Four: SCALE of DOCUMENTATION	No Scale	Ambiguous	Relative	Referential	Full	Taxon Five: MODE of DOCUMENTATION	Nonvisual	Electronic	Actualized	Expressive	Descriptive
■								■								■								■
					■				■								■	■				■		■
	■	■					■											■				■		
■	■							■	■			■					■							■
■	■							■	■					■			■						■	■
		■		■													■					■		
									■								■							■
	■	■							■		■					■					■			
	■				■		■		■							■	■					■	■	■
									■						■								■	
■	■	■		■					■			■				■						■	■	■
	■	■			■											■		■			■	■		
	■								■								■							■
								■	■								■							■
	■								■								■							■
■									■														■	■
		■			■													■				■		■
■	■								■						■		■							■
		■							■								■						■	■
■				■					■								■							■
	■							■	■								■							■
														■										■
	■	■		■			■										■							■
	■							■	■								■							■
		■		■										■									■	
■					■	■			■			■				■	■	■				■	■	■